Modernist Impersonalities

Modernist Impersonalities

Affect, Authority, and the Subject

Rochelle Rives

MODERNIST IMPERSONALITIES
Copyright © Rochelle Rives, 2012.

All rights reserved.

First published in 2012 by PALGRAVE MACMILLAN® in the United States—a division of St. Martin's Press LLC, 175 Fifth Avenue, New York, NY 10010.

Where this book is distributed in the UK, Europe and the rest of the world, this is by Palgrave Macmillan, a division of Macmillan Publishers Limited, registered in England, company number 785998, of Houndmills, Basingstoke, Hampshire RG21 6XS.

Palgrave Macmillan is the global academic imprint of the above companies and has companies and representatives throughout the world.

Palgrave® and Macmillan® are registered trademarks in the United States, the United Kingdom, Europe and other countries.

ISBN: 978-1-137-02187-8

Library of Congress Cataloging-in-Publication Data

Rives, Rochelle.
  Modernist impersonalities : affect, authority, and the subject / Rochelle Rives.
  p. cm.
  ISBN 978-1-137-02187-8
  1. Modernism (Literature)—English-speaking countries. 2. Literature, Modern—20th century—History and criticism—Theory, etc.

PN56.M54R58 2012
809'.9112—dc23   2012001767

A catalogue record of the book is available from the British Library.

Design by Scribe Inc.

First edition: September 2012

10 9 8 7 6 5 4 3 2 1

Printed in the United States of America.

For S.M. and E.M.

Contents

Acknowledgments		ix
Introduction: Modernism and the "Escape from Personality"		1
1	"The Dissociation of Personality": Space and the Impersonal Ideal	21
2	The Impersonal Contract: H.D. and the Limits of Poetic Authority	47
3	A "Peculiar Feeling of Intimacy": D. H. Lawrence, Modernist Violence, and Impersonal Narrative	81
4	Problem Space: Wyndham Lewis, Mary Butts, and the Impersonal Object	113
5	A "Solicitude for Things": Elizabeth Bowen and the *Bildungsroman*	149
Conclusion: Emotion after *The Death of the Heart*		175
Notes		181
Index		209

Acknowledgments

This book is about engagement and the meaningfulness of relationships, both personal and impersonal. That said, I owe many for their various engagements with this project. First, I extend serious gratitude to my colleague sisters at the Borough of Manhattan Community College, City University of New York, Joyce Zonana and Page Delano, who acted generously both as my friends and as readers of the manuscript. More than anyone else, they understood my desire to continue working as a serious scholar while juggling the demands of community college teaching and service. Another round of thanks goes to my mentors at the University of Illinois Urbana–Champaign (now elsewhere), who helped give life to this project and have continued as its advocates: dissertation director and baby whisperer Janet Lyon unearthed texts for me that reconciled pleasure with academic work; Tim Dean created the seminar that would ground the next ten years of my academic labors; Jed Esty is responsible for generating so much excitement about the *Bildungsroman* that the subject occupies two chapters of this book; and Joe Valente read every chapter of my dissertation with unparalleled attentiveness—at least three times. I would also like to give credit to my more informal advisors—originally peers from graduate school and now lifelong friends: fellow impersonalist Christina Walter deserves recognition for both her generosity in sharing hotel rooms and her instant answers to any hastily emailed bibliographic queries; Melissa Girard should win a special award for just listening; and Scott Herring never fails to indulge me with opportunities for laughter and perspective—as well as incisive professional advice. If the heart really is the seat of emotion, I thank him from the bottom of mine.

Through the efforts of the Professional Staff Congress of the City University of New York (CUNY), I was entitled to both contractual and awarded released time from teaching, without which it would have been impossible to finish this book. A Faculty Development Grant at BMCC also provided me with time and funds to pursue this project. CUNY's Faculty Fellowship Program not only aided the completion of my manuscript but was also a boon for my personal life, for it was within the small assembly of scholars it facilitated that I found my husband, Michael Garral. My thanks go to the participants of our writing group, who read and commented on portions of this book, especially to Mary McGlynn, who has proven an invaluable mentor, resource, and colleague. The responses I received after sharing work from this project with the Columbia University Irish Studies Seminar were also especially beneficial. I express my appreciation to this group and the Warner Fund at the University Seminars at Columbia University for help with publication.

At the University of Illinois, I owe the timely completion of my dissertation to several departmental fellowships, which granted me both released time from teaching and the funds for travel and research. Chapter 4 especially benefitted from time in the archives at the National Art Library at London's Victoria and Albert Museum and from larks to various Bloomsbury haunts in the English countryside.

I thank the two anonymous readers of the manuscript for their thoughtful and pointed commentary. Their observations were crucial for trimming the excesses of the manuscript and whipping it into shape. Thanks also to my editor at Palgrave Macmillan, Brigitte Shull, along with her wonderful assistant, Maia Woolner, for their support of this project and help with the mysteries of securing permissions. And on that topic, thanks also to Carcanet Press in the UK and New Directions in the United States for permission to quote from H.D.'s *Collected Poems*. While official permissions were not necessary, I also thank Paul Edwards of the estate of Wyndham Lewis and Bruce McPherson of McPherson & Company for their kind responses to my queries.

Portions of Chapter 4 were previously published as "Problem Space: Mary Butts, Modernism, and the Etiquette of Placement" in *Modernism/Modernity* 12.4 (November 2005): 607-627, and as "'No Real Men': Mary Butts Socio-Sexual Politics" in *Connotations* 18.1-3 (2008/2009): 246-58. Segments of the introduction and Chapter 1 appeared in "'Things that Lie on the Surface': Modernism, Impersonality, and Emotional Inexpressibility," in *Disclosure: A Journal of Social Theory* 16 (2007): 59-86. My thanks to Johns Hopkins University Press, the *Connotations* Society, and the Committee on Social Theory at the University of Kentucky, respectively, for permission to reprint.

Finally, I thank my husband and family for helping sync my life and body's demands with the last stages of manuscript preparation, especially as the project's "delivery" coincided (within days of my first writing this) quite literally with the "delivery" of a child. I owe much to my philosopher husband, Michael, and his ability to save me from impulse by patiently reflecting on all sides of a matter; to Douglas, Betty, and Amanda, expert furniture assemblers and caregivers; to my grandmothers, Martha Fern and Marcia Joyce, farmwomen extraordinaires, whose resourcefulness and dignity continue to astound me. And ultimately, I must borrow from George Eliot's *Middlemarch* to acknowledge "that unconscious centre and poise of the world" in the making of this book, the wondrously impersonal presence of our little one.

Introduction

Modernism and the "Escape from Personality"

> Generally speaking, it can be said that people wish to escape from personality. When people are encouraged, as happens in a democratic society, to believe that they wish "to express their personality," the question at once arises as to what their personality is . . . If they were subsequently watched in the act of "expressing" their "personality," it would be found that it was somebody else's personality they were expressing . . . It would be a group personality that they were "expressing"—a pattern imposed on them by means of education and the hypnotism of cinema, wireless, and press. Each one would, however, be firmly persuaded that it was "his own" personality that he was "expressing": just as when he voted he would be persuaded that it was the vote of a free man that was being cast, replete with the independence and free-will which was the birthright of a member of a truly democratic community.
>
> —Wyndham Lewis[1]

In *The Art of Being Ruled* (1926), Wyndham Lewis bluntly mocks the fiction of self-expression, or "personality," viewing it as a mimetic figment of the democratic imaginary. Lewis's feverish distrust of democratic ideals and their grounding in mass media points to an aesthetic as well as social debate that modernist studies has yet to articulate fully: what it means to escape from personality. Lewis's own brand of "impersonality," the term many modernists employed in their various critiques of "personality," invests itself in authority, and this connection has come to characterize the meaning of impersonality in modernist studies more generally. Particularly in addressing what appears to irk him most dramatically, the illusion of personality as a vehicle of individuality and a "libertarian sugar-plum," Lewis maintains that personality promotes the illusion of "free-will" and democratic political participation (*Art* 148). Given this critique of personality and its relation to democracy and individualism, the impersonal alternative Lewis imagines, recourse to authoritarian political and aesthetic ideals, presents serious ethical difficulties.

Lewis's disdain for personality and corresponding advocacy of an impersonal escape from it is further complicated by the somewhat contradictory idea that personality is flawed because it is too impersonal in the first place, too imitative and anti-individualistic. This contradiction supports the double bind that critics such as Edward Comentale have identified in texts such as *Blast* (1913), where Lewis actually "laments the impossibility of attaining true individuality in a cultural market that consistently appropriates all difference."[2] Ultimately, Lewis's attempt to restructure this environment, to reinstitute the authoritative organization of social order and true creative individualism, more explicitly accompanies the renowned misogyny and homophobia that emerge in his other essays. As I will argue at various points in this book, Lewis's essays continually manifest this contradiction; little difference appears between the authoritarian control of human subjects Lewis promotes, where invasive domination obliterates individuality, and the types of conformity he attributes to democracy.

Taking Lewis's diatribe as its starting point, this book examines the meaning of modernist impersonality—as a response to the increasingly explicit prominence of the "personality" in twentieth-century political, aesthetic, and literary culture—and its relation to the concept of authority, the "rules" that govern both social life and aesthetic production. This project also probes the contradictions of an impersonality that, in its relation to authority, can potentially reproduce the same mimetic structure of identification it critiques. In defining authority, I resist drawing connections between modernist writers and clearly defined political ideologies and regimes. Rather, I examine authority as it is more broadly articulated in modernist texts, whether it be in Lewis's preference for "some form of *fascism*" over democracy or communism, T. S. Eliot's reverence for tradition, or the fascination with violence shared by Mary Butts and D. H. Lawrence, each subjects of this book.[3] As Sharon Cameron has remarked in her influential book *Impersonality*, violence itself is a condition of the movement from personality to impersonality and the possibility of freedom that occurs when persons surrender to a power "that effaces what individuates them."[4] I suggest here that this move toward authority is a spatial problem. It emerges in the search for an organizational structure that might temper the loss of individualism and social order that, for thinkers such as Lewis, attend modern life. Impersonality, then, is both a rejection of modern individualism and a call for a truer sense of the term. Consequently, each text I examine in this book illustrates the tensions of an impersonality that, on one hand, promises the radical freedom of what Eliot terms "surrender" and "self-sacrifice"—from social constraints such as race, gender, sexuality, and more generally, "personhood"—while, on the other, it reinforces authoritarian paradigms that reproduce often violent scenarios of invasion and control.[5] For this reason, this book attends to a wide range of texts with often conflicting political and aesthetic ideals. As opposed to contrasting definitions that stress its neutrality, objectivity, and detachment, impersonality, I argue, is a theory of engagement, enabling forms of connection that both radically challenge authority and simultaneously sustain it.

My intention here is not only to grapple with the ethical difficulty and contradictions of impersonality in its abstract manifestations in modernist texts but also to expand the parameters of "impersonality" beyond the major authors and texts that have come to define it so rigidly. Because of Eliot's canonical status and his critical role as the spokesperson for the doctrine, impersonality has in many cases been advanced as a formalist theory of poetics only, exhibiting little relevance for the more "social" world of prose fiction and criticism. Consequently, the purpose of this book is not only to rescue impersonality from its resolute connection to authority but to uncover a broader literary-historical conversation and genealogy that incorporates texts that extend the meaning and practice of impersonality beyond the figures that have narrowly defined it: primarily Eliot, Yeats, and Pound, and less often, Woolf and Lawrence. In general, accounts of modernism have cemented Eliot so forcefully to the idea of impersonality that it is nearly impossible to examine its meaning in the work of other writers without recourse to Eliot's essay. While this project has obviously been unable to avoid this dilemma, it does seek to point out how figures such as Lewis, writing only a few years after Eliot "officially" articulated his version of the doctrine, clearly participated as much in its making as did Eliot, Pound, or Yeats, the three high modernists whose theories of masking, personae, and poetic surrender generally ballast critical considerations of modernist impersonality. Similarly, as I argue in the chapters that follow, figures such as H.D. and D. H. Lawrence articulated theories of impersonality that highlight their awareness of and distaste for "personality" as an established term in aesthetic and popular discourse well before the publication of Eliot's essay.

While Eliot's "Tradition and the Individual Talent" is renowned for its demand that the poet scientifically depersonalize, extinguishing his personality to impersonally inhabit the "form of tradition," the essay's and Eliot's centrality to modernist studies have obscured the more radical features of the doctrine it promulgates, which I attempt to trace here in this introduction.[6] The necessary connection critics have drawn between Eliot's dictum that the "progress of the artist is a continual self-sacrifice, a continual extinction of the personality" and his political conservatism can perhaps account for what still seems to be a rather hasty evaluation of impersonality in the new modernist studies and the term's overt omission from analysis of seemingly unrelated texts with ostensibly different political agendas, such as those I discuss in this book by H.D., Mary Butts, and Elizabeth Bowen (*Prose* 40). Admittedly, modernist studies is currently benefitting from a much needed reconsideration of the term "impersonality," initiated by critics such as Sharon Cameron, Tim Dean, and Colleen Lamos. Cameron's collection of essays on impersonality has catalyzed a renewed critical discussion of the term that unveils the radical potential of its contradictions. In addressing a loosely constellated range of texts in American literature by William Empson, Jonathan Edwards, Herman Melville, Ralph Waldo Emerson, and T. S. Eliot, Cameron argues that "[i]mpersonality (as a practice, as an ethic, as a representation), since it is undertaken by persons, could only be contradictory by definition," highlighting the radical possibility that impersonality might free "being" from "personality," disrupting "elementary categories we suppose to be fundamental to specifying human distinctiveness" (*Impersonality* 7, ix). For Cameron, impersonality disrupts the presumption that humans are unique and, as exemplified in William Empson's study of Buddhist iconography, elevates the enigma of "fully visible presence" over human distinction and depth (*Impersonality* 7). In general, Cameron's analysis does much to clarify the meaning of impersonality as a contradictory structure and philosophy that, according to Empson, engages "the other half of the truth about the world" (qtd. in *Impersonality* 2). This "truth" seems to result from the move beyond human particularity to a stranger, more indefinite world. However, Cameron's project does not theorize impersonality as a distinctly modernist phenomenon beyond Eliot (*Impersonality* 144). In this regard, my own project departs from Cameron's in attempting to theorize impersonality as a defining feature of a more coherent aesthetic and historical milieu. More specifically, I suggest that for modernists, the move away from the person toward a "world" occasioned its own sense of anxiety about the potential loss of personal authority and spatial dimension impersonality entails, a crucial underside that remains unexplored in Cameron's account of the term. Impersonality offered the potential of liberation but nonetheless emerged as a problem for modernists to negotiate.

In contrast to Cameron's assessment of impersonality as a radical concept that redefines the human through "dissociation" and "disintegration," earlier accounts of the aesthetic have tended to read it as a localized literary doctrine defined by its connection to authoritative masculinist aesthetics and formalism (*Impersonality* ix). For example, in *The Poetics of Impersonality: T. S. Eliot and Ezra Pound* (1987), a book that helped to establish high modernism as staunchly doctrinaire and antidemocratic, Maud Ellmann argues that Eliot resurrected the doctrine of impersonality for modernism as a "crusade against Romantic individualism in society."[7] Though Ellmann's formalist readings of Pound's and Eliot's poetry are often riveting, her failure to theorize impersonality beyond the purview of Pound and Eliot explains her assertion at the end of the book that the words "'impersonal' and 'personal' have probably outlived their usefulness" (*Poetics* 197). Impersonality, she argues, "was born conservative" (*Poetics* 198). This statement is not without its merit; the philosophical assumptions that inspire the doctrine can reach radically different ends, as I argue in this book. For Pound, as Ellmann provocatively suggests, impersonality "opens up the whole psychopathology of fascism" (*Poetics* 199). However, in ending on this dismissive note, Ellmann abandons the radical potential of what her pointed criticism often unveils. Her reading, for example, of Eliot's "The Love Song of J. Alfred Prufrock" highlights the more radical possibilities of impersonality, as she sees it in the authoritarian control the poem's diffuse yellow fog, "remorseless and impersonal," exercises over Prufrock, intensifying his "general unease of otherness" (*Poetics* 69). If the "yellow fog" of the poem surrounds Prufrock in the ultimate impersonal relationship, that fog can signify anything from the complete dissolution to the "apotheosis of self," depending on whether Prufrock experiences it as intrusive or as part of himself (*Poetics* 69). For Ellmann, the fog's threat to Prufrock's personal boundaries reflects the "interiorizing" gestures of the impersonal poem, which enables both "self-love" and "self-oblivion," where "the other always takes the subject by surprise" (*Poetics* 71). While Prufrock attempts to defend himself from the assaults of the voyeuristic Other, evident in his fear of "eyes that fix you in a formulated phrase," the ideal state of impersonality would result from his submission to this presence.[8]

Critics such as Tim Dean, still with reference only to Eliot, have investigated this radical potential more explicitly. Arguing that most misconceptions about impersonality stem from Eliot's "own contradictory and ambivalent pronouncements on the subject," including his focus on the mask as a tool for concealment, Dean claims that Eliot's theory instead enables "access" rather than "evasion" and is an "experiment with self-dispossession rather than self-advancement," thus disputing the claim that impersonality is necessarily concerned with advancing the authority of the poet.[9] For Judith Brown, this same diminishment of the subject defines glamour during the modernist period as it "inheres in the problem of modernist form."[10] While Brown does not engage the problem of impersonality explicitly, her study, *Glamour in Six Dimensions: Modernism and the Radiance of Form*, reaches further than any other recent account in linking an impersonal aesthetics to a wider modernist context. Indeed, the problem of impersonality underwrites her entire analysis of glamour as a "reformulation of feeling" in modernist culture (*Glamour* 16). Glamour does not promote "access," as Dean would suggest of impersonality, but is rather characterized by an aesthetic of restraint that moves away from "insistent subjectivity" in promoting an "impersonal style" (*Glamour* 7). Differences aside, Brown's impersonal understanding of glamour as it "shapes and reshapes the objects before us . . . by pressing them into an inhuman dimension" coincides with both Dean's and Cameron's assessment of impersonality as an affectively strange and mysterious condition that transcends, even transgresses, the limits of the person (*Glamour* 9).

It is important to understand these more recent accounts of impersonality—which credit it with altering the parameters of selfhood and subjectivity through novel forms of engagement that reimagine the self beyond humanist conceptions of the person—in relation to earlier critical accounts of the term, which reinforce the claim that modernism developed according to a humanist-inspired subjectivist tradition. These now classic arguments connect modernist anxiety to the possible loss of humanist individualism, not the desire to leave it behind, without considering the fact that this loss might indeed be productive, a form of "access," as Dean suggests ("T. S. Eliot" 45). For example, Daniel Albright's book *Personality and Impersonality: Lawrence, Woolf, and Mann* (1978) moves beyond Eliot (who is rarely mentioned) to read in modernism a "crisis of personality" that evinces paranoia of impersonal "de-capitation, disembodiment," and failure of self-expression.[11] Focusing largely on prose, Albright argues that the twentieth-century novel is characterized by "the personality of the author," where the drive toward "self-expansion" or "self-diffusion" is in actuality the outgrowth of the novelist's hope to achieve "a full reification of identity" (21). Judging from this presumption that personality is itself a goal, impersonality is a much lamented, not desired, state of being, and modernist writers nostalgically look backward toward a world centered by human subjectivity. In contrast, my reading of D. H. Lawrence's *Sons and Lovers* (1913) suggests how its reflexive meditations on impersonality disable the longstanding critical tendency to interpret such metaphysical interests in the service of humanism: of identity, self, and subjectivity. For Lawrence, "self-diffusion" functions as a critique of heterosexual romantic narratives that center on the self as a vessel for meaning and knowledge. Albright's own humanist logic, which posits a binary between the self and its own disintegration, limits a broader understanding of the dynamic that comprises Lawrence's version of impersonality.

Similarly, Michael Levenson's important work *A Genealogy of Modernism: A Study of English Literary Doctrine* (1984) identifies a crisis period in modernism when subjectivity, egoism, and individuality simply failed as a foundation for "literary advance."[12] According to Levenson, a "frankly egoistic" early modernism inevitably gave way to the objective demands of an "extreme formalist aesthetic" advanced by Hulme and his followers, such as Pound (*Genealogy* 133). As useful as Levenson's argument is, the shift he outlines positions Pound's imagism along with Eliot's rise to critical prominence as markers of a more objective, more impersonal literary direction. In this narrative of modernism, Eliot speaks for a formalist doctrine whose distrust of the individual can only be conservative, where the denial of "self-expression as the criterion of success" necessitates "a controlling intelligence behind poetic creation" (*Genealogy* 159). As Levenson suggests, Eliot's version of impersonality, with all its emphasis on poetic surrender and submission, is unable fully to relinquish its own vantage point of critical control and doctrinaire authority. However, Levenson draws the link between anti-individualism and authority too firmly without attending to texts that configure this dynamic alternatively.

Space and the "New Psychology"

The modernist distrust of "self-expression" and its connection to control and authority, to "being ruled," is especially typified in the texts by Eliot and Lewis I have already mentioned. They also conveniently, if not somewhat arbitrarily, allow us to set some historical parameters for this discussion of modernist impersonality, which I begin at 1919 and 1926, particularly because both Eliot's "Tradition and the Individual Talent" and Lewis's *The Art of Being Ruled* demonstrate just how explicit the terms "personality" and "impersonality" had become in modernist literary and cultural debate during the six years between the publication of the two texts.[13] They also link the question of impersonality to authority, to the rules that govern and produce talent, itself a dimension of aesthetic authority. Furthermore, Lewis's critique of popular psychology underscores a connection that characterizes many of the theories of personality and impersonality I examine in this book but that leads to different ethical and political ends: that between the psychological and psychoanalytic theories of "personality" and the illusory humanist ideal of individualism; he thus aligns the prerogative to dispel "personality" with a critique of democracy that includes his self-proclaimed preference for authoritarian regimes.

Taking Lewis as an example, I would suggest that Levenson is basically correct in reading modernism as it developed against ideas of individuality and subjectivity, but the story becomes more complicated when the terms "personality" and "impersonality" come into play. As Levenson's work suggests, particularly when read in the context of Lewis's wrathful disdain for personality, the development of the impersonal aesthetic in modernism appears as a response to the humanist ideals of personality that attended democratic modernity, particularly as they promoted a unified depth model of selfhood and psychology. In general, Lewis's specifically antimodern modernism points a suspecting finger at what is, according to Fredric Jameson, the modern equation of individualism with "consciousness as such," particularly as it "purports to characterize the inner climate of the liberated individual and his relation to his own being."[14] This book then addresses how this distrust of identity and reflexive individuality extends throughout literary modernism, even as modernist texts counterintuitively invoke concepts that have generally been attributed to humanism.

Humanism, as I use it here, describes the kind of "anthropological" associations that centralize subjects in terms of egos, psychologies, and subjectivities.[15] It is in many ways a spatial concept, and I argue here that modernists responded to it as such. For example, the modernist critic T. E. Hulme, writing in *Speculations: Essays on Humanism and the Philosophy of Art* (1924), defines humanism as bound to a "conception of personality," a "new psychology, or anthropology" characterized by "a temper or disposition of mind which can[not] look at a *gap* or chasm without shuddering."[16] Humanism is a mantra whose "fundamental error is that of placing Perfection in *humanity*, thus giving rise to that bastard thing Personality, and all the bunkum that follows from it" (*Speculations* 33). The emotional shudder Hulme identifies reflects the prefabricated copycat form of personality Lewis so virulently attacks, a "new psychology" where emotion exists only in the realm of its expression, and the subject, in his inability to cross boundaries or space, lives in perpetual isolation.

This notion of "psychology," based as it is on the notion that humans have depths to be plumbed or expressed, allows us to understand impersonality as a profoundly phenomenological reorientation of space. To think of impersonality spatially allows us to better comprehend how the term might be linked to relationships that reproduce asymmetry, authority, and domination. Given this line of argument, I consistently draw on phenomenology as a theoretical model, particularly as modernists, in their response to humanism, sought to reshape the person. In *Phenomenology of Perception*, Merleau-Ponty defines phenomenology as an anti-Cartesian critique of the "*detached* . . . subject, or consciousness," faulting the human tendency toward "analytical reflection," which always "goes back to the subject as a condition of possibility," not the "world," and further, knows "nothing of the problem of other minds or of that of the world, because it insists that with the first glimmer of consciousness there appears in me theoretically the power of reaching some universal truth, and that the other person, being equally without thisness, location or body, the Alter and the Ego are one and the same in the true world which is the unifier of minds" (*Phenomenology* ix, xi, xii). In other words, rather than orienting the subject around the world, humanism disregards the world by making the subject the center of truth. In doing so, it authoritatively invades the other, depriving it of location, or being in the world, at the same time that it locks itself in space. The notion of a detached, reflexive, and depth-oriented human subject thus enables authoritative domination and asymmetry. In contrast, as Merleau-Ponty elaborates later in *Phenomenology*, spatial orientation changes when an object is "stripped of . . . anthropological association" (*Phenomenology* 101). There is no longer a "top" or "bottom," an "on" or "under," no hierarchy of positions that places the object in an inferior position to the human. Space, or what Merleau-Ponty refers to as the "world," essentially equalizes all things so that "bodily content remains, in relation to it, something opaque, fortuitous, and unintelligible" (*Phenomenology* 101). That is, in an impersonally oriented world that rejects the singularized person as its center, the individual is without content, protected from the gaze of those who would, to borrow from Eliot's Prufrock, "fix," "pin," and "formulat[e]" ("Prufrock" 15).

As we shall see in the accounts of modernist impersonality that follow, this lack of intelligibility and phenomenological, often queer sense of spatiality characterize the modernist rejection of psychology and the corresponding desire to equalize, albeit in a sometimes limited way, specific hierarchical social relationships. As Scott Herring has observed, this sort of "unknowing" privileges the inscrutability of identity in ways that problematize sexual epistemology in particular.[17] Because impersonality collapses individual depth, it supports what Tim Dean (following Gabriel Rotello's *Sexual Ecology*) advances as "[e]cological thinking," which promotes the ideal of experiencing social and sexual relations horizontally rather than vertically; this function of impersonality simultaneously "unstraightens," to quote Sarah Ahmed, conventional forms of spatial and sexual orientation.[18] While Dean engages a psychoanalytic viewpoint, to think of relationships ecologically means to view them phenomenologically, in profile, creating a sense of interrelatedness that exposes the "radical limits of human autonomy" (*Beyond* 154). Similarly, in *Touching Feeling*, Eve Sedgwick also acknowledges the productive possibilities of emptying depth, of being "beside" each other, but she suggests that ecological positions often flatten space, so that relationships lose dimension.[19] In regard to modernism and impersonality, I argue that replacing a personal "under" with an impersonal "beside"—which is, as Merleau-Ponty illustrates, a primarily phenomenological position—disturbs conventional ideals of dimension while making room for new ones that diminish asymmetries in power.

In its focus on the shifting scales of space and dimension, this book then examines a modernist critique of humanism that proceeds by retaining some of its very concepts, particularly in the ideals of human relation and social engagement humanism supports. As I suggest in the discussions of Wyndham Lewis, Oscar Wilde, Virginia Woolf, D. H. Lawrence, H.D., Mary Butts, Elizabeth Bowen, and other modernist figures that follow, these versions of impersonality, though often problematic, do not necessarily preclude forms of affect and attachment that dismantle authority precisely by diminishing the "person" as the "condition of possibility" (*Phenomenology* xi). Many of these texts, particularly those by women, have yet to be addressed in terms of their explicit critical engagement with impersonality, which has generally been understood to be incompatible with feminism. Critical accounts of modernism such as Levenson's, for example, which read impersonality resolutely as a detached and conservative aesthetic that shuns all forms of affective expression, can be partially credited for this omission, along with the role of feminist criticism in privileging "subjective" or "experimental" aspects of women's literature over more "objective" and "masculine" forms of writing—that is, in privileging the person over the world. While feminist criticism has begun to move away from such binary critical templates, critics generally have not considered the question of how political and aesthetic imperatives that appear antithetical to feminist ideals might actually offer novel avenues for understanding these ideals, as I argue with regard to the modernist poet H.D. in Chapter 2.

While this book does not intend to concretize connections between "women writers"—or focus on gender specifically—it does stress the importance of a more nuanced understanding of impersonality that may be simultaneously compatible with and troubling to what are generally taken to be the aims of women. At the same time, it resists reifying these aims, particularly with regard to women writers and their relationships with their male contemporaries. As I discuss in Chapter 2, feminist critics have typically faulted the neutralizing effects of a masculinely inspired impersonality on the particularity of women's experience. I attempt to counter these conclusions by reinterpreting the dynamics of impersonality, focusing instead on the term as a means of reorienting the originally detached and reflexive humanist subject—the person—toward a greater "world." In this conception, gender can be thought of as one form of "personhood" that modernist intellectuals found both necessary and problematic. In my discussions of H.D., Mary Butts, and Elizabeth Bowen, I attempt to illustrate how impersonality, as a dialectical, spatial phenomenon, need not preclude personal experience. Indeed, the most progressive forms of the impersonal aesthetic link its demand for abstraction with both novel technologies of scale and space and distinct levels of emotion. For example, as I argue of H.D., the poetic masochism of the celebrated "poetess" produces an intense affective experience that requires rigorous maintenance of physical space. Such a practice enables the woman poet to dissolve the physical boundaries of personhood that define her gender without fully discarding the specificity of her social experience of gender. More generally, impersonality enabled the women who appear in this study to imagine new forms of intellectual affiliations that transcended gender as a feature of personhood. As I suggest in the analysis of "Tradition and the Individual Talent" that follows, Eliot's own concept of impersonality offers a model for how gendered particularity might be synthesized with the externalized collective forms of aesthetic perspective that characterize impersonality.

T. S. Eliot and Poetic Emotion

While this book reaches beyond Eliot in tracing the development of modernist impersonality, its point is not to diminish altogether his centrality to the concept. Indeed, in extending the critical discussion of impersonality to new texts and contexts, one must first interrogate the establishment of Eliot's impersonality as a conservative and authoritarian ideal. Colleen Lamos has persuasively identified the ways in which the "waywardness of gender identifications and sexual desires" contained within Eliot's writings "inform and deform their declared aesthetic aims."[20] "Tradition and the Individual Talent," she argues, condemns an error or "perversion," that is the "expressions of one's feelings," only to find "another way of indulging them" through the "act of renunciation" (*Errancy* 24). My own rereading of Eliot's "Tradition and the Individual Talent" takes a similar direction, particularly in regard to the issue of affect, but emphasizes how the potentially reparative, even progressive, arguments embedded in the essay might support a more nuanced, politically complex understanding of impersonality that interrogates the usefulness of locating emotion in the individual subject.[21] The point of my focus here on Eliot is also to establish some of the key contradictions of impersonality—particularly regarding emotion, self-expression, and authority—as they will appear throughout this book and in the work of other modernist figures. To begin, Eliot advocates an official doctrine of "impersonality" to address the problem that personality, as a product of humanist individualism, presents for literary form. Speaking of depersonalization as a productive factor in literary tradition, Eliot's counterintuitive turn recasts the humanist critique of an impersonal and alienating modernity in the service of art and tradition. That is, from Eliot's viewpoint, this very depersonalization will overcome modernity's fiction of individuality and lead back to the world of art, tradition, and true creative individualism. On one hand, then, what could be interpreted as Eliot's progressive call for poetic collectivity in the imperative to "transcend what is individual, what is the peculiar essence of the man" for a poetic community or the "medium" of tradition quickly bleeds into a more reactionary and authoritarian process of artistic selection designed to secure only those most fit for that community (*Prose* 42). On the other, however, "Tradition and the Individual Talent" theorizes a radical mode of affective engagement, "poetic emotion," which transcends individual psychology and subjectivity to gain intensity only in the absence of expression. This ideal of impersonal poetic emotion brings us once again to the modernist critique of humanism, as exemplified by Hulme's distrust of the "new psychology . . . or anthropology" (*Speculations* 33). Martin Jay has offered a provocative historical account of this widespread modernist distrust of "psychologism"—and its "unprecedented preoccupation with the interior landscape of the subject"—tracing it through the work of Kant, Husserl, Hulme, and finally to Eliot, arguing that the poet most fully incorporated this suspicion into aesthetic modernism in his ardent promulgation of "anti-psychological arguments."[22] These injunctions against the personality, Jay contends, championed a form of "self-absorption" that rigidly demarcated subject from object, working in the service of detachment and objectivity against the prospect of emotion ("MSP" 101). I suggest in contrast that Eliot's theory of impersonality, and his corresponding ideal of poetic emotion, allows both subject and object to escape their respective boundaries. Without referencing the term explicitly, Charles Altieri has articulated how an ideal of emotion in modernist tracts might act as an aesthetic alternative to psychology, crediting Eliot with fashioning an "alternative model of affective life" that critiques a "romantic expressivist" model of emotion and identity.[23] In opposition to this notion of a singular self that is the repository of emotion, modernists such as Ezra Pound most directly characterize emotion as disciplinary and aesthetic rather than romantic, a necessary aspect of managing impersonality, particularly in the claim that "[e]motion is an organiser of form."[24] If emotion is attached to the individual, then the statement is itself contradictory, since form is by definition not related to individualized expressions but instead generalizable ones. However, if impersonality dissolves the boundaries that separate individuals, then some device must exist to guard against the complete dissolution of literary form and space, as a means of retaining order.

Eliot more clearly illustrates how a specific type of "poetic emotion" might organize literary form, a concept he introduces by way of contradiction, describing the poet's mind as a type of catalyst that remains "inert," "neutral," and "unaffected" in the presence of two elements: "emotions and feelings" (*Prose* 41). Eliot does not explicitly distinguish between "feeling" and "emotion," but he does treat them as separate categories in poetic composition: "[G]reat poetry may be made without the direct use of any emotion whatever: composed out of feelings, solely. Canto XV of the *Inferno* (Brunetto Latini) is a working up of the emotion evident in the situation" (*Prose* 41). Judging from this passage, it is certain that Eliot distinguishes feelings from emotion; whereas feeling attaches itself personally to the poet, emotion arises from the artistic process itself, not the individual poet.

In other words, feeling, which enters the poet's mind and aids the creative process, is a means to emotion as an end. In no way does this emotion have an individual referent, such as the poet. Whereas "feelings" are integral to the poet's personal creative process, they have no place in the greater impersonal "medium" of poetry, which is controlled and organized by emotion.

Critics such as Ed Comentale have also noted Eliot's need to "transform the 'excesses' of emotion into a neatly organized, highly rational social structure" (*MCP* 84). Taking as an example Eliot's essay "Hamlet," which discredits Shakespeare's play because its emotion is in "*excess* of the facts as they appear," Comentale argues that Eliot's desire is to tame the "crude emotional material" and correspondingly, "all that is messy about the self" (*Prose* 48, italics in original; *MCP* 84). This reading of Eliot as vigorously engaged in disciplining excess and overproduction, whether it be in emotion, art, or the marketplace, into tight organizational principles, certainly characterizes one aspect of the poet's thinking about emotion. Yet emotion for Eliot is more than a passive excess to be structured, controlled, and disciplined; it is an organizing and controlling force in own right. For Eliot, emotion is wasted when it is not properly generalized in the service of art and tradition—and ultimately form—when it limits itself too specifically to one individual. That is, the impulse to discipline and organize the "excesses" of emotion is in actuality a means to catalyze its agency in the first place.

Eliot indeed distinguishes "ordinary," psychological emotions from poetic ones; these "feelings which are not in actual emotions at all" are personal "[i]mpressions and experiences" (*Prose* 42). Thus "personal emotion," or the type of emotion "provoked by particular events in [a poet's] life," is a necessary catalyst of poetic, impersonal emotion, even though no trace of the earlier form of emotion should appear in the latter state. Poetic emotion is, explicitly, "a concentration, and a new thing resulting from a number of experiences which to the practical and active person would not seem to be experiences at all; it is a concentration which does not happen consciously or of deliberation" (*Prose* 43). According to Eliot's logic, emotion is neither subjective nor personal. Rather, it is concentrated and amenable to order because of its role in uniting a cacophony of experiences—much like a less violent version of Pound's vortex.[25] In likening poetic emotion to a "concentration," Eliot's counterintuitive claim is that emotion moves outward, away from psychology as an interpretive depth model of selfhood in a form of affect that cannot be expressed, recollected, collated, or analyzed. Eliot thus promotes poetic emotion as a collective phenomenon that "does not happen consciously or deliberately," meaning it resists individualizing psychology or subjectivity at the same time that it holds the boundaries of individuality—and the very organizational parameters of poetry as an individualized form—intact.

Furthermore, Eliot's use of the term "concentration" is particularly crucial in describing a type of individuality or difference that does not accord with commonly held ideas of identity and selfhood. The concentration we see here also conforms to what Eliot designates as "the new" and the individual (*Prose* 38). In more general terms, this sense of newness or individuality could stand in for a number of designations, such as gender, sexuality, or race, all of which refer to "personal" experience. Therefore, despite its homage to tradition and poetic doctrine, Eliot's version of impersonality and poetic emotion ultimately enables a structure of emotional connection that transcends the individual identities of its participants. What this in some ways deeply conservative essay offers is a radical form of emotional connection that transcends the boundaries of humanist selfhood, psychology, and identity. However, this particular emotional register does not dismiss personal experience and identity altogether. Rather, it takes the form of a collective forum or "medium" that resists individual psychology but simultaneously emerges from the *trace* of individual experience. This miniaturist trace of individualized structure functions beyond psychology, allowing one to express the "grains" of difference within an abstracted impersonal space. Since this emotional plane is not subject to interpretation or expression, it provides an alternative to the conventional, anthropomorphic humanism both Hulme and Lewis denigrate. For the purposes of critical theory, this impersonal understanding of emotion refuses to center the subject as a repository of psychological depth that can be interpreted, collated, or analyzed. At the same time, this rereading of impersonality provides an alternative to a poststructuralist decentering of the subject that understands human depth and affect as constructed fictions. Since it addresses the question of depth, this impersonal emotion can, as I have suggested, be interpreted as a spatial phenomenon. The phenomenological process of "concentration" Eliot outlines narrows, even flattens "expressed" or psychological forms of emotion. Because this emotion does not apply to a centralized subject that can be the source of study or interpretation, it occasions a movement in space that disturbs the barriers that separate inside from outside. The poetic emotional interior exists externally and vice versa. Accordingly, Eliot's poetic emotion can be thought of as a surface or plane that exteriorizes collective emotional experience.

Because it extends beyond the individual as a mode of feeling, the poetic emotion, Eliot elaborates, allows us to see more clearly how impersonality might both decenter and build authority. On one hand, and as can be extrapolated from Eliot's ideas about poetic emotion, modernist impersonality supports distanced and strange intimacies, wherein subjects and objects demonstrate their attachment to each other while preserving specific boundaries. Given this regard for spatial demarcation, the ideal manifestations of this impersonality dispel authority by ensuring regard for the boundaries of other subject positions, offering an opening into the external world that extends beyond psychology, subjectivity, and personality. Authority, on the other hand, can be seen as an overt structure of invasion, a spatial situation that impersonality can also sustain, occurring precisely through the forms of interior "access" that enable impersonal connection, as texts such as H.D.'s *Sea Garden* illustrate (*Prose* 45).

One example that more clearly illustrates how this dynamic between impersonality and authority operates is the question of empathy, which I explore in more detail in my discussion of Elizabeth Bowen's 1934 novel *The Death of the Heart*. The title itself implies not only a concrete death of the heart but its symbolic death: the death of feeling for others and the death of empathic engagement with both humans and objects. Modernist discussions of empathy, such as Wilhelm Worringer's 1908 treatise *Abstraction and Empathy*, actually challenge the humanist ideal of empathy as a matter of individual psychology and subjectivity, where the self is idealized as a reflection of the world around it. This subjectivist view of empathy reproduces authority, invading other subject positions, including works of art, with the "world" of the viewer's personality. As an alternative to this kind of aesthetic subjectivism, Worringer advocates an alternative, "abstraction," a form of apprehension that envisions beauty in the subject's pantheistic communion with the forms around him or her, which occurs precisely through submission to them. This form of impersonal spectatorship abstracts the subject, such that viewing art decenters the self as it both alienates and affirms the viewer. While Worringer's treatise ostensibly centers on the world of art, it clearly outlines the perils of an overtly humanist, psychologically driven engagement with the world.

Read as a retreat from psychologically driven forms of affective expression, Worringer's version of abstraction coincides with Eliot's concept of poetic emotion and the form of interiority that emerges from it. Furthermore, Eliot's focus on the "surrender" of individuality, what is quite possibly the most radical aspect of his impersonality, aligns his work with even more radical practitioners of impersonality, most notably Yeats, and attests to the possibility of an impersonality that is invested as much in the dissolution of authority as it is in the defense of it. For example, Yeats's critical prose offers insight into a rather radical outgrowth of the forms of poetic collaboration suggested by Eliot's "Tradition and the Individual Talent." Works such as "A Packet for Ezra Pound" (1927), "A General Introduction to My Work" (1937), and "Magic" (1901) literally exemplify Eliot's imperative that the poet set himself "among the dead" (*Prose* 38).[26] Yeats's openness to the dead, whom he addresses as his "teachers," attests to his interest in diminishing his own authority ("Packet" 14). This mystical, occult vein of modernism links artistic creation directly to the living body as a channel or vessel through which the dead can speak. Through this "automatic script," the dead exemplify creative emotion; they speak in plural as a "we" from a variety of subject positions, yet with one concentrated voice ("Packet" 19).

My point here is not to discuss Yeats's impersonality in detail but to position him as an intermediary figure who connects the formalist authority of high modernist impersonality to its more radical spokes. In general, Yeats's particular version of impersonality provides important avenues into the meaning of the term as a theory of social and sexual relations. These variants include, but are not limited to, extreme theories of sexual submission, drug-induced torpors (in the case of Mary Butts), visits to mediums, ventriloquism, conjuring, gratuitous violence, somnambulism (as in the case of *Nightwood's* Robin Vote), fantasies of prosthetic selfhood, and poetic and sexual masochism. However disparate, each of these strains of impersonality is characterized by an ideological dimension that refuses a unified sense of self and psychology, a personality. The form of automatism and ventriloquism Yeats elaborates and all the variants of it that I mention earlier are automatic precisely because they deny individual psychology, resist a unified presentation of personality, and, to use Eliot's terms, flee "deliberation" or self-consciousness (*Prose* 43).

Beside and Beyond: Engaged Modernism

As a mode of engagement that moves beyond humanist understandings of selfhood and psychology, I argue that impersonality, despite its connections to some unpalatable political ideals, is a spatial dynamic that can potentially destabilize authority. The individual chapters of this book examine how the models of impersonality in modernist texts both fulfill and disappoint this ideal. Chapter 1, "'The Dissociation of Personality': Space and the Impersonal Ideal," establishes the historical groundwork for understanding the meaning of "personality," particularly as it developed in relation to concepts of space and popular authority in early twentieth-century Britain and America. Drawing upon a variety of literary, architectural, artistic, and quasiscientific texts, including those by Le Corbusier, Gaudier-Brzeska, Georg Simmel, F. W. H. Myers, and Morton Prince, this chapter gauges several artistic responses to the pervasive idea of personality as a social term, including the hypermasculinized version of impersonality Wyndham Lewis advocates in *The Art of Being Ruled* and the theory of personality as mask Oscar Wilde prizes in his famous *Intentions* essays (1891). The chapter finally looks to Virginia Woolf's ode to itinerant cruising,

"Street Haunting: A London Adventure" (1930), to identify an "impersonal spatial practice" that offers a more explicit alternative to Lewis's hostility.

Chapter 2, "The Impersonal Contract: H.D. and the Limits of Poetic Authority," extends this focus on space to the questions of dimension and boundary implicated in H.D.'s theories of poetic form and authority. In self-consciously exploring its own contractual relation to poetic impersonality—such that personal submission to impersonal aesthetic authority pays off—H.D.'s 1916 collection *Sea Garden* produces a poetics that is at once invested in authority and in its demise. In particular, the masochistic gestures I identify in her lyrics trouble feminist criticism by theorizing an impersonal interiority that denies a psychology of gender, especially as her poetic personae invade and inhabit variously gendered subjects. Ultimately, H.D.'s lyrics often collapse the distinction between interior and exterior dimensions of psychic life, subject and object, and active and passive subject positions. But more problematically, I suggest, this impersonal collapse imagines poetic authority and "voice" in the invasive takeover of other subject positions, honoring a poetic community that attempts to limit poetic access to a select few.

Chapter 3, "A 'Peculiar Feeling of Intimacy': D. H. Lawrence, Modernist Violence, and Impersonal Narrative," examines the same spatial questions about boundary and dimension that emerge from H.D.'s lyrics, but as they influence narrative form. In doing so, the chapter probes the relationship between impersonality and violence, arguing that, as a *Bildungsroman* (novel of development), Lawrence's *Sons and Lovers* embraces a code of action that both repudiates the heterosexual romance of the novel and aligns its project with work. For Lawrence's Paul Morel and his respective *Bildung*, an impersonal relation to the world offers a highly attractive but often dangerous, even fatal, means of altering the relational dimensions of the traditional heterosexual romance. In this capacity, the text reflexively meditates on its own impersonal strategies and the impersonal ideals of its hero, who continually resists assimilation into a psychologically based, hermeneutically oriented depth-model of character. Despite this seemingly progressive, queer critique of the *Bildungsroman* as a novelistic form, Lawrence's tendency to resort to violence as the agent for both forming interior bonds and eradicating psychology and personality from erotic relations demonstrates the ethical fissure in an impersonality designed to progressively equalize social relations. In general, the novel's violence appears as the logical outgrowth of the more general problem of an impersonal impulse that might potentially overtake the meaning of space and form.

Chapters 3 and 4 then suggest how an impersonal understanding of the object world, particularly as it appears in the work of Elizabeth Bowen and Mary Butts, might also counter this violence. Both writers, I argue, respond to what Christopher Reed has identified as the "anti-domestic tenor of avant-garde architectural theory" as embraced by figures such as Lewis and Lawrence, especially as it sanctions violence and repudiates the intimate values of domestic space in favor of an impersonal, deprivatized politics of living.[27] More specifically, Chapter 4, "Problem Space: Wyndham Lewis, Mary Butts, and the Impersonal Object," highlights the vexed relation Butts saw between the object and its relation to authoritative forms of ownership—from the literary authority of Paris' established salon set, a.k.a. Gertrude Stein and company, to the nationally condoned thievery of one of Britain's greatest institutional and imperialist titans, the British Museum. To set up the terms of this discussion, the chapter begins with a look at *Blast*, the 1913 literary publication that put the object at center stage, along with its editor and proponent of a highly masculinized avant-garde theory, Wyndham Lewis. Arguably as frustrated with the current status of the object in the art world as Lewis, Butts theorizes the object not as a detached entity but as a point of attachment and route to human connection. In stories such as "In Bloomsbury" (1932), "From Altar to Chimney Piece" (1938), and "With or Without Buttons" (1938), as in her best-known novel, *Armed With Madness* (1928), Butts's prose counterintuitively emphasizes the role of a grounded or situated object life in theorizing impersonality as an idealized synthesis of "passion and detachment."[28]

In making this argument, I deal not so much with the production of objects as with what situations and spaces objects produced for modernism. This focus is evident in Chapter 5, "'A Solicitude for Things': Elizabeth Bowen and the *Bildungsroman*," which, moving from the argument of Chapter 4, contends that Bowen's novel *The Death of the Heart* self-consciously advances an impersonal vision of the object world that critiques bourgeois social relations without repudiating domestic values of intimacy. It also returns to the issues of genre and form that ground Chapters 1 and 2—on H.D. and D. H. Lawrence, respectively—arguing that by dismantling subjectivity and personality, Bowen critiques and redraws the conventional *Bildungsroman* and its fantasy of bourgeois socialization—where personality is constructed through the authoritative and exclusive appropriation of objects. Ultimately, *The Death of the Heart* elaborates an impersonal vision of the object world that, neither detached nor sentimental, facilitates a space for empathic exchange.

However, as "Tradition and the Individual Talent" illustrates, some form of self and psychology, of "personality," is necessary for creating an interior—an affective "space" that positions subjects beside each other—such that dimension or structure exists in tandem with a flattened connection that promotes collectivity. As a means of negotiating this dynamic, the impersonal aesthetic offered modernists an attractive solution to many of the political and metaphysical problems modernity presented to them in imagining their own roles as artists and intellectuals. As an aesthetic practice, impersonality offered an antidote to the tedious individualist ethos apparent in modernity's bourgeois conceptions of progress, social development, and sexual norms. Yet the authoritative violence inherent to impersonality encodes serious contradictions and ethical problems. These are problems of space and organization. For example, how can women and other socially marginal groups impersonally efface their individuality without relinquishing their autonomy or the force of their political presence? This quandary exemplifies only one of the problems that arises in the wake of impersonality, particularly regarding the loss of emotional and affective connection that develops from modernity's failure to synthesize its reverence for impersonal mobility and its nostalgic attraction to the fixed self and personality: the literal death of the heart. In search of an antidote to this sense of loss, I ultimately want to articulate how an impersonal aesthetic that obliterates a humanist sense of self might maintain its "heart" through collective engagement with others. Sustaining this "heart" is especially important within an aesthetic that threatens spatial dimension as it dissolves boundaries between individuals and progressively challenges the very meanings of human particularity and literary form. Ultimately, impersonality's most progressive potential is also its most reactionary. In what follows, I discuss how modernist texts grapple with the problem of this impersonal condition, both in their attempts to reduce the social disparities of aesthetic creation and as a means of creating an engaged modernism.

1

"The Dissociation of Personality"

Space and the Impersonal Ideal

> If wandering is the liberation from every given point in space, and thus the conceptional opposition to fixation at such a point, the sociological form of the "stranger" presents the unity, as it were, of these two characteristics. This phenomenon too, however, reveals that spatial relations are only the condition, on the one hand, and the symbol, on the other, of human relations. The stranger is . . . the person who comes today and stays tomorrow. He is, so to speak, the potential wanderer: although he has not moved on, he has not quite overcome the freedom of coming and going. He is fixed within a particular spatial group, or within a group whose boundaries are similar to spatial boundaries. But his position in this group is determined, essentially, by the fact that he has not belonged to it from the beginning, that he imports qualities into it, which do not and cannot stem from the group itself.
>
> The unity of nearness and remoteness involved in every human relation is organized, in the phenomenon of the stranger, in a way which must be briefly formulated by saying that in the relationship to him, distance means that he, who is close by, is far, and strangeness means that he, who also is far, is actually near. For, to be a stranger is naturally a very positive relation; it is a specific form of interaction.
>
> —Georg Simmel[1]

As early as 1908, Georg Simmel articulated the potential value of impersonal spatial relations. The particular sociological impersonality of Simmel's stranger is not unlike the specific literary articulations of impersonality that arose just a few years later. Though he does not mention the term explicitly in this passage, Simmel theorizes something akin to what modernists would call "personality" as it develops from spatial and social interaction. As I will argue here, the aesthetic impersonality modernists would employ later was a response to this idea of personality as a sociospatial concept. According to this logic, having or possessing a personality entails the ability to socially demarcate oneself, to occupy a distinct unit of social space. For a sociologist such as Simmel, "personality" is linked to singularity and individuation. Furthermore, social space is not meaningful outside of the value it acquires from this sort of human organization. Within this spatial organization, the stranger inhabits the best of both worlds; his "personality" is made possible through a condition of spatial fixity that offers freedom of interaction without complete "liberation from every given point in space" (*Sociology* 402). That is, his fixed position within social space grants him a personality, but his "distance" ensures that that space is dynamic, neither overly static nor completely in flux. Like "the really new" Eliot praises in "Tradition and the Individual Talent," which "modifie[s]" and "alters" the "existing monuments" of tradition into a new order, Simmel's stranger also "imports qualities" into the existing social group, "which do not and cannot stem from the group itself" (*Sociology* 402).[2] Thus we can see how this sociological understanding of the stranger's relationship to the group might parallel the relation Eliot would later draw between the "new" and the order of tradition. Furthermore, as with Eliot's version of impersonality, Simmel's stranger demonstrates that personal and impersonal experiences are not mutually exclusive states of existence.

I begin this chapter with Simmel because his work most convincingly establishes connections between a sociological concept of impersonality and its manifestation in literary modernism. While my intention here is not to draw easy parallels, Simmel's stranger ideally resolves the principle dilemma of impersonality this book identifies—the question of how organizational structure is maintained in the wake of an aesthetic that operates by undermining individual distinction. As Simmel remarks, the stranger himself is a "principle of organization" that synthesizes the "nearness and remoteness" in every human relationship (*Sociology* 404). The stranger represents a "very positive relation." In two places at once, he offers an idealized "unity" between the impersonal distance that threatens to dissolve space altogether and the personalized nearness that threatens to too fully insulate it (*Sociology* 402). For Simmel, personality indicates a more fixed and isolated engagement with the social world. The word appears explicitly as a term of sociological analysis throughout his work and seems to indicate both the condition of social distinction and the means by which one achieves it; the ability to realize such distinction defines the "personality value of the individual," Simmel remarks, suggesting that the personality may be either weak or strong.[3] In this sense, and as Simmel explains in his analysis of adornment and personal style, personality builds upon an important contradiction; "personality value" is built by cultivating those altruistic relationships that ultimately threaten to undermine it. Simmel examines this characteristic of personality more intimately in his oft-cited essay "The Metropolis and Mental Life" (1903) where he explains how "the personality accommodates itself in the adjustments to external forces" (*Sociology* 409). Rather than singularity, this spatially oriented form of personality exercises no autonomy; it is defined instead by its malleability, existing only in relation to the "external forces" that sculpt and modify it.

In Simmel's account of modernity, "the leveling down of the [real] person by the social-technological mechanism"—and the resulting prominence of a personality characterized by its "adjustments" and modifications—accounts for the "deepest problems of modern life" (*Sociology* 409). In drawing attention to this claim, I do not wish to imply that Simmel is nostalgically lamenting some lost world of individual creativity or true personality. However, this understanding of personality as inherently weak allows us to distinguish between the depersonalization that, according to Simmel, characterizes life in the modern metropolis and the aesthetic impersonality employed by modernists. For Simmel, depersonalization results in a set of psychological conditions where personality falsely parades as individuality. This sociological conception of personality provides important context for understanding the more acute distress over "the escape from personality" displayed by modernists such as Wyndham Lewis, particularly in his injunctions against the "personality" as a market-driven, illusive "sugar-plum" of freedom and self-expression.[4] The connections between these critiques of modernity—one explicitly sociological and the other aesthetic—are driven, I argue, by a shared understanding of the meaning of personality as a spatial phenomenon tied to social authority and engagement. Consequently, the first half of this chapter explores the meaning of the term "personality" itself. In addition to Simmel's sociological model of personality, works in the developing sciences of personality by F. W. H. Myers and Morton Prince in particular elaborate a contradictory notion where the very authority of personality—derived from the ability to fix itself within social space—renders it vulnerable to fragmentation and chaos.

This contradiction is not unlike the dialectic of personal and impersonal experience that Eliot will later theorize in his own modernism. I thus argue in the second part of this chapter that this primarily spatial understanding of personality, particularly in its relation to authority, propels a number of modernist responses to the term by figures as diverse as Lewis, Henri Gaudier-Brzeska, and Virginia Woolf. I speak of authority here as it relates specifically to the magnetism and influence personality exercises within social and aesthetic space. This rather abstract idea of authority, as opposed to a primarily empathic relation to space, depends on the maintenance of personal boundaries and distinction. For sociologists such as Simmel, one must project a certain amount of authority for his "personality" to have "value" in the first place. However, as Simmel also illustrates, the various acts of engagement that personality entails render it vulnerable to fracture and fissure, such that authority and engagement work both in tandem and against each other (*Sociology* 49). Given this paradox, having a personality, as much as it is connected to social dominance, subjects one to potential deauthorization. Nonetheless, for Simmel, personality is also a necessary component in organizing social relationships. For this reason, modernists such as Woolf, Gaudier-Brzeska, and Le Corbusier attempted to liberate space from the very limits of its organization around the bourgeois individual or personality—the altruistic human relations that, for Simmel, make spatial relations possible. Despite the radical possibilities of these critiques, I argue that, in one way or the other, modernists such as Gaudier-Brzeska and Le Corbusier could not escape the paradox that informs Simmel's sociological critique of modernity. In their efforts to reimagine the human as a technology that exceeds "personal" organization or scale, they consistently return to the idea of personal authority in imagining meaningfully organized space. Only Woolf, I argue, advances a more ethical logic of impersonality that reorients space in the service of empathic engagement.

The Failures of Personality

The word "personality" appears so prominently in early modernist texts that its meaning is rarely explicitly articulated. "Personality" is so critical to the overall meaning of "Tradition and the Individual Talent" that Eliot does not define it; he rather gestures toward his audience, claiming that "only those who have personality and emotions know what it means to escape from these things" (*Prose* 43). Only a select few "know" what it means to have a personality, suggesting that "personality" is an acquisition, something one may or may not have. Within the strict parameters of the essay, the term comes to signify, quite broadly, something like literary individualism and self-expression. As with Lewis and Hulme, so troubled by that "bastard thing Personality," much of the modernist distrust of modernity and bourgeois individuality fastens to this version of "personality" as it connotes a sham individualism characterized by emotive messiness and disorder.[5] Here, the presumed authority and strength of personality as it relates to individualism and social singularity can quickly transform into a lack of self-possession catalyzed by self-expression and mimicry. That is, personality is weak. It is acted upon, modified, altered, adjusted, acquired, possessed, and often, for the sake of artistic authority, given up.

Personality as a function of ownership or possession implies both dominance and submission, activity and passivity, a problem that Warren Susman corroborates in his classic essay "'Personality' and the Making of

Twentieth-Century Culture." While its context is American popular and political culture in the 1920s, the essay allows us to imagine a specific social terrain to which modernists such as Lewis were responding. For Susman, the shift from a "culture of character to a culture of personality" rests on a "spiritual vision" of self-realization and self-making, new discourses of sociology and psychology, and the rise of self-help culture.[6] The link between personality and self-realization appears in the slew of self-help manuals circulating at the time, generated by the success of Samuel Smiles's *Self-Help*, which was published in 1859 but continued to sell in the early twentieth century.[7] In keeping with this literature, Susman claims that personality was to be built or constructed as opposed to character, which was generally defined in terms of good or bad. Consequently, words such as "*fascinating, stunning, attractive, magnetic, glowing, masterful, creative, dominant, forceful*" correspond to the condition of having a personality, of "being different, special, unusual, of standing out in the crowd," yet likeable at the same time (italics in original; "PM" 218). Implicitly, Susman's version of personality circulates around the spatial significance of the term. Certainly, the idea that having a personality requires the ability to stand out among others reflects a spatial, sociological notion of personal authority that takes us back to Simmel's stranger, who is "fixed within a particular spatial group, or within a group whose boundaries are similar to spatial boundaries" (*Sociology* 402). Moreover, the concept of personality as related to charm or charisma reinforces the meaning of the term as a function of one's spatial authority and, further, one's ability to influence others through effervescence and magnetism.

Susman's definition of "personality" coincides with Eliot's more implicit sense of the term: something that one acquires but that not everyone can have—an article of possession. As Sharon Cameron remarks, "*personality* stresses self-ownership, the of or possessive through which individuality is identified as one's own" (italics in original).[8] Following Hobbes's concept of the "person," Cameron argues that being a person establishes "intelligibility within a political and legal system," affording certain rights without presuming "anything of substance" (*Impersonality* viii). Since a person, according to Hobbes, is a "possessing agency," it follows that "personality" stresses one's possession of oneself (qtd. in *Impersonality* viii). In reference to Susman's analysis, one can then assume that one meaning of personality circulates around distinction, spatial fixity, and the forms of social demarcation that enhance personal authority or self-possession. Terms such as "dominant" and "forceful" announce the presence of a specific social relationship, often asymmetrical in power, contributing to the singularity of personality as a form of self-ownership. This connection between personality and authority over oneself and others is certainly important but also unstable, as it builds on social asymmetry and the domination of others. At the same time, this instability underscores the question of how those "personalities" less accepted by society—defined by racial, class, and sexual particularity—also came to be connected to the term, particularly for modernists such as Lewis.

That is, as much as its meaning circulates around social and political authority, personality also signifies a possible means of access to such authority for the disempowered. Perhaps this contradiction accounts for both the pervasiveness of the term in modernist texts and the anxiety it produces. Again, Simmel most convincingly outlines this dynamic in his sociological account of modernity, making explicit reference to the "personality" in his discussion of adornment, which, he argues, "intensifies or enlarges the personality by operating as a sort of radiation emanating from it" (*Sociology* 339).[9] Indeed, the "personality, so to speak, *is* more when it is adorned" (italics in original; *Sociology* 340). He observes further that "[a]dornment is the egoistic element as such; it singles out its wearer, whose self-feeling it embodies and increases at the cost of others . . . But, at the same time, adornment is altruistic: its pleasure is designed for the others, since its owner can enjoy it only insofar as he mirrors himself in them" (*Sociology* 339). Simmel's assessment here again hinges on the connection between personality and space. That is, the strength and authority of a personality reflects its mobility and its ability to permeate boundaries through an altruism that magnifies and mirrors the personality. However, this function of personality also contributes to its weakness, since adornment can be either put on or taken off. Like adornment, personality is an artificial matter characterized by its solubility, its tendency to dissipate after engorging itself too completely, particularly as it becomes subject to copy. This characteristic is essential to what Simmel calls "style," which "brings the contents of personal life and activity into a form shared by many and accessible to many" (*Sociology* 341). Personality functions analogously; whatever pretense to individuality and distinction it maintains, its accessibility renders it vulnerable to destabilization and deauthorization.

The historical notion of personality as accessible and thus vulnerable to invasion and, even more drastically, dissociation is a rather radical outgrowth of the dynamics of "style" Simmel identifies as well as the cultural trends Susman charts in his essay. Susman notes the popular fascination with Morton Prince's *The Dissociation of Personality* (1910) and its prolonged study of the famed Miss Beauchamp's multiple personalities; indeed, as similar texts suggest, this obsession with the sick self indicates an increasing cultural fascination not with the success or authority of personality but with its superficiality and likelihood to fail as a mode of self-presentation.[10] Asserting that such personality failures are productive, F. W. H. Myers's major work of "psychical research" *Human Personality and Its Survival of Bodily Death*, published posthumously in 1903 and best known for its influence on the modernist practice of automatic writing, argues that human personality, vulnerable to both order and disorder, is by nature a "much more *modifiable* complex of forces than is commonly assumed."[11] Myers advocates tapping into the integrated personality's capacity for "disturbances," particularly as a means for extending the magnetism of the personality beyond the confines of the body's physical boundaries. Ultimately, the text points to the radical potential of personality disturbance as it opens the possibility of new modes of relation among people, enabling forms of "supersensory communication" that extend beyond the various limitations of regular speech (*HP* 3). Myers explains this by stating that "each method of disintegration suggests a corresponding possibility of integration" (*HP* 47). That is, personal magnetism dialectically depends on the fractures inherent in the personality. This formulation is a quite radical precursor to the forms of occultism and automatic writing that modernists such as Yeats would advocate. By focusing on the fissures within the strong, authoritarian personality, Myers offers a version of personal magnetism and charisma that undercuts the domination of others.

Myers's work is part of what Ian Hacking has more recently termed the "sciences of memory," particularly in relation to the more current multiple personality movement, which he links to earlier practices of spiritism and beliefs in reincarnation.[12] Hacking emphasizes the role of "sexual ambivalence" in relation to "the disorder [of multiple personality] and its causes," arguing that the belief in multiple personality radically contests the "implicit definition of personality as a consolidation of self and identity" and enables one to break out of compulsory heterosexism and gendering by adopting other roles (*Rewriting* 69, 87). As with Myers and Simmel, Hacking's critique of personality rests on its relation to a defined sense of boundary or space. That is, the strength or authority of a personality depends on how well it "fixes" itself within the social space it inhabits as it simultaneously contacts and influences others. In keeping with Susman's definition of the term, a personality can charismatically extend into, inhabit, or dominate other social spaces besides its own. This particular characteristic distinguishes personality, especially in its importance to a modernist aesthetics, from the ego, the individual, character, or the self. While these concepts are related to personality, none are all-inclusive of what it means to have one. Personality both structures social space and is shaped by it. Myers takes this point even further by suggesting that supersensory communication "actually modifies a certain portion of space" as it "taps into" the fissures inherent in the personality (*HP* 151). He then appears to posit an objective space that exists outside of individual psychic space, where personality forms one point in a network of related entities. When personality displays its internal fissures, so does the space it inhabits.

Wyndham Lewis versus Oscar Wilde: Personality and the "Male-Invert Fashion"

In its debt to Simmel and the developing sciences of personality and psychology, the notion of personality as inherently modifiable—if not fissured and fragmented—attends the range of meanings it can adopt in modernist contexts, particularly regarding the explicitly negative reaction to the term that appears in the work of many modernists. As I mentioned earlier, within modernist thought, personality acquired very particularized meanings relating to sexuality, gender, and race; these meanings reflected a fundamental anxiety about access to authority within social space. Indeed, the strong, authoritative aspects of personality became the most likely to be subject to modernist attack, but oddly it was when these characteristics came to characterize minority identities. Modernist critics such as Lewis, for example, assault the bourgeois conception of personality Susman identifies, not simply in disdain for these characteristics, but also in his anxious desire to regulate access to this sort of social influence. That is, his contempt for personality and its authority in society was also fueled by his misogyny and homophobia. In essays such as "The 'Homo' the Child of the 'Suffragette'" and the "The Feminine Conception of Freedom," Lewis equates public political space with feminism, condemning suffragism and its creation of a political world that reflects only the demands of the feminist revolution.[13] Then, in a contradictory move, he seeks to invalidate democratic idealism by linking personality to private space, femininity, and women's situatedness within the private sphere.

Similarly, in *Blast* (1913)—Lewis's manifesto assaulting all things bourgeois and feeble—he employs the term "personality" as an index of spatial fixity to characterize the particular immobility of race. For example, in "The New Egos," Lewis claims that the "African . . . cannot allow his personality to venture forth or amplify itself."[14] He binds the African within a concretely limited form of emotional interiority that directly contrasts with that of the mobile "modern town dweller . . . who sees everywhere fraternal molds for his spirit" and for whom "[i]mpersonality has become a disease" (*Blast* 141). According to Lewis's misanthropic logic, neither of these new egos is admirable. The ideal ego would be neither too mobile nor too fixed in its location. In lacking or exceeding spatial containment or fixity, both the town dweller and the African evoke specific geographical topoi. Its abstract meaning aside, space generally connotes architectural structure, an outside and inside. Personal space conventionally evokes the inside, or the kind of interior that firmly embeds the highly embodied, racialized position of the African.[15]

In *The Art of Being Ruled*, Lewis also directs several of his polemics against the personality to certain partners in crime: the "feminist" and the "male-invert" or "homo" (*Art* 218). He observes in "The Role of Inversion in the War on the Intellect" that democracy requires "the greatest vanity for the greatest number," an imperative that governs "all the features of emotive life" (*Art* 216). That would be the emotive life of women and "inverts," who, if given the chance, would literally restructure space to cater to their needs: "First, the *salon* (the home of the *precieuses ridicules*) will be pitched next door to the nursery; then gradually the connecting door will become a large folding-door; and then at length all septum of any sort will disappear. The *precieuses ridicules*, dressed in baby frocks, will be on their floor with their dolls, or riding rocking-horses in Greek draperies" (*Art* 216). In this exaggerated reorganization of domestic space, Lewis envisions the triumph of "male inversion, the latest child of feminism . . . in these neighboring battlefields of the high and the low-brow" (*Art* 217). Such "refaynment . . . the *obligation* of culture, of a 'refayned' speech, and the unreality of millionaire luxury as a necessary background . . . goes with male inversion" (italics in original; *Art* 217). That is, certain personalized appropriations of domestic space make the "'homo' the legitimate child of the 'suffragette'" (*Art* 218).

It would be useful to find a starting point for the presumed collaboration Lewis posits between homosexuality and collective feminism. That point, as expressed by Lewis in "The Physiological Norm and the 'Vicious,'" would be Oscar Wilde, whose brilliant personality fully realizes Susman's list of adjectives: "[A]s he possessed to the full the proselytizing zeal that usually goes with sex inversion . . . he prepared the ground with his martyrdom, ecstatic recantations, eloquent and tear-ful confessions, and the great prestige of his wit, for the complete reversal of the erotic machinery that has ensued or is ensuing" (*Art* 209).[16] It is odd that Lewis attributes such noxious personal magnetism and authority to the "proselytizing zeal" of Oscar Wilde, a man so punished by the democratic system and clearly invested with a "personality" predicated on sexual meanings that were antithetical to bourgeois norms. Wilde did publish several tracts on decoration, including his influential *Decorative Art in America* (1906), which broached such topics as fashion, acting, and modeling.[17] But Lewis goes so far as to position Wilde directly alongside the "'Nancyism' of the joy-boy or the joy-man—the overmannered personality," complete with "the grating or falsetto lisp" (*Art* 210). Overall, Lewis counts "Oscar-Wildeanism" as part of "The Feminine Conception of Freedom," the topic of another short piece from *The Art of Being Ruled*, which gives little credit to suffragist ideology or Wilde's own musings on the nature of personality (*Art* 239).

Aside from its connection to Lewis's modernism, Wilde's own role as a "personality" and its relation to his legendary queerness is crucial to any genealogy of impersonality. Ironically, while Lewis's superficial and derogatory banter betrays serious anxiety about the contradictory power of personality in granting social authority to society's most marginalized members, and vice versa, it demonstrates little familiarity with Wilde's work. For like the modernists who would follow him, Wilde attempts to negotiate the contradiction that personality poses for aesthetic creation; he wants to do away with personality's weak forms—which are vulnerable to theft, imitation, and mimicry—but he is ultimately unwilling to discard the term in his idealization of true individualism in society and art. In essays such as "The Soul of Man under Socialism" (1891), Wilde opposes liberalist democracy and capitalism for promoting a network of sentimental property relations that obscures the "real" individual personality. The essay, which is ostensibly about how to solve the problem of poverty, advocates a socialist system designed to strengthen the personality by deprivatizing exclusive individual relations to works of art, sex, and social capital. In Wilde's vision, the thief, the "rebellious" and "ungrateful" poor man, possesses a "real personality," offering a healthy challenge to a strict matrix of privatized social relations.[18]

Wilde's use of the thief as a rhetorical lynchpin for the artistic personality in struggle is quite appropriate, considering the definition of personality as mask and the insincerity he endorses in his *Intentions* essays first published in 1891: "Pen, Pencil, and Poison," "The Decay of Lying," "The Critic as Artist," and "The Truth as Mask."[19] Despite Wilde's ostensible support of "personality," he is as vocal about the possibility of its degeneration into superficiality as is Lewis. As he remarks in "The Soul of Man Under Socialism," "so completely has man's personality been absorbed by his possessions that the English law has always treated offences against a man's property with far more severity than offences against his person" (*Plays* 20). Wilde rebukes a system that values material possessions over human beings, encapsulating the potential life of personality into a network of objects. Furthermore, he suggests that private property actually endangers personality. That is, if property is so important in concretizing personality, then what will prohibit others from appropriating one's personality as their rightful property? This threat of banditry, which masquerades as a legal acquisition of property, appears to be the real impetus behind Wilde's argument. One cannot build a strong personality within a system that values private property, because property objectifies personality and thus renders it prey to "the clamorous claims of others" (*Plays* 15). Personality, like property, can be stolen, manipulated, and manhandled. As in Simmel's assessment of the term, personality is vulnerable to overaccessibility. However, the ideal and truly authoritative personality performs a positive function like the rebellious thief who circulates outside networks of communicative exchange, successfully withholding "the private lives of men and women" from the prying and censorious public (*Plays* 35).

Wilde understands the limitations of personality but sees it as a useful tool, a contradictory "mask" of self-expression that protects one's privacy from extreme invasion. As mask, Wilde advocates a personality that progressively prefigures the variants of impersonality I discuss in this book, which emerge later in Yeats's, Eliot's, Pound's, and H.D.'s theories of lyrical masking and possession. In "The Soul of Man under Socialism," Wilde uses the term "personality" countless times as a seeming synonym for individualism and egotism. Private property, he argues, "has crushed true individualism, and set up an individualism that is false" (*Plays* 20). Consequently, "the full expression of a personality" is not possible (*Plays* 21). Rather, what results is an "impoverished personality" that must set itself in resistance to the community at large (*Plays* 44). Significantly, Wilde advances his analysis through the rhetoric of sickness and health; in a healthy environment—that is, one not driven by market forces—the work of art, and the artist, can project and express "personality" without the vulgar need for rebellion. For Wilde, the erasure of a market-based economy might solve this problem, as capitalism cements the artist into conflict with the community, creating a thing called "Public Opinion" (*Plays* 22). Rather than condemn him to crime and rebellion, to the status of the thief, socialism would restore the personal integrity of the artist by dispelling the "barbarous conception of authority" that attends "the natural inability of a community corrupted by authority to understand or appreciate Individualism" (*Plays* 34). Wilde is defining authority here as it relates to the pressures of public opinion, which results directly in a "morbid" relationship between the public and the artist who resists this authority (*Plays* 34). Under socialism, Wilde claims, community itself would be more meaningful and healthy in the light of this increased level of individualism and self-expression.

Personality, Wilde claims, should not be "tainted with ideas of authority," yet the ideal of personality Wilde advances is authoritative (*Plays* 20). His implicit assertion is that artistic personality grows weak and plastic under the capitalist system. The argument rather resembles Simmel's diagnosis of life in the modern metropolis; "the person," obligated to rebel, continually "resists being leveled down and worn out" by the money economy and the "social-technological mechanism" (*Sociology* 409). For Wilde, such perpetual struggle weakens and deflates the personality, reducing the work of art to a mere imitation of the public's desire to see. Directly evoking the "ideas of authority" he overtly critiques, he demands that, instead, the "work of art should dominate the spectator" (*Plays* 37). These sorts of injunctions certainly complicate Wilde's relation to modernists and their distrust of the romantic-expressivist ideal of personality, but they play on the same contradictions regarding the inherent volatility of personality as an asset required to produce literature and art. The personality itself is weak, but even in its erasure, it is required to produce a work of art that is distinctive and meaningful. Like Lewis, Wilde laments the loss of authoritative creative genius to the money economy. But unlike Lewis, Wilde offers an alternative version of personality that rests upon a deprivatized vision of the art world. However abstract, this concept contests normative forms of social privacy, the "false" ways people individuate themselves by adhering to bourgeois norms, which include marriage. Indeed, Wilde states in "The Soul of Man under Socialism" that "marriage in its present form must disappear" with "the abolition of private property" (*Plays* 24).

As an affront to the intrusiveness he sees in such unions, Wilde espouses the virtues of masking, an ideal that will erupt later in the impersonal cloaks of Yeats's and Pound's poetic personae. In this regard, Wilde's version of personality and individualism does not necessarily affirm the romantic individual. While Wilde clearly values personal expression, the expressive self—whatever or whomever hides behind a successive play of masks—is immaterial and unimportant. Rather, what matters is the *act* of expression. Personality does not require an authentic self; in advocating individuality, it does not reify the individual. For example, in "The Decay of Lying," Wilde notes that "[p]ersonal experience" is always "a most vicious and limited circle" (*Plays* 68). Since art rests upon the devaluation of "life" and values what is not experienced, the personality born of great art is impersonal. Consequently, Wilde's version of "personality" is most radical in that it is, like the personality Lewis detests, a fabrication, a falsehood. However, as a fabrication, it contests romantic, bourgeois ideals of singular selfhood and expression. One is not restricted to one personality. As he observes in "The Critic as Artist," "what people call insincerity is simply a method by which we can multiply our personalities" (*Plays* 149). For this reason, at the beginning of the dialogue, he praises Robert Browning and his famous dramatic monologues, which influenced the poetic techniques of both Eliot and Pound. Able to "stammer through a thousand mouths," Browning is a master of "fiction," not poetry (*Plays* 102). Born of lying, such "personality," Wilde later claims, is "technique," which explains "why the artist cannot teach it, why the pupil cannot learn it, and why the aesthetic critic cannot understand it" (*Plays* 157).

Ultimately, the sort of personal expression Wilde imagines, like Eliot's poetic emotion, cannot be taught or analyzed. As I am arguing, this version of "personality," since it does not sentimentally reify a singular creative self or individual, prefigures the aesthetic of impersonality that modernists such as Le Corbusier, Gaudier-Brzeska, Woolf, Lewis, and Eliot will later employ. Despite the subtitle of "The Critic as Artist: With Some Remarks on the Importance of Doing Nothing," personality is an action, a "technique" (*Plays* 157). Though the essay adamantly promotes individualism, this does not preclude collectivity. The new "critical spirit" will allow people to better "know others" and consequently "realise, not merely our own lives, but the collective life of the race" (*Plays* 138). This critical spirit, and the attendant concept of personality it supports, is impersonal. In a more radical enactment of the deprivatization Wilde urges in "The Soul of Man under Socialism," it entails that people give up possession of their "own" lives to enter the "lives of the dead" (*Plays* 139). Forecasting Eliot's "Tradition and the Individual Talent," Wilde's belief that criticism can "teach us how to escape from our experience" dismisses the social, the "familiar," for a much more radical mode of collective social modernity (*Plays* 139). To be "absolutely modern," according to Wilde, is not to be modern at all (*Plays* 138).

An "Arrangement of Surfaces": Modernism and Prosthesis

In the end, however, and unlike his modernist successors, Wilde's version of personality pivots around the matter of individual "style" and expression, personal flamboyancy, fashion, and influence. It promotes forms of imitation and copy that many modernists found unacceptable, as evident in Lewis's impatience with Wilde's "overmannered personality" (*Art* 210). In contrast to this version of personal style, which maintains faith in the effectiveness of "personality" as a mode of self-presentation, however inauthentic or fabricated, I examine in this section a variant of modernism that radically restructures the concept of the "person" altogether in its concern for the spatial dimensions of both the human body and things. While this strain of avant-garde thought preserves Wilde's valuation of "technique" or action over content or depth, it represents a further shift in values away from individualism, emphasizing uniformity as a means of reclaiming the weak, pliant, and modifiable characteristics of personality established in contemporary psychology and sociology. That is, the modernists I discuss in this section—the French sculptor Henri-Gaudier Brzeska and the Swiss-born French architect/designer Le Corbusier—preserve the basic structure figures such as Myers ascribe to personality, but reframe its ostensibly innate capacity for disturbance in the service of authority. Orchestrated through fracture and fissure, such a project entails a rescaling of the human organized around a paradoxically uniform vision of the human; an example of what Tim Armstrong and others have termed "prosthetic modernism," it "offers the body as lack at the same time as it offers technological compensation," knitting its parts together in a system of "virtual prosthetics."[20] My purpose in this section is to extend this notion of prosthesis explicitly toward an understanding of impersonal aesthetic form as it developed in response to the various discourses of personality circulating at the turn of the twentieth century. Prosthetic logic is impersonal in two senses. First, as Armstrong observes, it redefines the human from a depersonalized perspective as a form of technology itself. Second, a prosthetic logic both alters and extends the notion of the integrated self or individual in an explicitly spatial logic that expands the "fixed" nature of personality. While I focus here on the authoritarian, even fascist undertones of this reorganization of the person, I also want to open way for the radical possibilities of personhood such thought allows.

Critical analyses have generally pursued the ideologically troublesome aspect of this prosthetic logic, attaching it to Lewis and his embrace of authoritarianism and hypermasculinity.[21] By promoting the body as both lacking and technologically superhuman, the modernist logic of prosthesis showcases the ethical split that characterizes aesthetic impersonality more generally as found in its paradoxical leanings toward a progressive dissolution of social boundaries that dissolves the ego and, conversely, its authoritarian fantasies of control that magnify that ego. Established explicitly by contemporary psychology, this paradox linked alterations in the personality to literal bodily transformations. According to Prince's *The Dissociation of a Personality*, the famous Miss Beauchamp would lose control of her hands and limbs when her personalities alternated. More generally, in asking "what is personality?" Prince proposes looking into the "physiological alterations which determine the division of personality and permit one and the same individual to have multiple mental lives" (*Dissociation* 232). Here, the "division" of the personality into "multiple mental lives" represents a privilege that actually becomes the source of its potency while contesting the notion of a "normal real self" (*Dissociation* 232).

Like Prince, Le Corbusier and Gaudier-Brzeska, working in industrial design and sculpture, praise this multiplicity of function, but unlike Prince, they are interested in fracturing the personality only to reunify it through an impersonal vision of bodily scale. The question of appendages offers an especially important connection between Prince's ideas about personality and Le Corbusier's pronouncements on modernist design. Linking an impersonal aesthetic and material culture with prosthesis, Le Corbusier's *The Decorative Art of Today* first appeared at the 1925 Exposition des Arts Décoratifs in Paris. In this text, the designer's rhetoric, encapsulated in his famous imperative, "[m]*odern decorative art is not decorated,*" underlines the particular impersonality he advances as an explicitly spatial logic that compensates for human lack and inadequacy.[22] Objects should appear disinterested, functional, and designed for the service of humans. They should then reflect a human scale as a means of supplementing humans' "natural capabilities." Decorative objects are "human-limb objects," and decorative art comprises "the totality of 'human-limb objects'" (*DAT* xxiii). The book offers numerous examples of what Le Corbusier terms "type-needs furniture," which act artfully as prosthetic "extensions of our limbs" (*DAT* 75). More accurately, these items behave as additional limbs to perform tasks our bodies cannot fully handle; like Miss Beauchamp's contrary appendages, these limbs function independently of our ability to control them: "[F]iling cabinets and copy-letters make good the inadequacies of our memory: wardrobes and sideboards are the containers in which we put away the auxiliary limbs that guarantee us against cold or heat, hunger or thirst" (*DAT* 72). Such implements seek to master the physical vulnerability of the human body. Consequently, a scientific diagram of the skeletal, nervous, and circulatory systems of the adult male establishes the scale for these designs. The illustrations proceed to diagrams of items that most contemporary readers will find in any well-designed office or living space. Among the "technico-cerebro-emotional" objects pictured is a modern-day file cabinet, a lamp whose "neck" extends in multiple directions, an "[i]nnovation trunk," which, when turned on its end, becomes a chest of drawers complete with an accordion style apparatus for hanging clothing, and numerous tables, buffets, and filing systems whose "internal" organs, often hidden or secret, are as interesting as the external amenities that grace their form (*DAT* 70).

Le Corbusier's rhetoric explicitly thematizes the objects we tend to take for granted in our own living spaces as products of an impersonal material culture, redefining the boundaries of both the object and the person. This is clearly an abstracted, uniformly scaled personhood, as is evident in the violent response of "one of the big names in charge of the 1925 Exhibition," who claimed that Le Corbusier's ideas were "killing the individual!" (*DAT* 72–73). "Personality" is replaced by the archetypal and authoritative unanimity of design. Le Corbusier responds to this charge by reformulating a paradox that forms the crux of modernist versions of impersonality more generally; he insists that impersonal forms of abstraction support individuality and privacy, as represented in the secret organs of his creations. In its uncanny mimicry and extension of the male form, the "tool-object" makes space for the "elevated activity" of individualism, a life of "music, books, the creations of the spirit—that is truly one's own, truly oneself" (*DAT* 73).

While the overt guarantee of Le Corbusier's rhetoric is to place "the individual . . . on the highest level" within an abstracted and impersonal scale of design, one can see that his maxim-like precepts are deeply invested with an authoritarian ideology of how and what the individual should be. Again, this vision of authority rests on the ability to define or demarcate oneself within social space. Le Corbusier's "cold and brutal" furniture designs reference the masculine workspace or, at their most personal, the masculine boudoir. More directly, Le Corbusier suggests that decorative art is "orthopaedic, an activity that appeals to the imagination, to invention, to skill, but a craft analogous to the tailor: the client is a man, familiar to us all and precisely defined" (*DAT* 72). While the designer ostensibly seeks to reproduce a more democratic, efficient, and impersonal material culture, he links this to a "*folk culture of today*" that forges individual artistic judgments into a kind of "unanimous collaboration" (italics in original; *DAT* 32). Establishing such standards, Le Corbusier adds, will construct the "unanimity of a new sense of feeling, which reflects upon an epoch of precision dominated by the machine" (*DAT* 36). While Le Corbusier's statements represent one way of shoring up modernist universalism, they also reflect an authoritarian aesthetic in which the prosthetic, technologically replete body becomes a vision of unification and "unanimity."

Metaphorically speaking, furniture design resembles tailoring, a simple extension of the mechanical and ubiquitous proportions of the well-designed business suit. Le Corbusier directly contrasts the hygienic candor of the masculine workplace with the cluttered insincerity of the department store, whose wares hide "beneath decoration" to eclipse "flaws, blemishes, all defects" (*DAT* 54). Such spatial culture can only connote hysterical femininity: "Decoration, decoration: yes indeed, in all departments; the department became the 'ladies' joy!'" (*DAT* 55). If anything, Le Corbusier's adherence to this authoritative logic of spatial scale connects his work to the literary aesthetic of impersonality. In "Tradition and the Individual Talent," Eliot promotes literary form and authority as an explicit issue of scale, a matter of correct proportioning. Drawing on the language of geometry, Eliot argues that "for order to persist after the supervention of novelty, the *whole* existing order must be, if ever so slightly, altered, and so the relations, proportions, values of each work of art toward the whole are re-adjusted" (*Prose* 38). Impersonality is relational, but in a perfectly scaled, managed manner that, in the cases of both Eliot and Le Corbusier, perpetuates the authority of one form over the other.

Yet it is possible to argue that Le Corbusier theorizes an impersonality that emerges through new forms of bodily organization and alterations in the scale of selfhood. The radical potential of this form of impersonality emerges more clearly in the case of Henri Gaudier-Brzeska, who died in the trenches of World War I at age 23, and for whom sculpture actively produces a form of emotion that, in seeming opposition to Wilde's praise of self-expression, is not expressed. Indeed, the young sculptor's manifestic declarations about emotion capture both the progressive potential of impersonality as well as its authoritarian downside. Ultimately, the contradictory logic of Gaudier-Brzeska's statements represents a more extreme articulation of the contradictions in Eliot's "Tradition and the Individual Talent." The vorticist "celebration of annihilation as the fullest proof of manly life" not only "anticipates what has come to be called fascist modernism," as Paul Peppis has observed, but also functions as both a more reactionary and radical exaggeration of the kinds of submission and self-effacement that Eliot's own doctrine of impersonality would later privilege.[23] While Gaudier-Brzeska does not mention the terms explicitly, his conception of emotion is bound up within the same concept of aesthetic impersonality that Eliot would later articulate, where aesthetic disinterestedness and personal obfuscation are necessary conditions for creating an emotionally connected artistic community.

Pound's homage *A Memoir of Gaudier-Brzeska*, published in 1916 only a year after its subject's death, immediately calls attention to the emotional quality of the sculptor's work, counting it, more so than contemporary painting, "peculiarly a thing of the twentieth-century."[24] "Sculpture, of this new sort," he adds, is "more moving than painting" because of its ability to create an "austere permanence" with "some relation *of* life and yet outside it" (*Memoir* 29). In investing Gaudier-Brzeska's sculpture with the agency of emotional movement, Pound foregrounds the sort of poetic emotion T. S. Eliot would later theorize in "Tradition and the Individual Talent," implicitly suggesting that sculpture is more "emotional" or "moving" than painting because it is a multidimensional surface that flattens the distinction between inside and outside. Of course, this conclusion is contradictory, since painting is generally considered more flat than sculpture, which is three-dimensional. Gaudier-Brzeska, as Hugh Kenner explains in *The Pound Era*, also saw sculpture as an "expression of certain emotions," but only in so much as the work did not resemble its actual subject, as in his famous 1913 sculpture of the "Hieratic Head of Ezra Pound."[25] This conception of sculpture is impersonal because it obscures the physical characteristics that contribute to an actual identity in favor of a more general form of emotion present in the cold planes of stone. Indeed, it diminishes the sort of social and aesthetic authority I have attempted to define here, since having an authoritative personality requires singular definition, the ability to be recognized within a defined social space. "You understand it will not look like you, it *will* not look like you," wrote Gaudier-Brzeska to Pound. "It will be the expression of certain emotions which I get from your character."[26] But as with Le Corbusier, this concept of emotion as surface represents a new technology of scale that redefines the human altogether.

In doing so, such rearrangement disturbs the conventional distinctions between inner depth and outer surface, as with Le Corbusier's secret compartments and outer-appendages.

Quite notably, Pound's description of Gaudier-Brzeska's sculpture further establishes its impersonality in its suggestion that the work achieves "austere permanence" by demonstrating "some relation *of* life" at the same time that it remains "outside of it" (italics in original; *Memoir* 29). In the same way that, for Eliot, personal experience is a necessary catalyst for entry into a more impersonal poetic tradition, Gaudier-Brzeska's sculpture maintains a synthesis between the reality of personal experience and an autonomous, impersonal existence. Gaudier-Brzeska's "Written from the Trenches," which appeared first in *Blast* as part of his "Vortex" manifesto and later in Pound's memoir, reworks the distinction, if in different terminology, between personal feelings and the more impersonal poetic emotion that Eliot theorizes in "Tradition and the Individual Talent." Ironically, the essay, originally handwritten in a combination of lower and uppercase scripts, enunciates its message in a staccato format of objective injunctions that appear to chastise emotion rather than embrace it. Sculpture is an "ARRANGEMENT" or "SIMPLE COMPOSITION OF LINES AND PLANES" (*Blast* 28). Despite this point-blank mode of delivery, emotion is the manifesto's main subject. This form of emotion is not unproblematic, considering the sculptor's seemingly callous disrespect for human lives. Indeed, the essay definitely solidifies the connection between modernist intellectual elitism and cold authoritarianism by asserting that "THIS WAR IS A GREAT REMEDY," having taken "AWAY FROM THE MASSES NUMBERS UPON NUMBERS OF UNIMPORTANT UNITS, WHOSE ECONOMIC ACTIVITIES BECOME NOXIOUS AS THE RECENT TRADE CRISES HAVE SHOWN US" (*Memoir* 27). In its crude and utilitarian vision of the world and art as an efficiently functioning machine that must eradicate "UNIMPORTANT UNITS," one cannot overlook the connection between such a statement and the latter fascist leanings of figures such as Pound, Eliot, and Yeats. Again, far from conveying emotion, this statement appears to reflect cold disengagement from the surrounding human environment.

Nonetheless, the sculptor's thoughts about emotion prove quite radical, and as I have argued of T. S. Eliot's "poetic emotion," contribute to an antipsychological, impersonal form of emotion, which establishes collective bonds outside of shared personal experience and identity. This possibility is most evident in the sculptor's analogous positioning of wartime turbulence to artistic agency, claiming that "IT WOULD BE FOLLY TO SEEK ARTISTIC EMOTIONS AMID THESE LITTLE WORKS OF OURS" (*Memoir* 27). Furthermore, "the chaos of battle," does not "ALTER IN THE

LEAST the outlines of the hill we are besieging" (*Memoir* 27). Much like Eliot, the artist professes his disbelief that individual emotions, desires, and aspirations could affect his turbulent surroundings, which are ironically and imperturbably anchored by the earth's natural surface or form, the hills around him. Though the emotional machinations of war—the "volleys, wire entanglements, projectors, motors" and, significantly, the digging of trenches—might literally sculpt the earth, its surface remains unfazed by these human actions. Accordingly, like the aggressive turbulence of war, personal or individual artistic emotions are also "FOLLY" (*Memoir* 27). That is, an artist's narcissistic belief that artistic or personal emotion will materialize in a true aesthetic medium is as foolish as faith that man's battle will somehow alter the earth's impermeability.

As an alternative to the ineffectiveness of personal artistic emotion, the sculptor outlines an impersonal ideal of emotion that exhibits no pretense to "ARROGANCE, SELF-ESTEEM, [or] PRIDE," concepts linked to a depth-model of selfhood and psychology (*Memoir* 27). Rather, emotions "present" themselves as an arrangement of surfaces, so that depth itself is only an illusion (*Memoir* 28). Similarly, Gaudier-Brzeska refers to the "ARRANGEMENT OF MY SURFACES" as the means by which he "present[s]" his own emotions, indicating his belief that he is not a psychologically three-dimensional being comprising secret depths and recesses. He writes, "I SHALL DERIVE MY EMOTIONS SOLELY FROM THE ARRANGEMENT OF SURFACES, I shall present my emotions by the ARRANGEMENT OF MY SURFACES, THE PLANES AND LINES BY WHICH THEY ARE DEFINED" (*Memoir* 28). Significantly, his words reveal the same irritation with expression Wyndham Lewis conveys in his rants against personality and its expression. Rather than expressed, such emotions are "present[ed]" as surface phenomena that confuse any distinction between inside and outside. In stating that emotions are more accurately "presented" or "defined" through an objectively precise arrangement of surfaces, Gaudier-Brzeska denies the possibility of a coherent self that exists prior to their expression. Rather, the sculptor counts emotions as always and already on the surface, rearranging the romantic connection between emotional expression and psychological depth. The sculptural self is an impersonal "technico-cerebro-emotional" object, to borrow from Le Corbusier (*DAT* 70); a systematic "arrangement of surfaces," this self literally exteriorizes emotion, particularly in relation to others.

As with Eliot, this vocabulary of "arrangement" indicates that, for Gaudier-Brzeska, emotion is experienced collectively as an abstract aesthetic medium that diminishes the importance of the individual and personality. Gaudier-Brzeska's concepts of "[s]culptural energy," "[s]culptural feeling," and "[s]culptural ability," which he elaborates in other portions of his "Vortex" manifesto, further illustrate this position on emotion (*Blast* 155). Rather abstractly, Gaudier-Brzeska defines sculptural energy as "the Mountain," whereas "[s]culptural feeling is the appreciation of masses in relation" and "[s]culptural ability is the defining of these masses by planes" (*Blast* 155). My point here is not to exhaustively distinguish between these three modes of "sculptural" activity but to demonstrate how the sculptor conceives each mode as a form of collective relation or engagement, as he indicates quite explicitly in his definition of sculptural feeling. Indeed, sculptural feeling and ability depends on the existence of an intense empathy that draws spatial relations and connections between monuments of sculptural energy. These relations are purely immediate. They do not arise from any sense of depth, which must be represented or expressed. Rather, the relations between "masses" are defined "by planes," flat surfaces that, in their rejection of soul, psychology, and selfhood, are never "derivative or secondary" (*Blast* 156). Echoing the imagist ideals of Pound and foregrounding Eliot's latter version of poetic emotion, Gaudier-Brzeska's last paragraph defines the form of impersonal collectivity established through sculptural energy, feeling, and activity, "We have been influenced by what we liked most, each according to his own individuality, we have crystallized the sphere into the cube, we have made a combination of all the possible shaped masses—concentrating them to express our abstract thoughts of conscious superiority" (*Blast* 158). The "we" Gaudier-Brzeska invokes is not exactly a democratic community but a collective assembly of like minds, "the moderns" he affiliates himself with in an earlier statement in the essay: "Epstein, Brancusi, Archipenko, Dunikowski, Modigliani" (*Blast* 158). Most interesting here is the sculptor's use of terminology and its similarity to that of Eliot's "Tradition and the Individual Talent." As with Eliot's concept of poetic emotion, individuality is a catalyst that only exists residually in the emotional and aesthetic medium it produces. Suggestive of imagist rhetoric, Gaudier-Brzeska describes how each individuality is "crystallized" from a sphere into a well-defined cube. Whereas a sphere is composed of curves, a cube is an "arrangement of surfaces," an assemblage of flat planes that theoretically eradicates depth. Only in this arrangement is a collective assembly of like minds possible. As with Eliot's poetic emotion, these "possible shaped masses" have been "concentrate[ed]," reduced and flattened to an essence that exists both within and without, allowing them to realize their "conscious superiority" (*Blast* 158).

Despite the authoritative pretense of this statement, this model of surface and concentration points toward the possibility of a more empathic, engaged type of modernist tract. As such, it indicates the sheer range of political ideologies—from radically progressive to deeply authoritarian—modernist texts can accommodate, all in their critique of bourgeois individualism. Admittedly, one cannot deny that Gaudier-Brzeska's highly intellectualized, abstract theory of emotion exemplifies some of the more politically unpalatable currents that have conventionally been ascribed to high modernism. However, the tract progressively theorizes a form of emotion that is both antihumanist in its strong distrust of anthropological associations and impersonal in its desire to disable the boundaries of individual selfhood and psychology. The potential of such an impersonal logic lies in its capacity to reorganize spatial codes, ways of seeing and perceiving, and modes of placement while presenting the body as irreducible to transfer or exchange. Because it deals with emotional resonances, prosthesis is not merely an ornament that can be put on or taken off, as in Lewis' novel *Snooty Baronet*, where the protagonist unhinges his prosthetic leg before and after sex. In keeping with Le Corbusier's defensive claim that his abstracted scales of design protect the individual, the ideal forms of modernist impersonality I examine in this book are ideologically flexible enough to cradle a particularized and unalterable idiosyncrasy within its universalizing impulse.

Virginia Woolf and Impersonal Spatial Practice

For a text that realizes the progressive potential of Le Corbusier's and Gaudier-Brzeska's otherwise reactionary theories, I now turn to Virginia Woolf, who, in her essay and ode to itinerant cruising "Street Haunting: A London Adventure" (1930), moves away from personality by drawing a more concrete and socially reparative vision of the impersonality elaborated by Eliot, Lewis, and Gaudier-Brzeska. In contrast to the aesthetic and cultural superiority prized by the latter group, Woolf's impersonal ideals extend the scope of humanity itself, specifically to the deformed and disabled; her vision challenges the parameters of personality, but the end result privileges engagement rather than authority. To return to Simmel, the sociologist illustrates how altruistic engagements with others undermine the authority of personality, or an individual's ability to demarcate himself within social space. As I have argued, modernists such a Le Corbusier, Lewis, and Gaudier-Brzeska display a fundamental anxiety toward the potential loss of authority that such engagement entails. Moreover, their critique of personality accompanies the need to compensate for its presumed weakness through authoritarian ideals of aesthetic unanimity. For Woolf, however, the loss of personality occasions novel forms of engagement that fuel creativity. Indeed, Woolf reworks the same rhetoric of surface employed by Le Corbusier and Gaudier-Brzeska, but instead contributes to an anthropology of city life that envisions individuals as they emerge through entangled networks of care and support.

"Street Haunting" takes us back to Simmel's stranger, who synthesizes "nearness and distance" to both dynamize social space and guard against its dissolution (*Sociology* 404). For Simmel, this "fundamentally mobile person comes in contact, at one time or another, with every individual, but is not organically connected, through established ties of kinship, locality, and occupation, with any single one" (*Sociology* 404). Similarly, Woolf's impersonal spatial practice, unlike Le Corbusier's, which privileges a uniformly able-bodied human type, encompasses the specific forms of embodiment and situation that place her fellow creatures within, not without, the social matrix of humanity. In Woolf's case, an impersonal relation, facilitated by the "liberation from every given point in space," preserves a sense of "nearness," intimacy, and attachment (*Sociology* 402, 404). The stranger, like Woolf's urban *flaneur*, possesses the objectivity conferred upon him by distance, but this does not contribute to crude, authoritative detachment. As Simmel remarks, "objectivity does not simply involve passivity and detachment" (*Sociology* 404). Rather, the stranger is part of "a particular structure composed of distance and nearness, indifference and involvement" (*Sociology* 404).

In accordance with Simmel's description, Woolf quite famously opens her own treatise in a moment of conventional desire, of "involvement," where she is "set upon having an object," a pencil, which operates as a guise for the freedom of perpetual movement, of not "having an object."[27] "No one," Woolf writes, "has ever felt passionately towards having a pencil" (*Collected IV* 155). Nonetheless, this object, however frail the reality of its existence, occasions the author's movement from an interior architectural space to "part of that vast republican army of anonymous trampers" (*Collected IV* 155). Echoing Wilde's imperative that the new "critical spirit" can "teach us how to escape from our experience," Woolf remarks that upon leaving our homes, we "are no longer quite ourselves" (*Plays* 139; *Collected IV* 155). With this movement away from the "objects which perpetually express the oddity of our own temperaments and enforce the memories of our experience," Woolf's observations begin to detail a series of shifts in the urban phenomenological ground that visually individuate the objects around her while simultaneously dispelling them into the "vast" anonymity her essay celebrates (*Collected IV* 155). In other words, this mode of narrative perception places, or situates, the perceived object at the same time that it renders it mobile in its ability to defy normative visual regimes.[28] In this relationship, this fleeting but perceptible object actually determines the scale through which the narrating subject appears. Consequently, the movements and perpetual reconfigurations of space occasioned by Woolf's observations create points of connection that emphasize the role of the object in calling into being and creating the setting for its own existence.

Rather than absolute phenomenological certainty, the rhetoric of Woolf's cruising hinges on the term "atmosphere" as the grounds for visual display. This atmosphere ensures that scale is often perceived but rarely fixed beyond the moment of perception, in sharp contrast to Le Corbusier's designs, which erase individual distinction by authoritatively reifying an absolute human scale of every man. For example, the sudden appearance of a dwarf in the essay physically alters the scale of human perception. The "central oyster of perceptiveness, an enormous eye," resting originally "only on beauty," has altered, now taking in "oddities and suffering and sordities" (*Collected IV* 156, 157). In the process, the eye, satiated by pleasure, becomes empathic: "What, then, is it like to be a dwarf?" Woolf asks. Escorted into a shoe store by women of normal size, the dwarf, as the phenomenological marker that establishes the spatial scale of her surrounding environment, turns the women into "benevolent giants," while displaying her "perfectly proportioned," "arched," and "aristocratic" foot to the shopgirl before her (*Collected IV* 157). As Woolf remarks, the dwarf is not unresentful about her situation in life, but she demands to be observed, acknowledged: "Look at that! Look at that! She seemed to demand of us all, as she thrust her foot out, for behold, it was the shapely, perfectly portioned foot of a well-grown woman" (*Collected IV* 158). It is impossible to ignore her, and as a result, Woolf notes a change in the "angles and relationships" of observation; the dwarf had "called into being an atmosphere which, as we followed her out into the street, seemed actually to create the humped, the twisted and the deformed" (*Collected IV* 157, 158). While such an atmosphere is transient, itinerant, and subject to change, it also engenders an altered perspective that grants phenomenological certainty to those figures that alter and extend the scale of humanity.

Furthermore, the forms of itinerancy Woolf observes and the various atmospheres that surround them create a mode of social attachment, a being-with. That is, the dwarf can only access powers to create the atmosphere, both as an object of observation and in her departure from the conventional human object, through an attached relation to others. In the next scene, Woolf's observation shifts to another threesome, a company of two blind men, "brothers . . . apparently . . . supporting themselves by resting a hand on the head of small boy between them" (*Collected IV* 158). Once again, Woolf describes a "convoy" that passes by tremulously, as if evading objectification, yet "holding straight on" in a sense of absolute direction (*Collected IV* 159). Woolf seems rather deliberate in her choice of the word "supporting" to describe the relationship between the two men and the boy, who literally enables the men their direction; in a less cold version of Gaudier-Brzeska's sculptural activity, the boy prosthetically extends the two brothers, creating an impersonal, horizontally positioned surface that dissolves the meaning of a unified bodily ego.

Woolf's reference to the "angles and relationships" of observation parallels Eliot's assessment of impersonal form, where the emergence of the new modifies the existing order of art, "readjust[ing]" the "relations, proportions, values of each work of art toward the whole" (*Prose* 38). The convergence of these perspectives illustrates the contradictions of a spatially oriented impersonality that empathically champions the agency of humanity's outcasts to disable normative registers of visibility on one hand while buttressing the authority of tradition on the other. However, both accounts define the impersonal as it modifies and transforms the existing social and aesthetic terrain. This point of commonality does somewhat problematize the grounds of Woolf's observations, particularly at the end of the essay, as she frames the effects of her cruising. That is, however progressive, her perceptions tend to work in the service of her own aesthetic prowess, or authority. Seeing produces "delight and wonder," since, to "escape is the greatest of pleasures . . . the greatest of adventures" but one only has the "illusion that one is not tethered to a single mind" (*Collected IV* 166, 165). Unlike her "fellow men," she has the privilege of her mobility, her ability to revert back into the protective walls of her personalized domestic space.

However, in "Flying over London," Woolf's imaginative aerial cruising self-consciously contests what appears to be the implicit target of "Street Haunting," the authority of the "inveterately anthropocentric . . . mind," which creates a "welcoming, accepting" social "harbour" for the airplane's immanent landing (*Collected IV* 167). Rather than reinforce a human scale of proportion, the plane occasions a phenomenological shift away from the human business of personality: "Everything had changed its values seen from the air. Personality was outside the body, abstract. And one wished to be able to animate the heart, the legs, the arms with it . . . so as to collect; so as to give up this arduous game, as one flies through the air, of assembling things that lie on the surface" (*Collected IV* 172). Here, Woolf challenges a process of assembly that maintains an authoritative, "anthropocentric" spatial scale. While holding on to this scale is "arduous," letting go of it entails the loss of certain social comforts—namely, personality. Here, Woolf describes a more technologically advanced form of the street haunting she celebrates on her trip to buy a pencil. In doing so, she also acknowledges the potential ethical problems of impersonality in ways that her modernist contemporaries do not. On one hand, the change in values "seen from the air" references a form of impersonality that ultimately alters the idealized scale of the human subject, away from anthropocentric, humanist notions of selfhood toward a far more animated, prosthetic selfhood that positions "[p]ersonality . . . outside the body, abstract" (*Collected IV* 172). On the other hand, Woolf suggests that, as a technology itself, this change in values can go too far, toward complete dehumanization or depersonalization, foreshadowing her later anxiety regarding the Second World War, fascist domination, and the advent of technology, symbolized specifically by airplanes, as is evident in texts such as *Between the Acts* (1941).[29]

For Woolf, personality consists of a specific social consciousness of material scale, apportioned by one's property, the things in one's rooms, or "the objects which perpetually express our own temperaments and enforce the memories of our own experience" (*Collected IV* 155). Such personality can alter itself on a busy city street or in the cockpit of an airplane. By experimenting with shifting technologies of physical scale, Woolf at least momentarily resolves the problem of organization impersonality poses—unearthing a multidimensional social fabric that supports social cohesiveness and attachment by distinguishing individuals only as they acquire outline through literal connection to others. The dwarf appears only in the proximity of her cohorts, and the blind men appear only through the support of the young boy. Woolf's shifting visual scales then demonstrate how the subject might occupy a position of empirical certainty yet simultaneously alter normative registers of visual apprehension. Indeed, Woolf's scenario suggests most importantly that specific forms of empirical placement, of phenomenological grounding, must exist for space to cohere and for subjects to appear with dignity. The characters of Woolf's "Street Haunting" appear inextricably placed beside each other but in a way that unsettles conventional visions of placement, individualism, and depth assessment.

The essay thus underlines the value of phenomenology for my project and for theorizing impersonality more generally, particularly as it provides an alternative to poststructuralist critiques of essentialism and depth. According to Jean-Paul Sartre, a phenomenological relationship gets "rid of the dualism which in the existent opposes interior to exterior."[30] As Woolf's affectionately drawn trios suggest, a phenomenological perspective replaces relationships of depth, which depend on the opposition of interior to exterior, with relations of breadth, to some extent collapsing hierarchical social relations. Such a perspective assaults the Cartesian tradition and its authoritative impulse, according to Merleau-Ponty, "to disengage from the object."[31] In contrast, an impersonal understanding of relations in its most radical dimension, keeping with T. S. Eliot's imperative that emotion is neither conscious nor deliberate, "runs counter to the reflective procedure which detaches subject and object" (*Phenomenology* 198). Merleau-Ponty makes clear that the blurring of subject and object also erases the idea of a specific bottom and a top: "But what meaning could the word 'against' have for a subject not placed by his body face to face with the world? It implies the distinction of a top and a bottom, or an 'oriented space.' When I say that an object is *on* a table, I always mentally put myself either in the table or in the object, and I apply to them a category which theoretically fits the relationship of my body to external objects. Stripped of the anthropological association, the word *on* is indistinguishable from the word 'under' or 'beside'" (*Phenomenology* 101). Merleau-Ponty's description of the change that occurs when objects are "[s]tripped of anthropological association" mirrors Woolf's critique of the "inveterately anthropocentric . . . mind" in "Flying over London" (*Collected IV* 165–66). These charges to humanist individualism fault its lack of engagement for producing asymmetrical, hierarchical relationships. When one actually engages with the object, an anthropocentrically "oriented space" disappears and so does a top and a bottom, an active and passive agent, as we shall see in the next chapter on the imagist poet   For these spatial situations, the descriptive preposition "under" presents no difference from "beside." To move beyond "anthropological association" means to radically move beyond authority, beyond the ego, psychology, and personality to an impersonally invested relation that "discover[s] the origin of the object at the very center of our experience" (*Phenomenology* 71).

2

The Impersonal Contract

H.D. and the Limits of Poetic Authority

> A song, a spirit, a white star that moves across the heavens to mark the end of a world epoch or a presage to some coming glory. Yet she is embodied-terribly a human being, a woman, a personality as the most impersonal become when they confront their fellow beings.
>
> —H.D.[1]

Speaking of Sappho, H.D., the modernist poet, is at once concerned with the body and its ability to "terribly" sabotage the voice, the "coming glory," of the master poet (*Wise* 59). In this description from *The Wise Sappho*, H.D.'s guide to the poetic vocation, the poet aligns the "impersonal" with the disembodied "song" or "spirit;" conversely, she locates "personality" within the world of the body and social relations. In this state of impersonality, the poet holds the bard-like authority to "mark" or "presage" history and the future, but this ability does not preclude her place in the world among "fellow beings," a condition that also disables the scope of the poet's voice, or authority. In light of this contradiction, this chapter examines H.D.'s theory of impersonality as it self-consciously explores the poetic vocation and its relation to authority. As do her contemporaries, most notably Ezra Pound, H.D. promotes poetry as the subject of authoritative, impersonal mastery. In *ABC of Reading* (1934), for example, published well after *Notes on Thought and Vision* and *The Wise Sappho* (1919), Pound announces his intention of writing pages "impersonal enough to serve as a text-book" for how to study poetry.[2] This use of the word "impersonal" suggests that poetry can be objectively learned through meticulous study, by following a set of rules or principles that lead to poetic authority. Unlike the work of Pound, however, H.D.'s own oeuvre suggests her acute awareness of the potential problems of this sort of impersonality; she self-consciously explores the problems and dynamics of an impersonal method that erases individual distinction, or personality, precisely through an intense engagement with others that presupposes a personality in the first place. Thus, for H.D., Sappho's connection to the world of "fellow beings," where "she is embodied-terribly a human being, a woman, a personality," is a necessary condition of sustaining impersonal poetic authority (*Wise* 59). In H.D.'s particular conception of the impersonal process, poetic mastery, or the ability to performatively pronounce, "mark," or "presage" time, is born through a "personality," whose surrender is a requisite aspect of a cycle where the authorization of poetic voice is not complete without its corresponding deauthorization.

This dialectical process has been most famously articulated in T. S. Eliot's "Tradition and the Individual Talent" (1919), where he argues that the "extinction of personality" requires a "continual surrender . . . a continual self-sacrifice" to become "something which is more valuable" in order to enter the more authoritative "form of tradition."[3] While Eliot mentions this complication rather casually, as if it were not complicated at all, the poetic impersonality of H. D's early work actually prefigures "Tradition and the Individual Talent," exposing much of the ethical and conceptual difficulty that Eliot's pronouncements resolve so hastily. Her poetry and criticism explore this problem of authority quite explicitly, particularly as the question of personality and impersonality encompass a much larger social domain of exterior significations including gender, sexuality, race, and other forms of physical or bodily specification, evident in her concern with the problem of Sappho's embodiment. As she remarks, poetry itself does not function outside of "certain physical relationships" that "develop . . . along natural physical lines," both supporting and dismantling the authority of the individual poet (*Notes* 17).

This understanding of impersonality extends beyond the realm of poetics to the world of concrete phenomena: real space and real bodies. This pervasiveness is especially apparent in H.D.'s film criticism, where she explicitly outlines her theory of impersonality as a radical process of decomposition and transformation. For example, in "The Mask and the Movietone," her 1927 contribution to Kenneth Macpherson's journal of film theory, *Close Up*, the poet praises silent film as an impersonal medium that dissolves the boundaries between audience and actor, distilling the singular personality of the film star as well as the audience's attempt to objectify her. Whereas the poet credits sound technology with "accurately and mechanically weld[ing]" face and voice, this cinematic integration is limited, operating not as "a mask" but as a "personality."[4] The silent cinematic figure, however, is more radical, more impersonal, as it dispels personality and disrupts any rigid binary between viewing subject and viewed object; it is a "marionette around which one could drape one's devotions" in an effort to "add imagination to a mask, a half finished image, not have everything done for me" ("Mask" 116). In contrast to Walter Benjamin's assertion that cinema "preserves . . . the spell of personality" in exchange for having lost the "unique aura of the person," H.D. imagines cinematic pleasure as an intersubjective process of exchange circulating around the dissociated impersonality of the unwelded image; in this context, the subject viewing the film imaginatively ventriloquizes her own voice through the mask, defying the very concept of bounded personhood and personality.[5] Viewing film, like writing and studying poetry, most ideally entails an imaginative effort to incorporate or amplify one's own voice through the mouth of another.

I open this chapter with this example from H.D.'s film criticism because it illustrates what her version of impersonality seeks to accomplish: the disintegration and reconstitution of the "person" through the replication and amplification of both cinematic and poetic voice. However radical her thoughts may seem, especially as she envisions an unbounded community of film-viewing facilitated by the silent image, the resulting structure of invasion, self-amplification, and control her fantasy of intersubjectivity supports is hard to ignore, particularly in the image of the "marionette" film star. Yet it is also this less ideologically palatable, ethically difficult side of H.D.'s criticism and poetry that has been seriously overlooked in her critical "making" as a poet. I begin then with the idea of H.D. as an especially misunderstood figure in modernism. While feminist criticism in particular helped to establish H.D. as a serious modernist poet, it has in many ways obscured her contribution to a larger modernist discourse of aesthetic and sociological impersonality, which she first articulates in the 1916 publication of *Sea Garden* and a few years later in the 1919 publication of *Notes on Thought and Vision* and *The Wise Sappho*.

The critical response to H.D. not only reflects the politics of resurrecting female authors into the literary canon in the early 1980s, but it also points to a more general misunderstanding of impersonality itself.[6] My goal here is not to dismiss the importance of these accounts but to clarify some of the confusion surrounding H.D.'s connection to impersonality, particularly in its relation to masculinity and authority. One example, Casandra Laity's influential *H.D. and the Victorian Fin de Siecle: Gender, Modernism, Decadence*, reads H.D.'s work within a "personal" poetic tradition, arguing "foremost that H.D. eluded the male modernist flight from Romantic 'effeminacy' and 'personality' by embracing the very cults of personality in the British *fin de siècle* that her contemporaries most deplored."[7] Key to Laity's negative view of impersonality is the assumption that it is a "masculinist doctrine," a nondesiring, "non-sexual poetic of gender-neutral images" that prohibits "narrative strategies that might allow for a female I" (*HDVF* 5, 42). I take an alternative position here, arguing that H.D.'s impersonality is actually compatible with Laity's reading of the poet, emerging as a highly affective poetics that expands the very meaning of desire. This misunderstanding of impersonality and its attendant gender politics not only is limited to feminist accounts of H.D. but also occurs in more general studies of impersonality, where it is equated with the high modernist, masculinist aesthetics of Eliot and Pound.[8] And while studies such as Sharon Cameron's *Impersonality* have successfully dislodged the force of such arguments, there is otherwise no mention of H.D.'s foundational contributions to the doctrine as it informs modernism more generally. Certainly, the retreat from individualized voice Cameron identifies in Eliot's *Four Quartets* (1944), its "estrangement . . . from its constitutive properties," is the culmination of a three-decade-long series of experiments with impersonal poetic voice, experiments of which H.D. was a key initiator.[9]

This link between impersonal poetic voice and authority motivates the major claims I make in this chapter, particularly as I read H.D.'s *Sea Garden* as a work self-consciously invested in both monitoring and maintaining poetic authority. First, drawing from the claims of feminist critics responsible for the now visible position of H.D.'s poetry within the literary cannon, I read the poet's work as it theorizes novel modes of attachment and intimacy that emerge from a progressive model of aesthetic community that protects private interiority. However, in contrast to these accounts, which emphasize impersonality as a gender-neutral and authoritarian ideology of aesthetic conservatism, I argue that the very model of poetic community these critics value in H.D.'s poetry is actually a feature of her particular version of impersonality, characterized by an interest in moving beyond "personalized" expressions of identity and selfhood. Second, I suggest that this same progressive feature of H.D.'s poetics connects to more politically questionable practices and ideologies—such as masochism and eugenics—where the potentially progressive logic of community and cohesion formed by overcoming the boundaries of oneself often slips into fantasies of authority and control. These connections, I argue, problematize the overriding focus on gender as a tool of analysis in existing H.D. scholarship, particularly as it obscures the complexities of her own ambivalent relationship to impersonality. My point here is not to dismiss the importance of gender to H.D.'s work altogether but to offer a more nuanced reading of the role gender plays in her impersonal poetics, where one only accesses poetic authority through the decomposition of gender. H.D.'s impersonal aesthetic functions according to a principle of exchange, of "surrender," to use Eliot's terminology; in this dynamic, gender is only one aspect of the "personality" requiring disposal, if only momentarily, in order to exercise impersonal poetic authority (*Prose* 40).

As H.D.'s film criticism suggests, impersonality requires two agents, both of which exact certain transformations and demands of the other. In these "contracts," enacted literally in H.D.'s poetry, the female poet willingly—and masochistically, I contend—contributes to her own victimization and exploitation in order to access another kind of poetic authority or voice. Accordingly, we can see how H.D. could have interpreted her authentication as an imagist poet in Ezra Pound's attempt to produce a masculinist, avant-garde aesthetic not as an exchange necessary for securing gendered power, but as an acquisition of poetic power and voice at the expense of another kind of agency. This form of exchange is not merely instrumental and utilitarian. Rather, in H.D.'s lyrics, impersonality surfaces not as an objective and emotionless form of relation, but as an intense mode of affect that is related to both the act of surrender and the acquisition of poetic authority. As a mode of affective engagement, this form of impersonality reflects H.D.'s particular version of imagism, which is both distinct from and similar to Pound's own version of the doctrine. Much in contrast to Laity's characterization of a masculine modernist poetics that, in its asexual gender neutrality, dismisses its decadent precursors, Daniel Tiffany traces the emergence of imagism to an evolutionary moment depicting "the conversion of literary Decadence into a formation of the avant-garde."[10] He looks to Pound's "youthful experiments with death in poetic language," reframing the poet's concept of aesthetic disinterest as a "form of exquisite but aberrant mourning" (*Radio* 11). According to Tiffany, this modernist image paradoxically propounds a poetics of objectivity that turns on cryptic, hermeneutical, and mythological structures of meaning. This relation is paradoxical because objectivity presumes that meaning is immediately clear and does not require individual acts of hermeneutic interpretation.

While Tiffany's focus is Pound's imagism, his explanation has ramifications for H.D.'s version of the aesthetic as well. Of particular importance to H.D.'s poetry is the relation Tiffany draws between the detachment of the image and its function as a "radiant node or cluster," complete with, as Tiffany puts it, "telegraphic properties" (*Radio* 21). Given this discussion of the image, the figure of H.D.'s mute marionette comes to mind, with its ideal ability to ventriloquize, or telegraph, the voices of its audience. According to Tiffany's reading, in its ability to move beyond individual subjectivity, the image itself is highly objective, but not detached or emotionless. Indeed, Tiffany argues that Pound's imagism semantically inverts our general conceptions of subjectivity and objectivity: "The 'objective' image in particular raises interesting questions, since it emerges from a state of possession, an emotional seizure that Pound terms a 'vortex.' It is important to emphasize that the 'objectivity' of the Image occurs not by purging emotion, but through the agency of emotion" (*Radio* 80). Much like Pound's impersonal imagism, H.D.'s version of impersonality imagines itself as a contractual form of possession, a seizure of the other. This relation is contradictory, as contracts tend to connote objectivity, not emotion. But more so than Pound, in imagining this seizure or possession, H.D.'s prose and poetry stages and theorizes the instability of this impersonal relation. Her poems explicitly function as impersonal poetic contracts; the poet is not merely masked or in personae, as in Pound's poetry, but rather self-negation is literalized through a physical, bodily relation that catalyzes the fracture of lyrical voice.[11] In these examples of poetic impersonality, the maintenance of poetic authority requires an actual, concrete loss of self at the hands of the contractual partner.

In *Notes on Thought and Vision*, for example, the poet overtly emphasizes both the utilitarian and often underhandedly exploitative value of physical relation, asserting that "[a]ll reasoning, normal, sane and balanced men and women need and seek at certain times of their lives, certain definite physical relationships. Men and women of temperament, musicians, scientists, and artists especially need these relationships to develop and draw forth their talents. Not to desire and make every effort to develop along these natural physical lines, cripples and dwarfs the being. To shun, deny and belittle such experiences is to bury one's talent carefully in a napkin" (*Notes* 17). H.D.'s poetic treatise provocatively claims that sublimating "definite" sexually and erotically coded social relationships obscures one's artistic talent. Art develops, H.D. implies, not only from certain strategic affiliations but also from a flow of desire that implies highly gendered exchanges of power between "men and women." Later she claims that "the body like a lump of coal, fulfills its highest function when it is being consumed" (*Notes* 47). H.D.'s maxim-like assessment of the body suggests that its finest utility lies in its capacity to be consumed both by a desiring physical agent, as the object of desire, and in desire itself, as a subject. Thus however "reasoning, normal, sane, and balanced" this relation is, it is not without a form of consuming affect, substantiating the same sort of paradox Tiffany identifies in the "emotional seizure" of imagism (*Radio* 80).

In this impersonal "emotional seizure," self-destructing physical and social relationships engage and heighten creative activity. Furthermore, submission to these relationships paradoxically and dialectically produces aesthetic authority, the end product of the effort to "draw forth . . . talent" (*Notes* 17). In channeling an audience of both one and multiple voices, the marionette image suggests that singular creativity necessarily converges upon more collective acts of aesthetic creation. This theory of a paradoxically impersonal self-creation appears most explicitly in *Notes*. In this text, a private self or interior emerges as a condition of the body's "personal" destruction, in which the artist must submit to another body in order to achieve the desired outcome of distilling the singularity of "individual men and women" (*Notes* 48). As *Notes on Thought and Vision* intimates, the dissolution of personality arises through intense feeling, by simultaneously possessing and being possessed by another body in a scrupulous and ritualistic negotiation of physical and aesthetic space. As we shall see in the reading of *Sea Garden* that follows, poetry itself narrates these processes of possession, where the fantasies of incorporation and spatiality that erupt as rather troublesome political and ethical imperatives simultaneously sustain a progressive vision of gender and sexuality.

A Rose Is a Rose Is a Rose: Impersonality and Poetic Insecurity

This section of the chapter develops a more elaborate picture of H.D.'s theory of impersonality by tracing connections between the poetic theory of *Notes on Thought and Vision* and *The Wise Sappho*, and the first and last poems of *Sea Garden*. The first poem of *Sea Garden*, "Sea Rose," inaugurates the drive toward impersonality as it will appear throughout the collection; it enacts and typifies the dialectical double movement that will complicate boundaries between active and passive subject positions throughout the collection as it narrates the decomposition and recomposition of its poetic subject, the rose, a conventional symbol of femininity. This poem explores the meaning of impersonality through a series of dialectical tensions that continuously dissolve and subsequently reinscribe categories of identity such as gender, transporting its poetic personae or images away from the restrictions of gender without resolutely denying the particularity that accompanies such a category.

The poem begins with the speaker directly addressing the rose, willing this blighted organism into being as she assigns it a value, "more precious / than a wet rose / single on a stem," and narrates its movements:

> Rose harsh rose
> marred and with stint of petals
> meager flower, thin,
> sparse of leaf
> more precious than a wet rose
> single on a stem
> you are caught in the drift
> Stunted, with small leaf,
> you are flung on the sand,
> you are lifted
> in the crisp sand that drives in the wind

Can the spice-rose
drip such acrid fragrance hardened
in a leaf?[12]

Typically the poetic symbol of love and femininity, the rose is "stunted" and "flung on the sand" only to be ecstatically lifted both through and by the stinging medium of the "crisp sand" that actively "drives in the wind" (*CP* 5). This ecstatic "lift" must occur through an intervening agent that actually displaces the rose, dissolving it "in the crisp sand" to enter this process of flinging and lifting once again. In this operation, the rose reaches its impersonal, desymbolized state only to return dialectically to that condition, a movement reinforced by the repetitive structure of the poem. For example, the speaker's repeated reference to the rose as "you" contributes to this tension by demonstrating how the rose moves in and out of the speaker's range of control. This ubiquitous "you" is part of a relationship of command, as imperatives are issued and obeyed; the repeated pronoun reinforces the speaker's authority by confirming the rose as distinct from yet familiar to herself, as it identifies the flower with the speaker's exacting descriptions of its "stunted" and "small" proportions. However, this harshly punctuated "you" also actualizes the rose's "lift." The speaker's surrender of authority manifests itself in the poem's final question of whether this unlikely rose is actually a rose, which strongly contrasts with the confident declarations of its beginning: "Can the spice-rose / drip such acrid fragrance / hardened in a leaf?"(*CP* 5).

The speaker's now tremulous, even dismayed questioning of the nature of the rose positions it with power despite its "stunted" and meager existence. Consistent with Pound's ideal science of imagism, the poem verbally represents an exercise in observation of the image itself that ends with the speaker/observer questioning the likelihood of what she has seen to what that sight abstractly represents. The speaker's doubtful recognition of the rose, which so strongly counters her confident, apostrophic confirmation of the rose at the poem's beginning, suggests that the rose, with its "acrid," repellent fragrance, hardly resembles the abstracted version of itself, yet still holds on to that essential particularity that makes it a rose. Likewise, the rose, a poor specimen of an organism that would hardly survive in this parched and treacherous landscape, bears its most potent power as the image in its most decrepit condition. Yet somehow it does survive; indeed, in apostrophically affirming the rose, the speaker of the poem creates her own evolutionary schema, selecting it as most "fit" and suitable for the impersonal process of creative reproduction.

This enactment of "selection" exemplifies a movement toward control that occurs throughout H.D.'s poetry. In "Sea Rose," however, that very gesture confers power and autonomy onto the rose. Unsuited for the cultural taste for sweetness, the rose possesses the variability to survive alone, to exchange the sociability of the garden for the precarious vulnerability of isolation. Yet despite this absence of animate contact, the "stinted" garden supports the ideals of sociability and human connection that characterize H.D.'s version of impersonality. If sociability implies the "personal" experience arising from communal relations between individuals, then "Sea Rose" demonstrates the mutually constitutive nature of impersonal and personal experience. The impersonal experience, enabled by the rose's passivity and detachment, leads it back to a world of human social connection, of identity, of gender, and of personality.

Thus the "Sea Rose" is questionably a rose, as its identity is dispersed into "the crisp sand / that drives in the wind," which ultimate explains the speaker's final and lingering question: "Can the spice-rose / drip such acrid fragrance hardened / in a leaf?" (*CP* 5). If the speaker embraced conventional codes of gender as symbolized by the red rose, the answer to this question would be no. But the poem itself suggests that the answer is yes, that the rose, still gendered, survives its parched conditions as a misrecognized identity, leaving its conventional identity behind to crystallize its essential and impersonal being. As an image, this state is not a contradiction, but a synthesis. The poem demonstrates that this impersonal condition is but a distillate of the rose's social identity, its role in the world of "fellow beings," its existence as a symbol of sweetness, love, and femininity (*Wise* 59).

A poem such as "The Rose" defines H.D.'s theory of impersonality as dialectical, for the rose's impersonal state of being, its disparate misrecognized identity, does not preclude its original social existence. While H.D.'s impersonal poetic technique may indeed, as Susan Stanford Friedman claims, block direct autobiographical referents, this obstruction does not preclude the poem's evaluation of specified social relationships.[13] In *Notes on Thought and Vision*, for example, H.D. equates the body with personal and social experience, which simultaneously casts off and creates its concentrated essence, or self, much like the transformation of the "stunted" and "marred" rose. In *Notes*, however, the relationship of impersonality to the body is figured analogously to the way an oyster makes a spiritual "pearl of great price" (*Notes* 51). This aesthetic experience is only momentarily available, if at all, because awareness of the pearl automatically shifts "our centre of consciousness" to concern again "with the body," the shell that essentially makes the pearl (*Notes* 50). H.D.'s conception of this "shift" suggests how the state of impersonality depends on the constant exchange of one form of sociality for another, leading to a transhistorical form of experience characterized by permeable, undefined boundaries of the self.

This solubility, this "pearl," occurs both as an outgrowth of and in contrast to an embodiment that individualizes experience through social and personal interaction.

Consequently, H.D.'s poetry raises complex questions about identification, which manifest themselves both in the difficulty of determining the importance of gender in her work and in the dialectical nature of her brand of impersonality. If the dialectic between the self and its dissolution overlays a similar dialectic between "certain definite physical relationships" and creative productivity, the theory of impersonality H.D. elaborates in *Notes* posits personal experience as a condition of awareness and perspicuity that, experienced through the body, overrides the entire journey to the world of impersonal vision and back (*Notes* 17). Nevertheless, H.D. perceives this spiritual body, in which she is a "jellyfish and a pearl" as bound inviolably to a corporeal, worldly body. One can then extrapolate that this impersonal generation, this lifting and flinging, is not a process that one encounters alone. Rather, the creation of this "pearl" requires consuming physical relationships so that the body, as H.D. remarks in *Notes on Thought and Vision*, "gives off heat" (*Notes* 47). In this formulation, H.D. views the body as analogous to both personality and sociality. Like gender, the body is a social or personal element that is necessary for catalyzing the movement into personality, or ecstasy. Conversely, the fall out of ecstasy and back to the body represents an encounter with the incarnate world of human beings.

If this process seems somewhat abstract or cryptic in *Notes*, H.D. more concretely illustrates this inevitable movement from a cherished impersonality to socialized personality in *The Wise Sappho*, particularly by accentuating the paradoxical ethereality of the ancient Alexandrine poet, as evident in the epigraph to this chapter. In this case, H.D. appears to use the term "personality" to refer to the identity one acquires through specific social relationships and interactions and as a specific mode of spatial, social placement. H.D.'s enigmatic and paradoxical description of the tortured Sappho hangs almost tremulously on the word "[y]et," as it presumes simultaneity between impersonal and personal being. The passage seems to fatefully lament the fact that the world of social relationships, of "fellow beings," will consistently supersede and prevent full consummation of the desire to transcend it. However, H.D.'s portrait of Sappho also situates the ancient poet in a state of becoming or metamorphosis. The colliding states of impersonality and personality elicit this perpetually evolving condition, suggesting that the two modes of being violently generate each other through repeated confrontations.

Consistent with this rather conflict-driven philosophy, the poems of *Sea Garden* encode both the combative nature and simultaneity of personality and impersonality. The final poem of the collection, "Cities," which contrasts pointedly with "Sea Rose," meditates on the relation between impersonal creation and the personality that results from social interaction. As I discuss in the introduction to this book, specifically through the example of Wyndham Lewis, modernist impersonality can appear as a politically problematic response to the various effects of democratization and the fictions of individuality and self-expression it is understood to support. This recourse to impersonality as an antidote to the imitative qualities of "personality" and self-expression is also exemplified in a poem such as "Cities," where the crowding of foreign influences have essentially defaced and disfigured the perfection of the city. In saying this, I do not intend to merely reiterate the argument that high modernism vehemently opposed modernity's influx of mass cultural forms, especially since one can consider these forms impersonal in essence, particularly the cinema that H.D. celebrated and embraced. Instead, I wish to point out how the speaker of "Cities" confronts the difficulty, even impossibility, of finding an impersonal space amid the relentless presence of social spaces that the poem codes as "personal." While cities—for intellectuals such as Baudelaire, Whitman, Simmel, and so on—are often impersonally anonymous in essence, the poem envisions the city as distinctly personal in its banality, in the triumph of excessive quotidian prejudice over real beauty or poetic skill.

The poem trades the arid, diffuse space of the garden for the congestion of cosmopolitan life. The first stanza somewhat doubtfully ponders the speaker's ability to recast the social tedium, the bad impersonality that surrounds her:

> Can we believe—by an effort
> comfort our hearts:
> it is not waste all this,
> not placed here in disgust street after street, each patterned alike,
> no grace to lighten
> a single house of the hundred
> crowded into one garden-space.
> Crowded—can we believe,
> not in utter disgust, in ironical play—
> but the maker of cities grew faint
> with the beauty of temple
> and space before temple,
> arch upon perfect arch,
> of pillars and corridors
> that led out to strange court-yards and porches
> where sun-light stamped hyacinth shadows
> black on pavement. (*CP* 39–40)

In these stanzas, the speaker of the poem articulates her misgivings toward the power dynamic that comprises the poetic vocation—or "task" the poem refers to in latter stanzas. The repeated question, "can we believe," presages an anxiety that surrounds the poet's ability to assume poetic command, to correct the lack of beauty and "grace" that characterizes "street after street, each patterned alike." The initial insecurity of this discourse distinctly counters the confident voice of *Sea Garden's* first poem, where the speaker values, affirms, and creates the stunted "single" rose.[14] But in "Cities," the speaker closely aligns her own weakness with the maker of cities' loss of control of his product, his growing "faint" (*CP* 40). Ironically, this loss produces uniformity ("street after street / each patterned alike"), and the isolation of the singular rose's harsh atmosphere succumbs to a "hundred" houses "crowded into one garden-space" (*CP* 40). In this dystopic scenario, the serrated, hostile environment of "Sea Rose," which both impoverishes the stunted rose and supplies it with imagist intensity, is displaced by the human, "personal" need for shelter. This spatial crisis transforms the "garden-space" into a crowded influx of "houses," artificially constructed shelters designed to nourish personal needs. The poem then provides an ironic coda to a collection where shelter is almost always absent and even counterproductive, where exposure functions as the key to poetic mastery.

As a result, the poem continues to waver, uncertain in its project. "Cities" replaces the apostrophic imperative of "Sea Rose" with an explication of how the poet initially acquires such vocative strength. The poem illustrates a progressive movement, in which the questions that disclose the speakers' insecurity—for example, "can we believe?" or "is our task less sweet?"— transform into the more imperative tone of the poem's final stanzas, where the speaker apostrophizes her "love" (*CP* 42). As Jonathan Culler notes in his discussion of apostrophe, the vocative voice actually wills "a state of affairs," which it attempts to call into being "by asking inanimate objects to bend themselves to [its] desire."[15] Culler also remarks that poetic voice uses apostrophe "to establish with an object a relationship which helps to constitute him ... to establish images of its power so as to establish its identity as a poetical and prophetic voice" (*Pursuit* 142). Apostrophe is thus essential to creating a poetic persona and can "be read as an act of radical interiorization and solipsism" (*Pursuit* 146). In "Cities," the speaker initially resists such a merger with the subject of the poem—the city—which would appear to banish, rather than transform, the crowded city, creating a singular environment that resembles that of "Sea Rose." In contrast to the isolated landscape of "Sea Rose," a poem such as "Cities," where an explicitly external sociality induces a poetic crisis, draws attention to the problems of impersonal or apostrophic diffusion. In its incessant insecurity,

"Cities" could be read as a chronological precedent to the earlier poems of *Sea Garden*, as a dramatic declaration of the vulnerability necessary for accessing an authoritative poetic voice.

The speaker's quandary thus involves accessing the ideal type of influence from among a massive barrage of others while protecting herself from the exploitation of which she is, in fact, guilty. Her repeated and apprehensive concern for the growing faintness of "the maker of cities" represents a particular problem; the obfuscation of artistic talent necessitates the poet's hunt through a crowded rubble, a scene of mismanaged influence, where mere copies eclipse the real purveyors of cultural memory. A demented form of impersonality results from this city, crowded "so full / that men could not grasp beauty" (*CP* 40). Consequently, the untrammeled, almost toxic beauty of the *Sea Garden* can only surface through a specific, scrupulously managed, and highly exclusive contract that will provide the poet with a voice. Accessing the correct form of poetic voice depends on the poet's ability to decipher and sort through the debris of her acquaintances. How one takes maximum advantage of this congested social and personal space by judiciously culling out various modes of good influence ultimately determines one's success as a poet.

This anxious rhetoric, circulating around organicist concepts borrowed from the biological sciences, follows the specific patterns Erin Carlston has identified in her argument that fascism "often supplied the vocabulary of even the most vigorous anti-fascist critiques."[16] Despite these similarities, however, H.D.'s lexicon differs markedly from Carlston's description of a culture whose disdain for commercialism emerges in images of "commodified sexuality, particularly masturbation, homosexuality, and prostitution" (*Thinking* 39). H.D.'s lyrics extend beyond mere caricature and misogynistic finger-pointing as a means of disciplining the crude commercialist impulse that characterizes the new "city." Indeed, the poem questions how to authoritatively manage this aesthetic wasteland without necessarily appearing too undemocratic. The poet's solution to this dilemma is problematic in itself, as her resolve lies in the speaker's waning poetic authority, which actually increases the urgency of her mission. "Is our task less sweet," she asks, that the "larvae still sleep in their cells? / Or crawl out to attack our frail strength" (*CP* 41).

In invoking the cell, H.D. draws on discourse from the biological sciences to describe the trials of the poetic vocation:

So he built a new city,
ah can we believe, not ironically
but for new splendour
constructed new people

> to lift through slow growth
> to a beauty unrivalled yet—
> and created new cells
> hideous first, hideous now—
> spread larvae across them,
> not honey but seething life.
> And in these dark cells,
> packed street after street, souls live, hideous yet—
> O disfigured, defaced
> with no trace of beauty men once held so light.
> Can we think a few old cells were left—we are left—
> grains of honey,
> old dust of stray pollen
> dull on our torn wings,
> we are left to recall the old streets?
> Is our task the less sweet
> That the larvae still sleep in their cells?
> Or crawl out to attack our frail strength:
> You are useless: We live.
> We await great events.
> We are spread through this earth.
> We protect our strong race.
> You are useless.
> Your cell takes the place
> Of our young future strength.
> Though they sleep or wake to torment
> and wish to displace our old cells—
> thin rare gold—
> that their larvae grow fat
> is our task the less sweet? (*CP* 40–41)

Here, the speaker employs the scientific discourse of "cells" to convey the general interplay of active and passive subject positions in the poem. Her use of the term can refer respectively to a singular and microscopic building block of matter, to a space of imprisonment, or, considering her frequent references to "honey," a unit within a hive, a social space for reproduction and shelter. Whatever its specific meaning, the term most generically and importantly announces itself as a unit of space, a tool for exploring two larger units of space, the city and the poem itself. The constructed new people of this city space develop alongside the "new cells," which "lift through slow growth" artificially and robotically, too rapidly to develop properly, thus becoming "disfigured" and "defaced" (*CP* 41). The impersonal and, one could also argue, commercial forces of modern city life have erased the face itself; individuality evaporates leaving no particular "face" by which to measure beauty or difference. Consequently, space itself holds no meaning.[17] At this moment, the poem stages one of the primary problems of impersonality this book explores: how does an aesthetic that attempts to dissolve the individual personality of the poet in favor of a more collective medium guard against its own dissolution into a formless mass with no sense of distinction? What happens to boundaries, to space itself, when poetry becomes impersonal? What kind of poetic authority is needed to manage this spatial problem? This disappearance of any kind of marked individuality also erases memory, leaving only the "old cells" to recollect the "old dust or stray pollen" and "to recall the old streets" (*CP* 41). These cells are the artists, the purveyors and safe-keepers of cultural memory, floating within a sea of copies and commodified art forms.

The question "is our task less sweet?" suggests that the vulnerability of the old cells' position actually renders their task *more* sweet. Likewise, the question intimates that the task of poetry is always fundamentally sweet, despite the despair and anxiety that might accompany it. Much like the acrid stench of the "Sea Rose," "Cities" juxtaposes "sweetness" with the less savory aspects of poetic production. In the poem, the old cells' task is more sweet, because the larvae's attack on their "frail strength" ironically instills in these spent remnants the virility to take "the place / of our young future strength" (*CP* 41). Through this relationship, the poem both organically integrates and confuses the distinction between active power and passive inefficacy. This confusion works through a scientific process of grafting; the old, native cells actually succumb to, and thereby exploit, the new cells in order to reproduce themselves. This paradoxically submissive exploitation, or mutual parasitism, forms the core of H.D.'s impersonal aesthetic, coded erotically as a mode of oral transmission within the last stanza of the poem:[18]

> *The city is peopled*
> *with spirits, not ghosts, O my love:*
> *Though they crowded between and*
> *usurped the kiss of my mouth*
> *their breath was your gift,*
> *their beauty, your life.* (italics in original; *CP* 42)

Here, spirits "crowded between and / usurped the kiss of my mouth" to give the beloved "life." The spirits overtake the speaker's vocal space of transmission in a sacrificial gesture that revitalizes her beloved, quite possibly the "disfigured" and "defaced" she apostrophizes earlier in the poem. The speaker's return to that same apostrophic mode at the end of the poem ("O my love") to evoke the now vulnerable and disfigured "maker of cities" suggests that this sacrifice has restored her poetic confidence along with the beloved's, not the speaker's "life." In its startling turn into a love lyric that apostrophizes or speaks nostalgically through the departure of a once magnificent poetic authority, the masculine maker of cities, the poem stages a revival of the speaker's poetic authority, along with the new "race" she represents (*CP* 41).

The method of grafting the speaker uses to imagine "our strong race" differs from that of the maker of cities in that he constructs a series of clones. The form of poetic replication H.D. outlines in "Cities" preserves a mark of particularity within her collective "our," achieved through both submission to and manipulation of the new cells. Indeed, the speaker seems to imagine an aesthetic parthenogenesis derived precisely from the bad impersonality she laments at the beginning of the poem, a reproductive enterprise so exclusive that it creates and sustains its own strong "race," hidden like terrorists in cells, who "await great events" and are latently "spread through this earth" (*CP* 41). There is no mention of gender here. The poem details a mode of asexual, impersonal reproduction that disregards the gender of its participants. Rather, the speaker uses the term "race" to mark her marginal identity and her exclusive claim to poetic expertise.

The form of reproduction the poem imagines particularly evokes Remy de Gourmont's *The Natural Philosophy of Love*, which, though originally published in 1904, was translated by Pound in 1926. In his introduction to the text, Pound stresses the link between the "domain of aesthetics" and sex and defines reproduction as a process of prosthetic creation. In keeping with his general presentation of gender, Pound aligns parthenogenesis with maleness, famously asserting that the "mind is an up-start of sperm."[19] The mind, like sperm, is an "up-start," both existing and functioning through an ejaculative movement outward. A few pages later, Pound further illustrates this process by discussing a more observable specimen: "[A]n insect carries a saw, it carries it all the time. The 'next step,' as in the case of the male organ of the nautilus, is to grow a tool and detach it" (*Natural* xiii). This propensity toward outgrowth produces a more sensitive, feeling being; the organism can extend his body's boundaries of feeling through exteriorization to an antennaelike effect. This process is one of many "extravagances in nature," which can be reduced to a "single out-push of a demand, made by a spermatic sea of sufficient energy to cast such a form; to exteriorize" (*Natural* xiii). Pound's findings here, as he self-consciously asserts, are compatible with the domain of aesthetic creation and illuminate H.D.'s use of scientific discourse in her own poetry as a means of exploring and resolving issues of poetic instability and insecurity. Yet H.D.'s lyrics differ from Pound's process of exteriorization in that her poetry envisions these reproductive engagements as subject to human control, choice, and deliberation, even manipulation. Thus, while texts such as *Notes on Thought and Vision* and *The Wise Sappho* imagine an impersonality that occurs involuntarily through unselfconscious interaction, poems like "Cities" point to the importance of intentional decision making in initiating these contracts.

Both H.D.'s and Pound's respective sciences of poetry define impersonality as a process of exteriorization that occurs through a precise combination of voluntary and involuntary efforts. While my point here is to demonstrate how H.D.'s impersonality creates a sense of an impersonal interior, a movement beyond the body to a concentrated essence or "pearl," this interior is structurally similar to Pound's exterior in that it is not amenable to interpretation or psychological depth. Rather, H.D.'s poetic interiority moves outward, toward the exterior, in a replication of the poetic self. Both H.D. and Pound appear to derive this prosthetic version of modernism from de Gourmont, who identifies two modes of asexual reproduction, "division and budding" (*Natural* 10).[20] These processes blur the boundary between asexual and sexual reproduction, since the terms serve also to describe "the formation of animal colonies, when the new individual retains a point of contact with the generating individual" (*Natural* 10). In no instance does de Gourmont find these forms of reproduction so remotely impersonal that "contact" or connection is lost. Particularly regarding the version of impersonality H.D.'s "Cities" illustrates, where the old cells exploit the softly fattened new cells to strengthen their own "race," creating prosthetic but slightly altered versions of themselves, the poem maintains the importance of a connection that actually problematizes the exploitation involved in the poetic reproduction it enacts (*CP* 41). The last stanza, which lauds the speakers' sacrifice by referring to the effusive solubility of "their breath," reaffirms a more positive point of connection in an otherwise impersonally negotiated contract between the poem's speaker and her subject (*CP* 42).

In envisioning primarily parthenogenic modes of reproduction, "Cities" can read like eugenicist fantasy but one that discounts classicism (and the classical body) as a trope that offers no solution to the poet's current aesthetic dilemma because the aesthetic world is already swollen with its influence.[21] For the poet, the overuse of classical imagery, which leaves "no crevice unpacked with the honey" quickly transforms, only one stanza later, to "hideous, disfigured, defaced" souls "packed street after street" (*CP* 40). Such lyrics disclose H.D.'s territorial stance toward the world of classical beauty, which her poetry guards from those who would cheapen it. This stance may seem rather undemocratic, if not outright authoritarian. However, if we read "Cities" in conjunction with a poem such as "Sea Rose," we can see that H.D.'s goal is to limit the misuse of classical imagery by selecting those, like the "Sea Rose," who, in being unfit, are most fit for poetic community. What is important and valuable about the rose and the *Sea Garden* in general is that it is not beautiful, not worthy of the standards of eugenic manipulation or natural selection.

Additionally, the process of poetic replication "Cities" illustrates appears to disregard gender as a criterion for poetic selection. Rather, the poem ostensibly broods on the poetic vocation more generally as it develops through interactions with a personalized sociality. The poem suggests that, however wearisome and disappointing the world of personal contact, disconnecting oneself from it entirely proves impossible and destructive. However, the poem's anxiety surrounds the specific difficulties the poet faces in accessing an impersonal voice within aesthetic tedium. The speaker deliberately presents herself as a marginalized presence, referring to poetic authority, or the "maker of cities," as a "he" (*CP* 40). However, in keeping with the ambivalent gender relations that characterize H.D.'s poetry, the speaker does not stand either directly with or, conversely, in feminine contrast to the masculine maker of cities. Rather, the speaker is not a woman, not a man, but a particularized "our," where poetic authority is explicitly a "he." H.D. thus refuses a binary that situates a feminine poetics against masculine poetic authority, even though she still tends to align masculinity with aesthetic dominance. Similarly, H.D.'s theory of impersonality seeks to evade gender but cannot function without reference to it. The poet's assertion that the "body of a man is a means of approach to ecstasy" eroticizes the philosophy of "Cities" in terms of a masochistic contract that permits the passive body to "use" the "consuming" agent in catalyzing self-dissolution (*Notes* 47). If feminist critics are correct in aligning H.D.'s concerns with those of women in general, then such a masochistic contract must be decidedly heterosexual, positing the female poet as the passive but ultimately victorious agent in her contract with masculine poetic authority. Yet H.D.'s poetry complicates this interpretation, as I suggest in the following section, particularly in relation to the poem's various gendered personae.

Contractually Speaking: H.D.'s Poetics of Masochism

> Sexuality, it is said, is dramatic because we commit our whole personal life to it.
>
> —M. Merleau-Ponty[22]

In *Phenomenology of Perception*, Merleau-Ponty questions the dramatic view of sexuality that involves our "personal life" (*Phenomenology* 171). He argues that while the body serves as the "mirror of our being," we can never fully understand the forces that bear on it: "There is no outstripping of sexuality any more than there is any sexuality enclosed within itself. No one is saved and no one is totally lost" (*Phenomenology* 171). This view of sexuality also characterizes the impersonal sexual poetics of H.D.'s poetry, as well as the respective sciences of both Pound and de Gourmont, which both mark reproduction, however physical and impersonal, as a process of feeling. Through contact with another, the body exteriorizes itself, producing what Pound calls "feelers," to both heighten its own sensual awareness while paradoxically dispersing that awareness into another being (*Natural* xiii). Such a science of reproduction and exteriorization characterizes H.D.'s own poetic masochism, enabling the dialectic that occurs between intense feeling and anesthetized detachment. In this sense, I am defining impersonality as a theory of acute sensuality that heightens feeling to the point of erasure. Victor Smirnoff has elaborated extensively on this particular form of affect as a feature of masochism, which he finds "in almost any mythical representation of sacrifice."[23] By translating Sacher-Masoch's use of the German *ubersinnlich* as "beyond sensuality," Smirnoff argues that "masochistic 'pleasure' transgresses the borders of perception and sensibility, moving beyond the realm of vision, touch, pain or kinaesthesia" ("Masochistic" 66).

I have chosen the concept of masochism as characteristic of H.D.'s aesthetic because it best describes *Sea Garden's* often tedious embrace of reiteration, suspense, and bodily suffering. Furthermore, the formalized aspects of masochism, as illustrated by Freud, Deleuze, and Theodor Reik, among others, closely comply with the often rigorously formalized tenets of imagism and the modernist doctrine of impersonality more generally.[24] Freud, in *Three Essays on the Theory of Sexuality*, addresses this splitting more explicitly as a spatial phenomenon, arguing that "components of the sexual instinct which involve pain and cruelty" are necessarily related to the skin, "which in particular parts of the body has become differentiated into sense organs or modified into mucous membrane, and is thus the erotogenic zone par excellence."[25] In masochism, the sensory organs are remodified, sculpted as a reorganization of space. Masochism emerges from these accounts as a spatial dynamic that systematically and ritualistically builds and deconstructs boundaries between individuals.

As masochistic experiments, H.D.'s *Sea Garden* poems construct the poetic vocation as a contract that involves certain sacrifices on both sides, both cementing and perpetuating the poet's own authority. This relationship ostensibly presents a problem for feminist criticism, primarily because of the difficulty of reading feminine masochism outside of a framework that normalizes it in terms of women's subjectivity and makes it pathological for the male.[26] Even "utopian" rereadings of masochism, such as Gilles

Deleuze's anti-Freudian *Coldness and Cruelty*, privilege a purely heterosexual model of contractual relations that posits women as fetishized objects and thereby victims of the male masochistic educator. Despite its limitations, and its tendency to arouse ambivalence, even hostility, from feminists, Deleuze's theory itself is flexible enough to accommodate numerous alternative configurations of active and passive gendered subject positions. According to Deleuze, the masochistic contract reverses the ostensible relationship between the sadist as the active administerer of pain and the victim as the passive receiver. This interpretation serves the aims and interests of the victim, whose passivity allows her to "educate, persuade and conclude an alliance with the torturer" in a "contracted" relationship.[27] Desire emanates from both sides of this contract, necessitating a poetic trade whose payoff is impersonal power and authority.

H.D.'s depiction of the impersonal aesthetic experience best corresponds to this interpretation of the masochistic contract. While my point is not to reductively align H.D.'s poetic masochism with Deleuze's understanding of the term, my analysis proceeds from their common understanding of masochism as a ritualized, scripted progression from personal to impersonal states of being. Deleuze looks to fleshly pain as the catalyst for impersonal experience; impersonal violence, identifying itself with "an Idea of pure reason," always subordinates the "descriptive personal and individual taste of the sadist" (*CC* 20). By pairing the term "descriptive" with "personal" and "individual," Deleuze links the sadist with the limited world of social significations, of individual identity. In this scenario, the masochistic victim is the agent of impersonal transmission, prompting the torturer to do her will by incorporating her voice into the master's own, speaking "through the mouth of his torturer" and "prompting the harsh words she addresses to him" (*CC* 22). In a process akin to that elaborated in *Notes on Thought and Vision* as well as in Eliot's "Tradition and the Individual Talent," the supposedly passive victim strategically dilutes personal experience through ventriloquism, as if the torturer merely masks his own wishes and desires. This activity, much like poetic apostrophe, vocatively replicates and splits the self so that the imperative component of masochism "transcends itself"; according to Deleuze, the "personal element" thus turns "by reflection upon itself into the impersonal" (*CC* 23).

Additionally, the "transcendental" or impersonal feature of masochism contests the validity of the fetishized tormentor. The pleasure of masochism lies in this disavowal, realized as the masochist prompts and scripts her tormentor in a performance of ritual and reiteration. *Sea Garden* explores quite directly how this ritualized approach to sexual relation incorporates the torturer into the masochist's script, ultimately reversing active and passive subject positions. On this brutal stage, gender forms only one condition of the dialectical movement between embodiment and disembodiment, personalization and impersonalization. The poems are consistent in their slipperiness, their rockiness, as they teeter with curious regularity on the verge of collapse. One notes this vacillation not only in the poems' harsh accents and punctuations but also in the series of dashes H.D. uses to construct their more fragmentary moments. These constructions appear not only in poems such as "Sea Rose," where the punctuated "you" partitions poetic confidence and its dissolution, but also in poems such as "The Helmsman," where dashes perform the same function.

Fragmentary Sameness and the Problem of Difference

In keeping with this paradoxically constant unrest, the poems often confuse issues of sameness—of shared experiential or same-sex identification—and fragmentary difference, so that the cohesiveness of female community often develops through divisiveness. These relationships appear particularly in "The Helmsman," which exemplifies how H.D.'s poetry simultaneously magnifies and repudiates sexual difference, both defining what is at stake in sexuality and attempting to leave it behind. In addition, the poem extensively meditates on the relations between interiority, community, and the double-bind of sameness—what accounts paradoxically for both a shared social identity as well as the shared, impersonal poetic community that surpasses that identity. H.D.'s ambivalent relation to sameness, especially as it surfaces in this poem, both affirms same-sex connection and problematizes that very identity.

Feminist readings of "The Helmsman" have generally emphasized the issue of erotic suffering in the poem as it creates female community, focusing on same-sex identification as it corresponds to H.D.'s real-life bisexuality. Alternately, I propose here that suffering, as suggested in the poem's contractual movement, might indeed have its reward.[28] Indeed, as evident in the imperative tone of "The Helmsman's" first lines, the initiates fashion a contract with the helmsman that reinforces their desire as enabling, part of their own system of control:

O be swift—
we have always known you wanted us. (*CP* 5)

In this case, the consuming desire of the helmsman ritualistically enables the collective female voice. The first two lines of the poem specify that the speakers already know of the helmsman's desire for them, locating it formally as a component of a returning, ritualistic cycle. The speakers' urgent clairvoyance also suggests that the entire poem (and the helmsman) follow a script of their own devising. As the inaugurating gestures, this scripting and prompting establish the poem as a masochistic contract. In Deleuzian masochism, the masochist disavows the world, an action that creates an impersonal reality through a "double suspension," since the victim merely detaches himself or herself from that world, without "destroying [it] nor . . . idealizing it" (*CC* 32). Sustaining such double suspension—which surfaces in the dialectical movement between a personalized world of social relations and an impersonal condition—requires strict formalization. Similarly, masochistic pain and pleasure depend on a highly ritualized series of repetitions that delays and suspends pleasure, a formality that manifests itself in the dictates of imagist law.

"The Helmsman" reinforces its speakers' ritualistic command of events by focusing on his desire as a part of their own script. Their focus on their own desire, and their corresponding control of it, suggests that they do not "decline in the sensuous trap of consuming male desire" (*HDVF* 112). In this dramatic and self-conscious production, the speakers conjure the helmsman with erotic expectation—"O be swift"—according to their previous knowledge of his desire: "[W]e have always known you wanted us" (*CP* 5). As they apostrophically will into being their own submission, they essentially create the helmsman's desire for them. This action reverses the Deleuzian masochistic scenario of woman as fetishized and disavowed object while engaging the male as masochistic "educator"; it ultimately contests the validity of his desire by turning him into an object of disavowal, or masochistic fetish. Likewise, the poem reverses the connection between femininity and masochism, which both Freudian and Deleuzian accounts sustain. Rather, the poem's scripting mechanism incites the helmsman's pursuit and explicitly identifies his desire as a lack that will never see fulfillment.

Sea Garden obsessively catalogues this restless spirit of the hunt not only in "The Helmsman" but also in other poems, such as "Pursuit" and "Huntress." The masochistic economies of these poems deliberately instigate states of suspension and expectancy that define the apparent cohesion of the female community as difference. That is, the idea of sameness in this context cannot necessarily be interpreted as a homoeroticism that affirms female community or lesbian identification. What critics have ultimately read as female community is less important than the greater sense of poetic community *Sea Garden* attempts to establish. In the instance of "The Helmsman," extreme communal insularity implies geographical partitioning and aesthetic death, as suggested in the remaining stanzas of the poem:

> We fled inland with our flocks
> we pastured them in hollows,
> cut off from the wind
> and the salt track of the marsh
> We worshipped inland—
> we stepped past wood-flowers,
> we forgot your tang
> we brushed wood-grass
> We wandered from pine-hills
> through oak and scrub-oak tangles,
> we broke hyssop and bramble,
> caught flower and new bramble-fruit
> in our hair: we laughed
> as each branch whipped back,
> we tore our feet in half buried rocks
> and knotted roots and acorn-cups
> . . .
> We forgot—
> for a moment tree-resin, tree-bark,
> sweat of a torn branch
> were sweet to the taste.
> . . .
> But now, our boat climbs—hesitates—drops—
> climbs—hesitates—crawls back—
> climbs—hesitates
> O be swift—
> we have always known you wanted us. (*CP* 5–7)

When the initiates "fled inland with our flocks" and "pastured them in hollows, / cut off from the wind / and the salt track of the marsh," they separate themselves from the helmsman and reduce their sensory capabilities. They prevent themselves from moving "beyond sensuality" by closing the boundaries of their bodies too tightly in intensive worship that is, paradoxically, a form of forgetting ("Masochistic" 66). Nonetheless, the initiates define the terms of the chase as they perpetually dissociate themselves from the threat of the helmsman's desire. However, this separation, which excessively restricts the personality, produces too much sameness. In the case of "The Helmsman," the difference the initiates vigorously maintain from their follower arises from the action of forgetting, both a restriction of their conscious world and an elaboration of their unconscious world. Yet the active nature of verbs such as "forgot" and "brushed" simultaneously suggests that such movements are anything but unconscious, if not intentional. As they tread inland, away from the helmsman, the initiates lose the aesthetic sensitivity born through erotic pain—stepping "past wood-flowers, / we forgot your tang, / . . . we brushed wood-grass" (*CP* 6). Their own oblivion, reflected in the repeated phrase "we forgot," ignites their compensatory search for aesthetic sensibility and fulfillment, which, as a ritual, must blend self-conscious deliberation with unconscious movement. However, the group's solitary worship and unified enchantment with their "personally" gendered female environment dims a higher aesthetic experience that depends precisely on their reflexive openness to the helmsman's desire.

Much like the poetic reproduction of "Cities," the shared identification that arises from this forgetting both queers the poem and encourages its ethical difficulty. The apparent sameness of same-sex "choric" identification endures only through a lapse of memory or, in a more deliberate gesture, a refused awareness of the helmsman's pursuit. In its attention to this cohesive forgetfulness, even irresponsibility, the poem regretfully mourns the lost pleasure of the initiates' shared identification, which it must trade for the form of relation that enables impersonal experience. On one level, the poem, and the queer politics that arises from it, suggests that relation with the same does not function as relation at all. It thus looks toward the problem of difference that a poem like "Cities" explores; how does one selectively create a truly impersonal poetic community that renounces individualism while preserving a sense of difference? Furthermore, how does this selective management of poetic community end up reinstituting individual power? "The Helmsman" does not provide a solid answer to these questions. The initiates' deliberate willing of the pursuit blurs the distinction between the difference of the helmsman and the sameness of their own community, victim and victimizer; the last stanza's "[b]ut now" demonstrates how the initiates remember this willing as a difference between past and present as it reinscribes a sense of the unconsummated distance between themselves and the helmsman. Simultaneously, this transition alerts them once again to the intentionality of their call, their scripting of the chase—in effect, their own construction and maintenance of the helmsman's desire. In Deleuzian terms, this coercive ventriloquism is an impersonal act of linguistic splitting that paradoxically severs and fragments the initiates' body. It also contests the helmsman's desire by bringing him into sameness with them.

In incorporating the helmsman into the initiates' own linguistic economy, the poem offers a more radical exploration of sameness that refuses a distinction between heterosexuality as difference and homosexuality or homoeroticism as love of the same. This coin has two sides; on the first, the poem clearly codes same-sex love and identification as a problematic limitation of the personality whose very emphasis on superficial forms of community prevents true, impersonal communal existence.[29] On the other side, however, the poem disturbs the conventional sexual and gendered binaries that stabilize heteronormativity. To make matters more difficult, this disturbance only arises through the initiates' authoritarian invasion of the helmsman's subject position. Particularly as it links sexuality to poetic form, the poem then enables a critique of the boundaries that create sexuality in the first place. Yet this very critique consolidates the initiates' identity in the same manner that same-sex love does. The initiates suspend themselves between their desire for difference, which occurs in relation to the helmsman, and their desire for self-replication, which functions as an ethically problematic invasion of the helmsman's subject (or object) position. Ultimately, the poem collapses this suspension, since the impersonal state the initiates enter by accessing difference in their relation to the Helmsman works as self-replication. However much the initiates direct their desire toward an other, they actually desire the same—characterized by the repetitive nature of ritual and delay that will dissolve and reconstitute their own bond. The poem's gender dynamics subtly contemplate the nuanced relations of poetic power, radically envisioning ritualistic submission as essential to maintaining poetic authority.

The poem links its own enmeshing of sameness and difference to its play with active and passive subject positions. A protean familiarity with either subject position is the goal of the poem's drive toward impersonality. The series of reversals and suspensions that occurs in the last stanza of the poem narrates the dialectical operations of such desire. The boat "crawls back" in a restriction of the ego, of personality, of the sensation that arises through bodily fracture, on to move forward again. This dialectical romp, like similar stanzas in "Sea Gods," "The Shrine," and "Sea Rose," refuses to consummate the relation between the helmsman and the initiates. The interminably incomplete nature of this partnership suggests that impersonality never functions merely as an end. In reaching this impersonal moment, the initiates' call for the helmsman paradoxically splinters them into union with him, producing the ethical kernel of discord in the poem. Does this decisive action fuse their separate identities in an authoritarian invasion of the individual, or does it progressively emphasize their connection? Like the "old cells" of "Cities," the initiates extend H.D.'s use of scientific and reproductive metaphor, grafting themselves into the body of the helmsman to establish a clone-like base of power.

To invigorate their ability to inhabit the helmsman's subject position, the initiates autoerotically script their own pleasure to disavow the helmsman and his desire. Yet the poem's scripting mechanism, which itself reveals the desire to disavow, codes that desire as productive by commissioning their self-dissolving yet self-replicatory takeover of the helmsman's body. This productivity occurs because the poem's suspension works by collapsing the division between subject and object, what traditionally constitutes lack in the Hegelian logic of desire, and reinstilling that division. This suspension bolsters the initiates' passive expectancy, which allows them, in kinship with the parasitic "new cells" of "Cities," to stunningly invade and replicate themselves through the helmsman's body.

In its concern for gender, the poem exchanges collective female pleasure for a fractured condition that permits the speakers to occupy multiple subject positions. This polymorphous motility occurs both as sameness and as difference, since the same voice occupies two distinct speaking positions, producing a transgendered poetic subject and speaker. The resulting form of poetic community transcends both the body and gender identification but cannot exist without dialectical reference to those very categories. As a consequence, the impersonal dialectic overrides a movement beyond and then back to gender identification that also encompasses sexual desire. The oscillations of the last stanzas not only represent the dialectic between impersonal and personal being but also point to the continual processes of desexualization and resexualization that necessarily attend this dialectic.

I have argued here that H.D. uses this theory of impersonality to irrevocably link same-sex love with heterosexuality, since the poem codes the contractual bond that produces such vocative and sexual mobility as decidedly heterosexual. However, the heterosexual relation ultimately collapses in the poem, because the contract it enacts with the helmsman produces an obligatory and invasive sameness, the prosthetic replication of the speaker we see in poems such as "Cities," at the same time that it repudiates it. The poem's progressive logic is equally reactionary; the heterosexual contract gives way to domination and authority, and its disavowal of the paternal order only maintains a logic of control, which in its disdain for the individual denies autonomy and difference. Whatever dialectic the poem wants to maintain between impersonal and personal being crumbles because it tends to reproduce exactly the kind of power and desire it repudiates.

Authoritative Exchange and the Vulnerability of Form

Poems such as "Cities" and "The Helmsman" allow for a more succinct definition of the impersonal moment as that act of self-replication required to incorporate one's poetic voice into other subject positions. This particular moment can be interpreted as either potentially invasive, designed to manufacture poetic authority and control, or supremely empathic. A provocative poem such as "Cities" suggests that impersonality does not initiate a break into multiple personalities but actually clones one particular poetic personality into a number of subject positions. This process alters the original parameters of the invading personality without eliminating what is essential to both subjects. In their repetitive dialectical structures, the poems demonstrate that the culminating moment of this scientifically coded poetic project is always its reversal. If disembodiment, and thus poetic replication, occurs through the intrusion of another body or poetic voice, then the impersonal payoff allows the sacrificial poet to commit her own violations. Her poetic voice perpetuates itself through future generations only by channeling itself through a string of other voices. This ventriloquistic multiplication effectively reverses her previous submission to poetic authority; she now occupies the sadistic position of "passive" torturer—to be used like a man as a means of achieving ecstasy. Taken together, the poems of *Sea Garden* reveal a self-conscious, gendered anxiety that arises in reference to the work's very project of authoritatively delineating true poetic community. As works such as "Cities" and *Notes on Thought and Vision* illustrate, poetic authority need not only perpetuate and establish itself, but it must also limit access to its own influence.

Sea Garden explores this vulnerable yet sadistic side of the masochistic contract through the gendering of the poems' poetic personae. For example, while the personae of poems such as "The Gift" or "Prisoners" arguably acquire a masculine gender, they also examine the debilitating effects of poetic authority as it becomes too rigorously formalized. I argue here that the speakers of these poems are masculine because, unlike poems such as "The Helmsman," these poems tend to destabilize an authority that the speaker of the poem possesses from the beginning. As I argued in my reading of "Cities," the poems of *Sea Garden* often masculinize poetic authority but do not necessarily support a binary relationship between masculine authority and a feminine poetics. Like the "maker of cities," an explicit "he," these speakers initiate their poems through their possession of the script that grants them authority. However, in keeping with *Sea Garden's* interest in poetic authority as it is both destabilized and rebuilt, the poems generate an inherently unstable poetic authority, as they stage a spatial collapse that contests their own formalization.

A poem such as "The Gift," where the masculine personae of the poem self-reflexively frets over his own authority in scenarios that evoke Pound's own masculinization of H.D.'s poetry, even more scrupulously attends to this gendered trade of poetic authority. As in "Cities," the masculine speaker of the poem attenuates his apostrophic power by drawing attention to the possible denial of his request:

> Instead of pearls—a wrought clasp—
> a bracelet—will you accept this?
> You know the script—

> you will start, wonder:
> what is left, what phrase
> after last night? (*CP* 16)

Here, the speaker reinforces the passivity of the recipient by positing himself as the agent of giving. She may passively accept the gift, but the speaker's self-deprecation qualifies his own power by making the acceptance conditional and by anticipating his beloved's ability to "know the script," which suggests that scripting has no use when his addressee foresees it (*CP* 16). This implication reverses the scripting mechanism of "The Helmsman" by suggesting not only that the speaker creates and possesses the script but also that the addressee can deauthorize his performance. The "script" is useful only in so far as access to it is limited.

H.D.'s poetry consequently theorizes impersonal poetic form in both its simultaneous dependence on a series of formalized and masochistic scripts and its constant destabilization of them. In "The Gift," the speaker believes his formal knowledge of the script guarantees his mastery of its ritual, just as one can master poetic form. However, the addressee's knowledge of the script destabilizes that ritual, instilling this type of deauthorization as a necessarily painful prerequisite to poetic creation. So while H.D.'s lyrics emphasize rigorous, almost excessive formalization as necessary for an impersonal poetics, such scripts are ultimately knowable, so she must also continuously challenge that formalism to maintain her "members only" policy. Her poems carefully qualify Pound's assurance in *ABC of Reading* that one can learn poetry through copious study and rigorous attention to poetic "method" (*ABC* 11). However, her lyrics must continuously deauthorize that authority in order to maintain it, to ensure that real talent separates itself from those who have simply learned to mimic it or, in the words of "Cities," from spaces too resplendent with beauty and honey.

This duality of the script, manifest in its ability to deauthorize itself, augments the speaker's paranoia:

> Do not think me unaware
> I who have snatched at you as the street-child clutched
> at the seed pearls you spilt
> that hot day
> when your necklace snapped.
> Do not dream that I speak
> as one defrauded of delight,
> sick, shaken by each heart-beat
> or paralyzed, stretched at length, who gasps:
> these ripe pears
> are bitter to the taste,

> this spiced wine, poison, corrupt,
> I cannot walk—
> who would walk?
> Life is a scavenger's pit—I escape—
> I only, rejecting it,
> lying here on this couch. (*CP* 16)

The speaker's vulnerability, his acute awareness of his paralyzing denigration, results from his relation to the image itself, which he has only "clutched" or "snatched at" vehemently but helplessly. The beloved in this poem personifies the poetic subject par excellence, manifested in the image, which is itself when it is not like itself. Thus the "ripe pears" that would accompany the beloved are actually "bitter to the taste" (*CP* 16). Likewise, this "spiced wine" is "poison, corrupt," continually sabotaging the speaker's attempts to appropriate it (*CP* 16). The image, and the beloved, actualizes a type of misrecognition that the speaker, whose interest is in command and authority, does not understand. Like "Sea Rose," the poem is not so much an exemplar of imagism but a self-conscious enactment or a didactic tool. Returning to Daniel Tiffany's reading of Pound's image as cryptology, which "sustains a poetic language" characterized by a decadent obsession with "dead bodies and ghosts," one can see that the poem both inverts and reinforces this perspective (*Radio* 20). As a distant memory or ghost, the image appears as the passive object of the speaker's active quest, which soon renders him pathologically passive, "sick, shaken / defrauded of delight / or paralyzed / stretched at length . . . / lying here on this couch" (*CP* 16). In general, the absence of apostrophic address in this poem suggests that the speaker cannot incorporate the poetic image; rather, he can only mimic it, in keeping with Tiffany's claim that at its earliest state, "the image presupposes a profound state of passivity" that enacts its own disappearance (*Radio* 52).

Rather than disappearing, the speaker of the poem appears to adhere to the script that he references at the poem's beginning, which requires that he revert back to his personal self to sustain his own poetic authority. This deliberate exercise entails that he must trade places with his poetic subject. Significantly, H.D.'s "The Gift" appeared a year before the 1917 publication of T. S. Eliot's "The Love Song of J. Alfred Prufrock" with its "patient etherized upon a table."[30] Her "paralyzed" patient appears "stretched at length . . . / lying here on this couch" (*CP* 16). While this moment clearly predates the famous sessions with Freud she records in her memoir, *Tribute to Freud* (1956), her reference to this mode of prostration presages her discomfort with psychoanalysis and its hermeneutical objective of mapping the self.[31] However passive, the speaker appears unable to transcend the outlines of his own body: he is stretched, but not broken. His passivity does not bring him to impersonality. Rather, the speaker has followed the dialectical tenets of impersonality too rigidly and consequently backs into his personality without moving out of it. He has desired to the point of anesthetization, acknowledging the addressee's power by envisioning himself as the ineffectual hunter of a "street-child" who covets the impersonal shower of "seed-pearls" falling haphazardly from a broken thread. Whereas H.D.'s theory of impersonality demands a codified contract between two individuals, "The Gift" illustrates the dangers such exclusivity presents to the impersonal poetic state its speaker mourns.

However, in the final stanzas of the poem, the speaker suggests that impersonal knowledge depends on shared rather than exclusive memory:

> Sleepless nights,
> I remember the initiates,
> their gesture their calm glance.
> I have heard how in rapt thought,
> in vision, they speak
> with another race,
> more beautiful, more intense than this,
> I could laugh—
> more beautiful, more intense?
> Perhaps that other life
> is contrast always to this. I reason:
> I have lived as they
> in their inmost rites—
> they endure the tense nerves
> through the moment of ritual.
> I endure from moment to moment—
> days pass all alike,
> tortured, intense. (*CP* 17)

Judging from its reference to the "initiates," "The Gift" arguably frames its speaker as the helmsman himself, whom the initiates have manipulated as a means of channeling and reproducing their own strength. As a sequel to "The Helmsman," the poem boasts a masculinized speaker and envisions the sea garden as a memory from the present day standpoint of sociability and civilization. While the speaker philosophizes and fantasizes about such a state of boundless and communal being ("I have lived as they"), he only envisions it as another life, in "contrast always to this" (*CP* 17). Whereas this other "race" persists transcendently "through" the moment of ritual, the speaker endures "from moment to moment," unable to shed his personality: his historical and bodily specificity. The initiates endure "the tense nerves" with detachment and ritualistic purposefulness, whereas the speaker is only "tortured, intense," prey to bodily impulses (*CP* 17). To intensify this agony, the speaker also misreads the very nature of impersonality, interpreting the dialectical retreats and advances of *Sea Garden*'s worlds only "in contrast" (*CP* 17). Lacking the oblivious inattentiveness of the initiates in "The Helmsman," who forget laughingly, his excruciating personal consciousness prevents him from apprehending another world, "more intense than this" (*CP* 17).

The speaker cannot forget because of the intensity of a "clutch[ing]" desire that the poem links to heterosexuality and, further, his attempt to control the poetic image. As I have argued, H.D.'s impersonality in general is coded heterosexually in the service of undoing that heterosexuality, particularly as the poetic subject and speaker occupy numerous subject positions, both male and female. The poem protests the unilateral desire of the speaker, favoring instead a desire that spills or splits, like "seed-pearls . . . when your necklace snapped" (*CP* 17). Whereas "The Helmsman" problematizes a narrow desire for the same, as appears in a subject/subject relationship, "The Gift" censures the strict demarcations of subject and object that mark heterosexual desire. Both poems progressively question sexuality as such, as both heterosexuality and same-sex love impede the gesture of interiorization necessary for reaching an impersonal world.[32] In the last two stanzas of the poem, this failure finds itself in the frustrated if not hollow command that follows his unconsummated wish for a "still," impersonal "place":

> Only a still place
> and perhaps some outer horror
> some hideousness to stamp beauty,
> a mark—no changing it now—
> on our hearts.
> I send no string of pearls,
> no bracelet—accept this. (*CP* 18)

The speaker's final gesture is to demand that his addressee accept his poem, his gift—in essence—his poetic authority. His failure relinquish authority ultimately prolongs his suffering while contributing to his failure to get to "another life" which "holds what this lacks" (*CP* 18). He thus refuses the masochistic contract, rejecting the dialectical cycle of deauthorization and reauthorization that sustains poetic balance.

Conclusion: Interior Dimensions

"The Gift" codes the speaker's refusal of the contract as a denial of interiority that develops from an impersonal state. The poem unveils the sea garden as an interior space, necessitated by but ultimately distinct from the reflexive position of the therapist's couch and the congested city with "no beauty / to distract—to crowd madness upon madness" (*CP* 18). The interior, impersonal space of the sea garden also defines itself by limiting access to a privileged few. In this sense, the interior is not limited to individual psychology but represents a highly managed form of collectivity. As a space whose legitimacy rests on its isolation, this geography suggests, as in "Cities," that the multiplication of "beauty" actually promises its demise—that true poetic voices are and ought to remain few. This separatist sentiment forms the crux of H.D.'s theory of impersonality and disconnects her vision from any necessary intimacy with women in particular. I have argued thus far that this theory of impersonality dictates an active surrender to poetic authority, which the poems often code as masculine. Furthermore, an impersonal poetics requires that one successfully exploit that violation as a disavowal of authority and as a means of perpetuating one's own poetic voice.

H.D.'s neat and concise execution of her poetry does not characterize her theory of impersonality, which, as I have identified in this chapter, produces a number of political and ethical problems. The poems of *Sea Garden* code the impersonal moment as an act of invasion or incorporation that replicates the poetic self through access to other, often variously gendered, subject positions. The result is an impersonal series of alterations of the original personality, a new kind of interior born of various forms of connection rather than mere invasion. Since the original personality actually moves outside itself to paradoxically submit to those it invades, the gesture of interiorization that H.D.'s poetry often illustrates is also a gesture of exteriorization, as with Pound's imagist poem, characterized by a "precise instant when a thing outward and objective transforms itself, or darts into a thing inward and subjective."[33] Similarly, H.D.'s very definition of the interior weakens the distinction between the exterior and interior, both corporeally and socially.

In his discussion of Ezra Pound's cryptology, Daniel Tiffany claims that the spatial fragility of these distinctions also forms Pound's theory of image making. According to Tiffany, "the hypothesis of externalized organs and faculties," quite evident in Pound's introductory remarks to de Gourmont's *The Natural Philosophy of Love*, not only forecasts Pound's embrace of the new technical media he would use to telegraph his fascist broadcasts but also "reveal[s] the corporeal dimension of the image" (*Radio* 171).

This "corporeal dimension" is literalized in H.D.'s theory of impersonality, where the body acts as an active medium for the amplification of the poetic voice. The body produces images, turning itself "inside out, externalizing a fragment of its mysterious inner life" (*Radio* 171). This particular aspect of H.D.'s imagism exposes a previously unnoted political problematic that is crucial for understanding H.D.'s work. For H.D., the image is tantamount to the self, and to the interior, which must be simultaneously made and unmade to assume a repetitive and strange form of stability. H.D.'s version of impersonality is committed to such a strict and rigorous program of formally managing the ego, of ritually guarding its periphery even in its most intense states of dissolution. This strict vigilance contrasts markedly with the ostensible detachment of her lyrics. In its most general form, an impersonal poetics is an increasingly reflexive poetics, both objectively detached and meticulously attentive to the individual poem. But if so much of H.D.'s masochistic impersonality depends on the poet's execution of her poems as scripts, complete with props and settings, to what extent does the detachment of H.D.'s lyrics really amount to a theatrical staging of poetics? Because its context is the stage, the marionette is a particularly appropriate symbol of the conceptual problem that accompanies this aesthetic. The silent cinematic figure is the image *par excellence*; it performs but only as it accepts the influence of those who "drape [their] devotions" around it ("Mask" 115). Paradoxically, this sort of reflexively scripted impersonality restricts the intentionality of the doll to facilitate the lack of deliberation that characterizes its performance.

To assess its importance for feminist or queer political practice and for modernist studies more generally, one must understand the kind of interiority that develops through a script. In its challenge to identity and sexuality, H.D.'s version of impersonality broaches the question of how one selectively creates a poetic community of like minds that renounces individual distinction and intention while preserving important differences. Furthermore, her poetry self-consciously stages the question of how one creates and manages such an interior, without reconstituting the power dynamics such a selection attempts to dispel. This is also a question of form.[34] These questions will appear more centrally in the next chapter, which explores the relationship between the hermeneutical impulse to interpret or map the self and the further development of impersonality in the work of D. H. Lawrence. In this regard, the central problem of H.D.'s poetics, and the source of their political instability, lies in her attempt to create a poetics of interiority or depth that does not comply with a system of hermeneutics or interpretation. H.D.'s lyrics thus prefigure T. S. Eliot's claim that impersonal poetic emotion "does not happen consciously or of deliberation" (*Prose* 43). That is, poetic emotion is instantaneous and unselfconscious; it does not support the possibility of a depth that can be analyzed or interpreted. This apparent interior state must remain subjectively private yet essential at the same time, prohibiting hermeneutic access to its various dimensions. H.D.'s lyrics then create a double-bind, since her vision of impersonality rests on its production of an interior dimension that embeds private experience in a collective body. This interior, however, arises from a specific kind of emotional seizure, an act of possessive engagement that encourages interpretive practice. Her lyrics, then, like the marionette, attempt to synthesize private and public experience, the incommunicable, sublime knowledge of being and the modes of self-presentation available to all. In this respect, imagism produces an interior that continuously exteriorizes itself, particularly in its attempt to create an impersonal aesthetic community that maintains the illusion of public values, at the same time that it limits access to a select few.

3

A "Peculiar Feeling of Intimacy"

D. H. Lawrence, Modernist Violence, and Impersonal Narrative

> One thing I know, I am tired of this insistence on the personal element; personal truth, personal reality. It is very stale and profitless. I want some new non-personal activity, which is at the same time, a genuine vital activity. And I want relations which are not purely personal, based on purely personal qualities; but relations based upon some unanimous accord in truth of belief, and a harmony of purpose, rather than of personality. I am weary of personality . . . I am sick and tired of personality in every way. Let us be easy and impersonal, not forever fingering over our own souls or our acquaintances, but trying to create a new life, a new common life, a new complete tree of life from the roots that are within us. I am weary to death of these dead dry leaves of personalities which flap in every wind.
>
> —D. H. Lawrence[1]

As early as 1915, four years before the publication of T. S. Eliot's "Tradition and the Individual Talent," D. H. Lawrence would characterize himself as an impersonalist. Writing to Katherine Mansfield in regard to her husband John Middleton Murry's scheme for "authors to be publishers," Lawrence praises an "easy and impersonal" life that resists the reflexive impulse to psychologize it by "fingering over our own souls or our acquaintances" (*CL* 395). Lawrence inveighs against the prominence of "mental decisions," aligning these reflexive acts with the "*personal* element" that fatigues him so desperately. For Lawrence, this "personality" is built upon the humanist presumption of expressive and unique individuality, an attitude toward selfhood that produces only stasis. Like other modernists such as Lewis, Lawrence's protest against individualism in society actually reflects his desire to protect the individual from the deindividuating forces of bourgeois social modernity; a truly "common life" born of "some new non-personal activity . . . a genuine vital activity" will rescue the individual from the contemplative quagmire of "personality," which, in individualist society, falsely parades as individuality. In much of Lawrence's work, and as I argue here of his 1913 novel *Sons and Lovers*, this understanding of activity and its corresponding attack on the "personal" links the individual to a progressive communal practice that dispels "personality" and the impulse to analyze it—an impersonal aesthetic.

Lawrence's attacks on "personality" are a pervasive feature of his work, extending from his diaries, poems, and letters to his novels, as Daniel Albright has observed in his classic study *Personality and Impersonality: Lawrence, Woolf, and Mann*. Albright reads Lawrence's "impersonality," his "contemptuous" attitude toward "all aspects of experience which cannot be resolved into some impersonal and universal force," as a conscious retreat from the author's "enormous ramification of . . . identity."[2] In this authoritative drive toward utter "self-expression," the author's consciousness subsumes that of his or her characters in the attempt to express the "self's repleteness" (*Personality* 1, 2). Given this description, Lawrence's questioning of Murry's proposed plan to efface authorial identity by turning authors into publishers makes sense: "[A]re there either books or authors . . . at the present moment?" (*CL* 395). Supposing that there are authors, impersonality, as Albright suggests, develops from the "furious evolution" of the individual author, whereby his personality diffuses to a point of exhaustion; boundaries between individuals dissolve as "the aggregate can never constitute self-definition" and "all identities are equally valid" (*Personality* 6). Albright suggests here that the impersonal aspects of Lawrence's work, in which universal forces trump individual agency in shaping human behavior, exist only in reference to very particular and personal social aspects of existence (*Personality* 3). That is, though Lawrence professes to dislike "personality," it is nonetheless a prominent feature of his writing.[3]

Particularly in light of his letter to Mansfield, the notion that Lawrence's impersonality necessarily arises from the magnitude of his desire to express his own personality seems somewhat flawed. An even more serious omission from Albright's argument is the larger ethical problem of impersonality in Lawrence's work. As is now well known, the impersonal ideals of activity *Sons and Lovers* supports reinforce some rather unpalatable political ends. More specifically, the text cannot sustain an impersonal narrative structure that undermines bourgeois aspiration without recourse to violence, particularly violence toward women but between men as well. In general, the novel is ripe for a rereading that makes connections between its impersonal aesthetic, its obsessive ruminations on sexuality, and its complex political and ideological investments. While Albright made a clear case for Lawrence's impersonality in 1978, the subject, so pervasive in his entire body of work, has since disappeared from critical discourse about the writer. Albright admittedly does not trace Lawrence's connection to impersonality beyond the three figures of discussion in his book, themselves rather loosely constellated. However, in positioning Lawrence beside Woolf and Mann, whatever impetus Albright provided for imagining the complexities of Lawrence's affiliations and intellectual investments had to contend with the already well-established feminist dismissal of Lawrence, spearheaded by the publication of Kate Millett's famous *Sexual Politics* in 1970.[4] My point here is not to target feminism solely for limiting the breadth or nuance of Lawrence criticism or for the larger political dismissal of his work but rather for the pigeonholing of the author into intractably defined moments of literary critical history, most notably second-wave feminism and Marxist and psychoanalytic criticism.[5] I suggest here that a return to Albright, and a renewed sociocritical focus on Lawrence's impersonality, could possibly unite and reinvigorate these arguments without invalidating their claims about gender and class.

In contrast, critics such as Tony Pinkney have suggested that these seemingly disparate lines of argument need not exclude each other, arguing that "fear of women in Lawrence is always at least shot through with other, equally fundamental anxieties, and can even at times become a kind of mask or code-word for the other."[6] Following Pinkney's assessment, I suggest in this chapter that Lawrence's misogyny, however brutal, as well as his particular class politics, responds to fundamental assumptions about the operations of literary structure and the way that sexuality underwrites narrative. As critics such as Judith Roof and Joseph Allen Boone have observed, narrative itself is linked with a fundamentally heterosexual ideology that focuses on "ends": marriages, deaths, orgasms, and so on.[7] More in conjunction with the sorts of "perverse" narratives that, according to Roof, actually reconfigure or even dispose of these "ends," *Sons and Lovers* ultimately narrates the dissolution of the novel as it reflexively undermines the primacy of individual or personal development (*Come* xxiv). Nonetheless, the perversity of the novel's rejection of normative, heterosexual, narrative ends comes at the cost of reinforcing other troublesome ideologies grounded in the repudiation of women and their presumed connection to Oedipal dynamics of the novel more generally. As Boone has pointed out, Lawrence's fiction is shot through with anxiety surrounding the tension between the desire to liberate "female sexuality" and fear of its "potential threat" to his own narrative mastery (*Libidinal* 116). Similarly, the dissolution of conventional narrative structure that ironically characterizes the "ending" of a text such as *Sons and Lovers* cannot take place without a corresponding challenge to author's own narrative design.

In manifesting this tension between narrative dissolution and authority, I argue, *Sons and Lovers* explores the ethical difficulties of impersonality as they arise particularly in prose. As I remark in the introduction to this book, impersonality (with the exception of Albright's study) has generally been understood in relation to poetry, most markedly because of the aesthetic's generally undisturbed connection to Eliot's "Tradition and the Individual Talent" and, further, the poetics of Yeats and Pound. Even H.D.'s poetry, for example, is generally considered more "impersonal" than her prose.[8] Whereas critics often connect modernist poetry to art or theory, prose stands as the more confessional, autobiographical genre, most invested in personal or individual development. Impersonal prose, however, as I am defining it here in relation to the novel more generally, stakes itself against individual development, ultimately elevating the impersonal experience of "common life" over the hermeneutic revelations of self that, for Lawrence in particular, characterize an Oedipalized heterosexuality and more generally fuel the novel's trajectory (*CL* 395). This form of narrative questions our impulse to interpret it, reflexively trading psychology as a mode of character development for a sense of interior that extends beyond individual subjectivity. Since it privileges novel forms of engagement based on knowing—rather than reading—the subject, Lawrence's project in particular engages with the same logic Eliot advances in "Tradition and the Individual Talent," where emotion is not "expressed" but is rather a "concentration which does not happen consciously or of deliberation" (*Prose* 43). As his letter to Mansfield indicates, it is precisely this conscious deliberation that Lawrence wants to eradicate from his own social and professional relationships and, as I am arguing, from his own fiction. This desire is, of course, highly ironic, since anyone who has read Lawrence's novels cannot fail to note the self-consciousness of their construction. However, this reflexivity, as I have argued, more generally characterizes a modernism persistently involved in investigating its own relationship to impersonality. That is, while modernists often approached impersonality as a necessity for authoritative authorship—for achieving, as Lawrence puts it, a "unanimous accord in truth of belief, and a harmony of purpose"—they were also acutely aware of the ethical and theoretical difficulties it posed (*CL* 395).

As with H.D.'s poetry, Lawrence's impersonal prose explores the problem of its own construction: the difficulty of negotiating a relationship to the social world without a personality. As I have illustrated, this is primarily a spatial or phenomenological problem, where the loss of individual boundaries initiated by impersonal engagements threatens to erase space and position altogether. Similarly, *Sons and Lovers* self-consciously explores the hazard its critique of personality presents to narrative form. And while this critique operates similarly to that H.D. (or Pound or Eliot, for that matter) commences in her own subtle manipulations of poetic form, I would argue that prose, or the novel more particularly, socially concretizes concerns that often remain abstract in poetry, even more explicitly linking individual personality to its own narrative development and coherence. Consequently, in its attempt to sustain an impersonal form of the novel, a text such as *Sons and Lovers* must vigilantly manage the injuries it inflicts on its own organization.

One could argue that such claims are equally true of poetry, but I suggest here that impersonal prose, generally the focus of this book, explicitly critiques the importance of personality to a narrative organization that elides material forces. Lawrence's logical vehicle for this critique of personality would be the particular novelistic form most concretely and ideologically invested in it, the *Bildungsroman*, or novel of development. In stressing the importance of the *Bildungsroman* or *künstlerroman* (which details more specifically the growth and development of the artist) for Lawrence, I am also emphasizing the centrality of the form to modernist impersonality more generally. I consequently return to this subject in my discussion of Elizabeth Bowen's 1938 novel *The Death of the Heart*. Indeed, the shift I am identifying here can be located in a number of modernist and protomodernist texts that seek to reclaim the narrative pattern of the *Bildungsroman* by undermining the importance of personality to individual development, ranging from Oscar Wilde's *The Picture of Dorian Gray* (1890), Virginia Woolf's *The Voyage Out* (1915), James Joyce's *Portrait of the Artist as a Young Man* (1914), to Jean Rhys's *Voyage in the Dark* (1934). These texts parley reflexively with the *Bildungsroman* as a narrative form whose project, as Franco Moretti has observed, is to centralize the value of "personal identity" in an "inevitable repugnance to change"—or tragedy, in particular.[9] Given this definition of the classical *Bildungsroman* as perpetually invested in the erasure of conflict, one can see how the very violence feminists have faulted in *Sons and Lovers*, along with Lawrence's own characterization of the novel as a "great tragedy," directly challenges the normative stability the *Bildungsroman* typically reinforces (*CL* 160).

"A New Non-Personal Activity"

Lawrence then proposes "activity" as opposed to the movement toward stasis that governs the operations of culturally normative projects such as the *Bildungsroman* (*CL* 395). In general, the term "activity" constellates a number of ideological and ethical problematics that have thwarted both modernists and modernist critics alike, particularly in their efforts to defend modernism from accusations of ideological conservatism. As Douglas Mao argues, one such dilemma is the violence between subject and object that activity implies. Employing a slightly different critical vocabulary than

Lawrence, Mao suggests that in emphasizing production, or "making," as a means of countering the cultural connections between nonproduction and the hyperrefinement of aesthetic idleness, modernist texts harbor a fundamental "anxiety about human violence against the object world."[10] The ethical difficulty of this turn toward "production" is particularly evident in a more masculinely inspired modernism that appears to trade any anxiety over the potential violence of "production"—or activity, to use Lawrence's term—for the assertion of its value.[11] For example, Lawrence's anti-Freudian treatise of 1923, *Fantasia of the Unconscious*, again links activity to the disastrous effects of personality, advocating "action, all kinds of action in place of mental activity" to avoid the stultifying quagmire of "dwelling on [one]self."[12] The connection between this text and his letter to Mansfield reflects the schematic, obsessive nature of Lawrence's thought. The action Lawrence proposes as a replacement for the "gnawing, gnawing disease of mental consciousness" is impersonal in essence and resembles the version of activity T. S. Eliot advances in "Tradition and the Individual Talent," where impersonal poetic emotion results from a "concentration ... of a very great number of experiences which to the ... *active* person would not seem to be experiences at all" (my italics).[13] For Eliot, the "active person" does not reflect upon or register personal experience as an individual. Rather, his experiences accumulate with those of others to form a greater, impersonal aesthetic medium. Eliot's claim here is counterintuitive if not contradictory; his version of activity entails "a passive attending upon the event" that affectively separates the artist from living experience through a sensibility that cannot be analyzed or interpreted (*Prose* 43). Lawrence also advocates a turn away from the psychological dimensions of personality, which he claims to be "sick and tired of ... in every way" (*CL* 395). However removed from the drama of self-knowledge and revelation, this form of impersonality carries more concentrated energy than do the "personalities," who, for Lawrence, are nothing more than "dead dry leaves" (*CL* 395).

Activity thus counters personal reflexivity. Lawrence's version of a "common life" built from "roots that are within us" imagines human connection as proceeding from the emptying out of psychological or hermeneutic depth (*CL* 395). By ascribing an "easy and impersonal ethos" that refuses to posit the soul at the ontological "roots" of human existence, Lawrence deflates the notion of the humanist subject as a vessel for interpretation, consequently melding the exterior into the interior while confusing traditional binaries of inside and outside (*CL* 395). In articulating desire for "common life," Lawrence again is not dismissing the individual but is instead emphasizing his hope for a common medium that preserves the integrity of the individual against the bourgeois ethos that threatens to engulf him. This "common life" positions itself against the invasive nature of hermeneutics, systems of interpretation that can apply to both humans and literary texts. In *Fantasia*, for example, Lawrence dismisses the "knowledge" gleaned from hermeneutic systems altogether as related to the individualism he deplores in society, which centralizes the human as a vessel for analysis and interpretation. "Knowledge," he claims, "is not even in direct proportion to being," or true individualism. Later he suggests that the "supreme lesson of human consciousness is to learn how *not to know* . . . how not to *interfere*," how to respect the privacy of other subjects and oneself without drawing interpretive conclusions about them (italics in original; *Fantasia* 67). In *Fantasia*, Lawrence's distrust of psychology underlies the new system of education he proposes for the young, one that foregrounds "dynamic activity" instead of reflexive thought (*Fantasia* 69). What emerges from this activity is an intimacy grounded not in the depths of the individual but from a common knowledge available to all.

This logic, however contradictory, to some extent redeems Lawrence from the oft-repeated charge that his radical individualism entails an anti-communal, even authoritarian rejection of humanism.[14] Instead, as I argue here, at least as it applies to *Sons and Lovers*, Lawrence faults humanism for an intrusive, psychological focus on the individual that ultimately hampers true individuality, cordoning it away from a common sphere of work shared with others. In response, Lawrence then uses the concept of "activity" to forge a link between the impersonal world of "universal force[s]" he admires and the social world of work. Ultimately, this social concretization of aesthetics distinguishes Lawrence's own version of impersonality from the poetic impersonality of H.D., Eliot, and Pound (*Personality* 3). But this connection also accounts for the ethical difficulty of Lawrence's project. As an attempted *Bildungsroman*, *Sons and Lovers* reveals the same anxiety over production that Mao diagnoses in other modernist texts, particularly as the text works to conceal the violence that literal forms of making entail. Lawrence's novel metacritically reflects upon this anxiety as the latent violence in the text ruptures the narrative through direct, physical entanglements. In these examples, activity then becomes linked to both the fruitfulness of aesthetic labor and the direct physical violence of Paul Morel's father, the coal miner. To summarize, the text follows the seeming development of its protagonist, Paul Morel, and his shifting and antagonistic attachments to his mother, Gertrude, a "woman of character and refinement," and his father, Walter, a man of the "lower class," as Lawrence describes them in a letter to Edward Garnett (*CL* 160). The narrative then follows a series of what Lawrence repeatedly terms "split[s]," where the son "casts off his mistress" and other women in his life as his mother's impulse to husband her son subsumes his retreat from her (*CL* 160–61). Whatever development and growth Paul experiences in the novel is always accompanied by a movement backward toward the small world of home, represented by his mother. Ultimately, Paul's entrance into the world at large, catalyzed by the novel's violent ending and the death of his mother, leaves him, as Lawrence remarks, "naked of everything, with the drift towards death," not personality (*CL* 161).

In investigating this uneven path of development, the novel then functions as a critical exploration of the *Bildungsroman* and its attendant narrative of bourgeois self-development, challenging normative narratives of self-formation, especially as they relate to sexuality. The movements of Paul's development are, as Lawrence remarked to Garnett, visibly manifest in the form of the novel itself: "If *you* can't see the development—which is slow, like growth—I can" (*CL* 161). This "slow . . . growth" specifically triangulates the subjects of intimacy, violence, and work and, as with other modernist texts I discuss in the book, supports impersonal modes of strange intimacy that do not develop from psychological or hermeneutic understandings of selfhood. But however effective in restructuring intimate life to challenge bourgeois modernity and its cloying forms of personal intimacy, this "growth" occurs at the expense of women. Lawrence, like Lewis, explicitly connects "personality" to the feminine. For example, Lilly, D. H. Lawrence's autobiographical mouthpiece in *Aaron's Rod* (1922), brusquely denounces his wife for taking on a "beastly personal tone," announcing his hatred for a "slimy, creepy, personal intimacy."[15] His wife's tremulous request for affirmation—"I'm not personal at all, am I . . . ?"—suggests that no self-respecting man or woman would willingly admit to "personal" behavior (*AR* 73).

Violence, Depersonalization, and Modernity

Lawrence's particularly harsh, masculine attacks on "personalized intimacy" underscore a second claim in this chapter; as a narrative and political strategy, modernist impersonality counterintuitively follows modernity's own impulses toward "depersonalization" to revise humanist ideals of intimacy and interiority. In making this argument, I refer to the process of depersonalization very specifically, and I am distinguishing between impersonality as an aesthetic, on the one hand, and depersonalization as a social process, on the other. Impersonality, as it appears in "Tradition and the Individual Talent" and in numerous other modernist tracts, describes both a process and a condition in which the distillation of individuality and singular authorial authority produces a common aesthetic medium. In its most progressive sense, a poetics and politics of impersonality exchanges individual forms of expression for a collectively experienced aesthetic, as exemplified in Lawrence's hope for a "common life" (*CL* 395). In contrast, I use the term "de-personalization," following Anthony Giddens, to describe a process that is consequent upon modernity's restrictive focus on the individual, which cordons off intimacy into the privatized sphere of self-realization and expression. According to Giddens, modernity has transformed intimacy into a self-reflexive project to be "worked at," compartmentalized away from abstract institutions into the proper sphere of "personal" time.[16] My claim here is that Lawrence's particular aesthetic impersonality confronts the strict partitioning of life that such depersonalization entails, a division reflected in the conflict between the privatized, bourgeois social aspirations of Paul Morel's mother and the public life of his father. In other words, Lawrence's logic posits the personality and "personal-life" as products of modernity's depersonalizing impulse.

This rather contradictory understanding of "personal-life" as developing from depersonalization is related to Lawrence's similar view of the individual. In *Sons and Lovers*, as in *Fantasia* as well as his letter to Mansfield, Lawrence's critique of individualism in society emerges from his desire to protect the individual from absorption into the larger social organization supported by bourgeois domesticity.[17] Such institutions support the development of personality, which, for Lawrence, amounts to a false construction of individuality. Giddens offers further insight into this relationship, arguing that depersonalization is a state of social affairs resulting from the humanist celebration of individuality, in which individuals, fearing depersonalization themselves, retreat into the presumed protection of private life, or bourgeois domesticity. Given this illustration, personality, as the presumed bridge between one's interior, private life and the public presentation of self, is a function of this compartmentalization of social space. Consequently, personality itself is part of the social structure that isolates intimacy within the private sphere of intersubjective relations. *Sons and Lovers* responds to such forms of depersonalization by locating Paul's most productive intimate relations in the workplace with female coworkers during his work below the "dismal stairs" of Jordan's Surgical Appliance Factory, where he actively makes or produces (in the modernist sense Mao identifies) prosthetics and surgical gadgets that literally alter the parameters of the human body. The place, however, quite literally defined by its "regulated system of values," its "impersonality," also robs him of his aesthetic vitality: "It seems monstrous also that a business could be run on wooden legs."[18]

This odd job, however, along with the ironic control it gives Paul over the physical exteriors of human beings, ultimately strengthens the division between the private life of home and the slightly more sociable, yet more impersonal, world of work. Indeed, the factory specializes in manufacturing prosthetic, artificial, mass-produced, extensions and approximations of the individual body, such as a "flesh-pink leg" (*SL* 139). This job exemplifies a rather hollowed out version of the prosthetic modernism I discuss in Chapter 2, which technologically and impersonally alters the definition of personhood by conjoining the body through a system of lacks and eventual compensations. Lawrence presents this prosthetic logic rather ironically, as employees exercise their aesthetic proclivities by making "weird little drawings of legs and thighs and ankles" (*SL* 131). However, the depersonalization this workplace inspires displaces the values of intimacy from the private sphere and reconstitutes them within a third, impersonal, often utopian aspect of existence that ideally collapses the public and private dimensions of life. In this form of modernist impersonality, the depersonalization that generally banishes intimate connections in public life is reworked into intimate connection in the space of work.

Giddens's logic implicitly connects conventional forms of intimacy—which base themselves upon carefully scripted revelations of the self—with heterosexual intimacy.[19] Throughout *Sons and Lovers*, Lawrence contests these heterosexual forms of intimacy through his representations of violent activity, whether in Walter's violence toward his family, the psychological violence that takes place in Paul's heterosexual relationships, or the violence between men. During these incidents, violence explodes conventional dyadic intimacies, working to open the closures that create exclusive, or "personal," social spaces. Narratively speaking, the violent event, with its lack of premeditation or deliberation, the "mental decisions" Lawrence detests, itself catalyzes this dissolution of narrative and social space that Lawrence's impersonal aesthetic demands, dissolving the sense of individual distinction that attends bourgeois development (*CL* 395). In this sense, violent activity also serves narrative more generally by producing and necessitating certain structural transformations. Leo Bersani has extensively examined this function of violence in *The Freudian Body*, where he argues that the violent spectacle in art acts as a disturbance freeing an "unmappable and fierce marginal force" that "coerces and finally paralyzes a highly conscious civilized 'central text.'"[20] In *Sons and Lovers*, these oddly productive tendencies of violence appear when seemingly incompatible narratives of development compete for narrative primacy, as when Walter Morel threatens his wife and children or when Paul Morel feels unbridled animosity toward the coal miner, Baxter Dawes: "He hated Dawes, wished something could exterminate him at that minute" (*SL* 388). Here, violence between men functions reparatively to resolve the antagonisms the text reflexively constructs. The psychic violence of intimacy and the literal violence in which it culminates redefine the intimate in relation to marginal sexual and class identities. Accordingly, Bersani emphasizes the role of violence in deflating interpretation to thereby make room for "counternarrative organizations and identifications" (*Freudian* 68). In novels such as *Sons and Lovers*, this anti-interpretive bent denies the role of self-disclosure in creating meaningful literary character and form. These texts work to deprivatize the self, rather than amplify it as the repository of meaning.

Lawrence, Impersonality, and Psychoanalysis

The question I examine here regarding novelistic impersonality more generally, concerns how *Sons and Lovers*'s violent and repetitive depersonalizing gestures, which it aligns with the "new," stake themselves *against* normative development in the novel, or the "old." This dynamic, reflected in the dialectic between the novel's movement toward impersonal human relations and its consequent reversion into more privatized models of attachment, comprises the novel's impersonality—which also accounts for the often tedious and at times tiresomely repetitive nature of the novel. This repetition, according to Peter Brooks, is characteristic of narrative itself, which "tells of" previously occurring events in a "going over again of a ground already covered."[21] Brooks links the narrative function of retelling and return more specifically to Freudian repetition. For Freud, Brooks argues, patients continually "return" to a "beyond" that is incommensurable with the pleasure principle that governs the present moment. This neurosis is strikingly similar to the patterns of intimacy that characterize Paul Morel's relationships with women, creating a Freudian style of narrative that resembles *Beyond the Pleasure Principle*'s oft-cited *fort/da* game, where the young patient, who stages and repeats the experience of his mother's disappearance, is "obliged to *repeat* the repressed material as a contemporary experience instead of . . . *remembering* it as something belonging to the past."[22] My intention here is not to create a reductive analogy between the Freudian game of *fort/da* and Lawrence's narrative strategy, but to draw attention to the impersonal, active nature of this form of Freudian repetition. This sort of impersonal, unconscious means of registering experience also accords with Eliot's version of impersonality, where experiences are not "recollected" but finally "unite in . . . a passive attending upon the event" (*Prose* 43).

It is arguable here whether Eliot intends to directly engage with Freud, especially since *Beyond the Pleasure Principle* was written in 1919 and published one year later. Regardless, Eliot's theory of impersonality maintains a notion of form that is based on repeated, and therefore generalizable, elements of literary structure, since it demands the erasure of personal authorship and other forms individual literary distinction, such as character. This process, elemental to impersonality as an aesthetic practice, is probably what would lead Lawrence to assert upon finishing *Sons and Lovers* that "it has got form—*form*" (italics in original; *CL* 160). Nonetheless, Lawrence's repetitive emphasis on "*form*," development one can "see," suggests the he values his work in its individual distinction. That is, as he professes to his individual effort in having written "it again, pruning and shaping it and out of sweat as well as blood," he also intimates that his artistic product is bound up in a more generalizable, or impersonal, phenomenon that makes it recognizable—form.

The difference between the impersonality employed by modernists such as Eliot and Lawrence and by psychoanalysts such as Freud is that the latter party tends to value repetitive behavior negatively as a form of compulsion. For Freud, the desire to repeat is a neurosis that both complicates and enables his own project of psychoanalysis as an "art of interpreting" (*BPP* 18). In contrast, Lawrence's distrust of romantic revelations of the self points to a modernist theory of impersonality that scrutinizes this very project of interpretation, however often it actually confirms various aspects of Freudian thought.

Despite this overt difference, Freud and modernists like Eliot and Lawrence think alike in staking repetition against interpretation. An additional link between a Freudian version of repetition and impersonality lies in the explicit nature of the term *activity*. Whereas Lawrence hopes for a "genuinely vital activity," Freud explicitly links activity to neurotic repetition (*CL* 395). In speaking of the *fort/da* game, in which the child repeatedly stages his mother's departure as a "distressing experience," Freud argues that the child takes on an "*active* part" by repeating an experience that originally reinforced his passivity (italics in original; *BPP* 15). Brooks confirms this interpretation by adding that the child's repetition of the game affords him "mastery in a situation in which he has been compelled to submit," allowing him to occupy both active and passive subject positions (*Reading* 98). Similarly, the repetitive aspects of Lawrence's texts, privileged above meaning or knowledge, reinforce passivity as a form of active narrative mastery precisely by refusing to honor change or development, the notion of a turning point.

Lawrence's antipathy to psychoanalysis has been widely discussed, as has the ironic amenability of his work to psychoanalytical models of interpretation. Terry Eagleton, among others, has quite famously evaluated the potential issues surrounding psychoanalytic readings of *Sons and Lovers*, which, he argues, is the most overtly Freudian example of Lawrence's fiction. Despite the objections to Freud that Lawrence voices in texts such as *Psychoanalysis and the Unconscious* and *Fantasia of the Unconscious*, Eagleton remarks that *Sons and Lovers* "might be taken as a striking independent confirmation of Freud's doctrine," especially since there appears to be no evidence that Lawrence was directly acquainted with Freud's work at the time of writing the novel (*Literary* 151). Even when Lawrence explicitly announces his disagreement with Freud, as he does in *Fantasia*, he also tends to confirm Freud's own theories. This argumentative tendency appears especially in Lawrence's constant need to alert his audience to Freud's fallacious thinking about sex. According to Lawrence, Freud errs in planting sex at the basis of all human relations and behaviors. He then revises and confirms Freud's thesis, judging the limitations of sex in its ability to extend beyond the individual self.

What is most interesting about *Fantasia*, particularly in regard to *Sons and Lovers*, is that Lawrence's musings about education make little room for parenting in a child's development. For Lawrence, action precludes both "self-expression" and intimate nurture (*Fantasia* 88). In fact, Lawrence advocates that parents, particularly fathers, take a distanced yet stern relation to their child's education and development, "forgetting" rather than "forsaking" their children (*Fantasia* 70). A child "must learn to be alone, and to play alone" (*Fantasia* 70). However, in *Sons and Lovers*, the fact that Paul Morel ends up so hopelessly alone, "naked of everything," unable to negotiate any relationship with others, suggests that solitude must be tempered by specific alternatives to an "interfering" Oedipal intimacy that solidifies knowledge of the self (*CL* 161). For Lawrence, this negative form of intimacy is always repetitive. Even the chapter titles of the novel, which literally organize and direct the progressing narrative's "development," support this claim. For example, "The Birth of Paul, and another Battle" as well as "The Casting off of Morel, the Taking on of William" suggest how the ending of one event coincides with the repetitive beginning of another (*SL* 37, 61). Similarly, the "Defeat of Miriam" relates Paul's various intimacies to an impersonal and repetitive structure of struggle and defeat, despite the individual ways in which those intimacies are distinguished or personalized (*SL* 254).

The Oedipal plot of *Sons and Lovers* also unfolds as a narrative of bourgeois aspiration that is subject to the novel's deliberate critique. In *Sons and Lovers*'s frequently polemical narrative, it is no coincidence that a boy who "loved to sleep with his mother" is part of a family who "felt quite select" (*SL* 92,100). Paul's early love for his mother, Gertrude, is a reaction to his father's brutality toward her. This exclusive bond arises through the mother's patterns of consumption, which enhance the environment of the working-class Morel household by aestheticizing it according to bourgeois, middle-class sensibilities. Gertrude's delicacy regarding their aesthetic domain leads Paul to love her "homecoming" upon the close of her shopping trips, where she "was always her best so, triumphant, tired, laden with parcels, feeling rich in spirit" (*SL* 99). Gertrude's fervent claim that she is a "wicked extravagant woman" is perhaps voiced ironically, since her purchase consists of one dish with cornflowers painted on it. However, the text does suggest that such wickedness lies in the isolated intimacy this extravagance confers upon the mother and her son, both of whom draw closer in the "fear of having robbed the pot-man" (*SL* 100).

While this relationship reflects Lawrence's misogyny, it also serves as a critique of the novel itself, in which bourgeois personal development often subsumes or elides larger material forces. *Sons and Lovers* then attempts to deform this focus on individual development by staging a dialectical tension represented in the conflict between Gertrude and Walter. In her attraction to bourgeois materialism, the intricately meshed attachment Gertrude nourishes within her home pulls the Morel children away from the working, and thus, in Lawrence's world, truly social community. The various modes of intimacy we see in this novel then closely follow the conflict between Paul's allegiances to his father's and mother's divergent class backgrounds. The sexualized psychic antagonism of class also follows a narrative of sexuality, which circulates around the passionate, possessive love of Paul's mother and the frequent punctuations of his father's impersonal yet frustrated violence. The repetitive, often brutal tones of this narrative disruption (or return) both revise and confirm Freud's thesis in *Beyond the Pleasure Principle*, along with its version of intimacy. In that text, a binding intimacy develops from the ego's sadistic impulse to eliminate everything external to it. In the case of a lost sexual object, the ego attempts to transform its erotic cathexis into an alteration of itself. Yet according to Freud, the subject repeats this loss as both a self-annihilating and affirming gesture. In Freudian narrative style, the text appears to double back on itself, narrating the movements of the "lover each of whose love affairs with a woman passes through the same phases and reaches the same conclusion" (*BPP* 23). But rather than as a compulsive and pathological desire to repeat, Lawrencian repetition, whereby the structure of the novel works through a series of complications that both dissolve and repeat intimacies, presents itself as progressive movement against normative trajectories of personal development. This is not necessarily a chronological movement forward, but a movement *against* aspects of conventional narrative itself, which tends to sequence a character's development according to specific turning points, or distinct and unique moments of maturation. According to this logic, what Freud terms "the perpetual recurrence of the same thing" foregrounds the falsity of distinctive individual change, the turning point itself, particularly as evidenced in the traditional narrative of the *Bildungsroman* and the marital closure that generally marks its ending (*BPP* 23).

As it develops against the heterosexual romance that often structures the *Bildungsroman*, *Sons and Lovers* maps Paul's ambivalent sexuality—characterized by his repulsion from the women in his life and his primal attraction to the coal miner, Baxter Dawes—onto a narrative of class loyalty, where Paul's artistic vocation merges with the vital fecundity of work. Paul's alienation from the public community of the rural working class results from his reclusive intimacy with his mother. Despite Terry Eagleton's claim that this is a "profoundly Oedipal novel," the text refuses a "personalized," ego-intensive intimacy in its almost maliciously anti-Oedipal sentiment (*Literary* 151). Whatever Oedipal leanings the text displays are repetitively and often deliberately disrupted, much in the way that, in *The Ego and the Id*, Freud couldn't help but "de-form" the supposed centrality of the Oedipus complex by speculating that "an individual's first and most important identification" is with the father.[23] The violence of the novel translates Paul's early antagonism with his father quite queerly onto Paul's "painful nearness" to his rival in love, Baxter (*SL* 423). That this union literally transpires as a result of Paul's sexual intimacy with the miner's estranged wife problematically points to the instrumentality of these relationships as they lead to the focal point in the text, where violent rupture erases class boundaries and displaces heterosexuality with a new, socially conscious form of "strange" and impersonal intelligibility.

In *Sons and Lovers*, the Oedipally inspired intimacy of Paul and his mother creates this illusion of individual change, which is then disabled through Paul's compulsive backtracking toward the intimate relations that revive his connection to his father. This second type of class-coded intimacy undermines individuality and personal identity. As a reader, one begins to expect certain occurrences. For example, as soon as Gertrude and Paul are "knitted together in perfect intimacy," or "brought exceedingly close together, owing to their isolation," this proximity soon ruptures (*SL* 171). In foregrounding these repetitive dynamics, the novel critiques a culture of modernity that centers on the individual personality and the illusion of its development. Conventionally speaking, personality supplies intimacy with meaning, but moments of intimate coupling in *Sons and Lovers*, where the self apparently gains "intensified meaning" through another's interpretation, frequently collapse; the project of making the self intelligible too often submits to preexisting narrative requirements of "intimate" conversation (*SL* 178). It is no surprise that Miriam, Paul's first lover, thought the boy "looked something like a Walter Scott hero" in an intimation that even the unconventional aspects of her intimacy with Paul might falter from the pressure of a prior novelistic script (*SL* 173). But rather than build personality, this intimacy works to disperse it.

Here, I refer to personality not only as it reflects the stabilized ego but also more particularly as the force with which one determines a relationship to a social totality. Through repetition, however, *Sons and Lovers* empties personality and development of its individualized meaning—and of its ability, as Franco Moretti has noted, to resolve the antagonism between self and society that underlines the project of the conventional *Bildungsroman*. Rather, as a dilemma of self-definition, romantic intimacy in *Sons and Lovers* exposes the repetitive elements of the nineteenth-century *bildung*, structured as it is according to presumably distinct trajectories of maturation. In rather disdainful homage to the traditional *Bildungsroman*, the homoerotic, if not explicitly homosexual, element of *Sons and Lovers* actualizes the contradictory project of socialization Moretti deems essential to the *Bildungsroman*, which harmoniously synthesizes individual aspirations with a "happy acceptance of bonds" and the "stability of social connections" (*Way* 26). Oddly, *Sons and Lovers* familiarizes social and personal trajectories of development through the literal violence that erupts in the distanced union of Baxter and Paul, reflecting Lawrence's feelings toward the various modes of intimacy and sociability that accompany, respectively, heterosexual bonds and the alternatives to them. Paul's quest for a socially useful work counters heterosexual and normative kinds of intimacy that seek to privatize it; it asks for far more than the mere reproduction of personality, which simply reconciling his individual social aspirations with an acceptable public venue could accomplish.

Work, or "the Actual Doing of Something"

We learn throughout the novel that, as an artist, Paul's need for his work to permeate larger social forms increasingly accompanies his withdrawal from those intimate relationships that overly personalize it. Paul's relationship with Miriam actually begins as an impersonal alternative to the personalized intimacy he experiences with the overly protective mother who is often his bed partner. The text also indicates that the exhaustive aspects of the pair's later intimacy arise as much from Paul's alteration as Miriam's emotive powers. In its particular idiom, the text states that "[p]ersonally, he was a long time before he realised her" (*SL* 179). The earlier intimacy between the two is "subtle" because Paul has not yet internalized the "personal" relationship with his mother as an index of relations with all women. Miriam is still an extension of a larger social body, a family whose impersonal appreciation of Paul's artwork counters the demanding presence of his mother. Despite Gertrude's essential role in the forming of Paul's aesthetic sensibility, Paul's sketches "would interest the Leivers more than they interested his mother" for "[i]t was not his art Mrs. Morel cared about, it was himself, and his achievement" (*SL* 179). Gertrude, and the drive she instills in Paul toward individual distinction, or personality, contributes to the artist's alienated and troubled social life. The fact that Miriam is strangely less individualized before Paul personalizes her is part of the novel's larger critique of a heterosexual, Oedipal socialization that envisions the strength of dyadic intimacy in the mother's power to individuate her son.

In other words, *Sons and Lovers* directs its critical gaze more fully toward the Oedipal bond as an accepted process of socialization than toward women specifically. While such larger theoretical categories of analysis certainly do not resolve the problem of Walter's violence or Paul's sadistic withdrawals, the novel's critique of Oedipal socialization destabilizes a form of heterosexually coded intimacy that it sees as confining and even debilitating for women as it is for men. Nonetheless, the text reductively subsumes its specific gender dynamics within the larger metaphysical conflict it illustrates between a lack of an adequately social work and the privatized personality that such a social situation tends to create. In depicting this conflict, the narrative development continually strains *toward* larger social visions but within a modernist vein. Tony Pinkney reads this basic conflict between aesthetic autonomy and communal solidarity as reflective of the novel's location in literary history. Much in *Sons and Lovers*, he argues, straddles a realist balance of private interest with social good and a modernist-inspired fascination with Paul's dissociated sensibility. Miriam represents, in Pinkney's eyes, a different kind of text the novel must eradicate as it begins to disturb the possibility of *Sons and Lovers*'s "would-be classic realism" (*DHL* 36). As a condition of this reading, Paul's accusing hatred of Miriam indicates the novel's failure to align itself with the "ordinary, human, unexaggerated, common, normal, restraint, reserve," its deformation into a modernist narrative (*DHL* 36). The brittle imagism of the novel's language, Pinkney contends, positions itself against Morel, and thus community, in favor of the mother (*DHL* 45).[24] While Pinkney correctly deems *Sons and Lovers*'s interest in the closure of private and public spaces a realist project, this interest should not be incompatible with modernist style.

In contrast to Pinkney's assertion, Paul's disdain for Miriam does not lean as much toward realism as toward the disruptive possibilities of moving away from the exaggerated, even scripted, intersubjectivity Miriam tries to create. Furthermore, Pinkney's reading of the novel's "process of expulsion" as related purely to literary genre and form fails to accurately connect the formal analysis with the thematic, overlooking how sexuality underwrites *Sons and Lovers*'s transformation into a modernist text (*DHL* 36). Pinkney very accurately diagnoses the structural trend of the novel as a whole as moving toward modernism, but he errs in observing that the novel's major tension, and its move away from realism, plays out in the choices Paul must make between his mother and his female sexual partners. In keeping with the deforming realist narrative, each sexual relationship merely repeats, with slight distinction, the Oedipal one, resulting in the "slow growth" Lawrence identifies in the novel's development (*CL* 161). The real tension in the novel, which occurs between Paul's Oedipal socialization and his identification with his working-class father, maps onto the choice Paul makes between his female sexual partners and the intimacy he feels for Baxter Dawes. As a same-sex object choice, Dawes is more like Paul, and thus comes closer to fulfilling the novel's goal, which, as Pinkney correctly explains, aims toward achieving a "totality of subject and object" (*DHL* 32).

Regardless of whether the novel actually accomplishes these aims, its project is not merely to reproduce the structure of the realist novel, as Pinkney indicates. The form of the *Bildungsroman* itself sabotages this hoped-for totality, throwing Paul into exceedingly close solidarity with his mother while suggesting that his father's work is neither "aesthetic" nor "humanizing" enough to transcend the given social realities of his community.[25] Morel, who "*can't* understand rules and regulations," represents an alternate public vision that is bawdy, sentimental, loud, and lax in bodily discipline (*SL* 127). After his mother's death, for example, Paul harshly criticizes his father for "sitting sentimentalising over her . . . in the public houses" (*SL* 445). Paul is critical of Morel's sentimentality and the sociability it entails, characterized by his inarticulateness, his ignorance of the cultural rules of self-expression, and his disregard for privacy. On one hand, Paul criticizes his father because his sentimentality is too personal, a candied form of expression that evokes only false emotion. On the other hand, Paul's reversion from public forms of expression in favor of private ones suggests that he still adheres, at least in some respect, to the personalized, often isolated, intimacy he shares with his mother. The strangely expressive affective life of Walter, who "never thought of her, personally," amplifies both the anti-sentimentality and the personalized feelings of intimacy that foster Paul's dual repulsion for and attraction toward Miriam (*SL* 445).

Ultimately, Walter's impersonal sentimentalizing—which takes place outside of the privacy of the home, where it becomes something more like a ritual—counters a personalized, ego-intensive intimacy and moves the novel toward the system of communal values Morel represents. Morel's inability to communicate, brought on both by his educational deficiency and by his feeling that "his son did not want him," is itself a form of impersonal affective engagement that paralyzes the novel's more central narrative, which develops Paul's apparent interiority hermeneutically through excruciating dialogues with women (*SL* 91). Paul tends to discount his father's affectionate, soft addresses of "my darlin," "my beauty," and "my duckie" not only for their sentimentality but also for their strangeness; the terms represent an affective dimension that reveals no "personal" or interpretive knowledge of their subject. Such words evoke silence rather than conversation, the latter of which, Moretti claims, functions as a key novelistic mode for developing personality. Nonetheless, these points of silent intimacy consistently punctuate the earlier portions of the novel. Morel enters again the "life of his own people" when he works, reuniting his children with a living sense of their past: "Sometimes, in the evening, he cobbled the boots or mended the kettle or his pit-bottle. Then he always wanted several attendants, and the children enjoyed it. They united with him in the work, in the actual doing of something, when he was his real self again" (*SL* 88). While Terry Eagleton argues that this way of "establishing human contact with his children through his practical skills about the house" renders a "reduced" and diminished Morel, I would suggest that the text visually magnifies these moments of utopian solidarity, particularly in relation to the relatively small portion of narrative space they occupy (*Literary* 152). In contrast to Gertrude's psychological dilemmas of consumption, the immediate, reparative nature of these acts of making, the common work of mending and cobbling, shields them from the intrusion of interpretation. While the text observes that Morel is his "real self," he is only that self in the "actual doing of something" (*SL* 88). This self exists in relative relationship to the father who bullies his family and makes them "writhe with hate of the man," producing an affective environment that shuts down the possibility of communication with his children (*SL* 87). As an alternative conception of selfhood, his "real self" enables a regenerative intimacy shared, not in speaking, but in "the actual doing of something." This impersonal model of intimacy moves Paul forward in search of a social context for his own work, away from exacting definitions of individual selfhood that the *Bildungsroman* demands.

The struggle between the story's Oedipal dynamic and the concentrated communal action that nullifies it discloses another kernel of discord between a narrative progressing primarily through the intimate displays of a hermeneutic journey toward exclusive heterosexual attachment, on the one hand, and a *proairetic* code of action, of "doing," that solidifies social community through a humanized work, on the other. This antagonism follows the two codes that, according to Peter Brooks, constitute plot—the *proairetic* and the *hermeneutic*. For Brooks, working from Barthes, the *proairetic* code concerns the logic of actions, "how their completion can be derived from their initiation, how they form sequences" (*Reading* 18). The hermeneutic code, by contrast, "concerns rather the questions and answers that structure a story," including the "revelation of meaning that occurs when the narrative sequence reaches full predication" (*Reading* 18). Following Brooks, I am proposing a relation between the hermeneutic as a form of intimacy in a novel that traces the development, or unveiling, of an individual's interiority. If the novel administers to Paul's increasing individuation and consequent dissociation, then it must also develop hermeneutically through the "questions and answers that structure a story" in order to reach a "revelation of meaning" (*Reading* 18). Yet the presence of the positively valued *proairetic* movement suggests that the novel reflexively problematizes Oedipalized hermeneutics and, more particularly, the relation of heterosexual intimacy to narrative development.

While Paul's relationship with his mother provides the model for his heterosexual romances, Paul's aesthetic consciousness, the possibility of his inhabiting an artistic medium, lies with his father; Lawrence's utopian fantasy resides in the possibility that the two might unite in humanly useful work. When Walter Morel makes fuses for the coal mine, the text does not gravitate toward his merits "personally" but toward the impersonal, *proairetic* community that he represents:

> But the best time for the young children was when he made fuses. Morel fetched a sheaf of long sound wheat straws from the attic. These he cleaned with his hand, till each one gleamed like a stalk of gold. After which he cuts the straws into lengths of about six inches, leaving if he could a notch at the bottom of each piece. He always had a beautifully sharp knife that could cut a straw clean without hurting it. Then he set in the middle of the table a heap of gunpowder, a little pile of black grains upon the white-scrubbed board. He made and trimmed the straws while Paul and Annie filled and plugged them. Paul loved to see the black grains trickle down a crack in his palm, into the mouth of the straw, peppering jollily downwards till the straw was full. (*SL* 89)

Tony Pinkney, arguing that the language here exemplifies the "stylistic hardness" of Ezra Pound's imagism, deems this a "crisply visualized" episode that aligns itself with Gertrude's rigidity despite its registering of the father's "sensuous" merits (*DHL* 46). The gunpowder fuses, he contends, ultimately subordinate the figure of the miner, reinforcing his connection to destructiveness, the "underground, darkness, night" (*DHL* 46). But the *proairetic* focus of the scene on activity—and the anxiety it betrays over the "violence of making"—weakens Pinkney's interpretation, along with its covert characterization of Pound's imagism as reactionary and conservative (*Solid* 21). This is a scene where action as an aesthetic practice, the "doing" of something, registers not "Gertrude's rigidity" but the utopian possibilities of work in common. The link between work and aesthetics here unites Paul's own artistic vocation with that of his father, rescuing the aesthetic from the world of mere idleness and leisure. In celebrating these values, the scene aligns itself against the mother, not the father, demonstrating how action forges community and aesthetic perception in a way that directly opposes the tightly "knitted," privatized intimacy of mother and son (*SL* 171). The crystallized severity and lyrical compactness of the language here runs in tandem with the scene's activity; the strong actions of making, trimming, and fetching signify the *proairetic* nature of group intimacy. That this intimacy builds around gunpowder fuses foreshadows the later violence of Paul's entanglement with Baxter and testifies to the class antagonism that supplies this eroticism with such energy.

The "Bodily Me": Interiority, Exteriority, and the Defeat of Meaning

So far, I have been examining how the impersonal sociability of an action-based intimacy alters the *Bildungsroman* and destabilizes the hermeneutically based narrative production of interiority or self. And while *Sons and Lovers* progresses dialectically through those ruptures in which the narrative of social aspiration that unites Paul with his mother meets the aggressive energy of his father, the text does not manifest this contestation quite as explicitly as my earlier analysis might suggest. Rather, as Morel's real presence becomes more ineffectual and impotent in the text, Paul's relations with women register the antagonism of this loss and begin to suffer more intensely. Terry Eagleton underlines this logic, arguing that the very organization of *Sons and Lovers* registers Morel's presence and his consequent diminishment. Nonetheless, while Lawrence blames "the predatory capitalism which can find no better use for [Morel] than a cog in the wheel of production," the novel, according to Eagleton, does not "confront these truths," as Lawrence's interest lies not in writing about the working class but in "writing his way out of it" (*Literary* 154). Here, Eagleton's overt class politics does not account for other ideological concerns embedded in Lawrence's critique of capitalism, thereby obscuring the novel's basic conflict: that between the Oedipalized, middle-class intimacy of bourgeois aspiration and the consistent textual "return" to Morel. Eagleton's pithy diagnosis of Paul's (and Lawrence's) desire to escape these confines not only erases the element of real conflict in the novel but also ignores the narrative and formal developments that (though not unproblematically) explore the possibilities of diminishing class barriers through a heightened medium of common work. The violent hate and cruel intellectuality Paul so frequently directs toward women, not solely "predatory capitalism," is the bitterly sexual outgrowth of class antagonism, of Morel's diminished yet pervasive presence. As Morel's explicit centrality to the narrative dwindles, Paul's relationships with women suffer most acutely. Rather than "writing" Paul (or himself) out of the working class into bourgeois sensibility, Lawrence preserves the violent sensibility of Walter to problematically actualize Paul's hope to "be rid of our individuality" in an "effortless" motion toward the beauty of "our after-life, our immortality" (*SL* 331–32).

In emphasizing Paul's move *forward* or *toward*, I am suggesting that the *proairetic* mode of the novel, as represented by Morel, moves toward life, reproduction, and immortality, while the hermeneutically oriented narrative connected to Gertrude reflects stasis and eventually death. While this reading may seem overtly schematic, it is no less schematic than the novel itself, in which the controlling maneuvers of the author seemingly contradict its impersonal aims. In forging relationships with Miriam and even Clara, Paul repeats not only the pattern of intimacy he understands with his mother but also the traumatic antagonism it breeds with his ever-diminishing father. Morel, then, adds a third dimension to the Freudian game of *fort/da*. His own ineffectuality, and his disappearance from the text's central narrative, pushes Paul backward in favor of intimacy with his mother. This intimacy enables Paul, just as it does Gertrude, to hold himself socially superior to his father and thereby renounce his communal orientation.

Consistent with *Sons and Lovers*'s dialectical structure, this feeling of superiority drives Paul's quest to establish relations with an absent father and problematically transpires in Paul's psychic cruelty to the women in his life. This dynamic reflects both Paul's torn class identification with his father and his withdrawal from the Oedipalized model of intimacy that his relation with his mother fosters and perpetuates. For example, after personalizing Miriam according to the model of his mother, Paul finds it necessary to escape, "to be almost unaware of her, as a person: she was only to him then, a woman" (*SL* 330). The text denounces Paul's depersonalizing impulse as having grown too strong, striding too far in the wrong direction. By taking Miriam only "as a woman" rather than a "person," he heightens the gap between subject and object that tends to fuel conventional narratives of desire. This brutal *withholding* of intimacy awards him demonic control, leading Miriam to ever more pointed and fruitless pursuits of his intelligibility.

Even within his more decidedly impersonal relationship with Clara Dawes, Paul strains even further from the close intimacy that characterizes the mother-son bond, inducing her to ask if it is "*me* you want, or is it *It*?" (italics in original; *SL* 407). In this relationship, even the most private acts absorb the impersonal flavor of public anonymity. Their energy emanates not from the individual discretion of a discerning subject but from a larger, more pervasive "strong, strange, wild life," much like the "daemonic" power Freud identifies in *Beyond the Pleasure Principle* (*SL* 407).[26] Such intense force, in its movement beyond the boundaries of individual bodies, trades private or individualized space for a more open one. An explicit textual logic directs Paul's progress toward this impersonality, which, to adopt Freud's terms, is "a *passive* experience, over which he has no influence" (italics in original; *BPP* 24). Simultaneously, this passive movement forward, predating Eliot's claim that impersonal poetic emotion develops from a "passive attending upon an event," intensifies Paul's violent and "wild life" precisely as it transforms it through more public forms of expression (*Prose* 43).

Yet Paul's reaction to this looming public and impersonal force is, once more, to backtrack, as he attempts to curtail the dissolution of corporeal boundaries that accompanies his father's public life. He consequently restores Clara and himself "to respectability" after they have sex outdoors, polishing their shoes and washing his hands (*SL* 355). His desire that Clara be "irreproachable" not only points to a wish to sanctify the adulterous affair but also aspires to protect the dignity of the appropriately private couple, transporting sex as an impersonal action back to its normative and private domain (*SL* 355). Paul's affectionate styling of his lover restores her to his distinguished and chosen possession, rescuing her from the animal logic of his impersonal sexual detachment. Despite this detachment, Paul's relation to heterosexuality is often possessive and "personal." For example, the absolute dissolution of individuality and the invasion of privacy that characterizes his relationship with Miriam renders any private sense of interiority meaningless, leaving Paul with the claustrophobic feeling of having "no barriers between us," as if his "body were lying empty" (*SL* 232). Miriam sucks the life out of Paul's body precisely by dismissing his physicality, suggesting how a "personally" coded, heterosexual model of intimacy can lead to bodily death.

Paul thus laments that in Miriam's intimate proximity "the individual bodily me is discarded," suggesting that Miriam's interpretive projects deny an essential part of his being: a discrete interiority that arises through the exterior, the "bodily me" (*SL* 232). This exterior, consistent with the impersonality of Eliot, Woolf, and Gaudier-Brzeska, is a source of essential and impersonal knowledge in the text, an equally intimate knowledge that defies interpretation through its relation to the code of action that accompanies Morel's waning narrative and Paul's relations with men more generally. The immortally inspired body of Paul's father, still "wonderfully young ... muscular, without any fat" provides a point of distanced identification that consistently impedes the narrative development of the privatized romance (*SL* 235). Paul's attraction to this body, which leads him to find it "strange that they were of the same flesh," generates the model of distanced intimacy that marks his desire for Dawes, the estranged husband of Paul's lover, Clara (*SL* 235). In contrast to the conventional *Bildungsroman*, Paul's heterosexual, romantic choices reverse or at least reclaim a narrative pattern that progresses by moving from a prohibited or "improper" desire to a legitimate or "proper" one that "marks the end" of a narrative.[27] In this case, the perversely violent "proper" desire that marks the end of the novel is that of Paul for Baxter Dawes.

The text further complicates this pattern by prohibiting the "proper" desire that ultimately centralizes itself, that of the boy for his father, as it punctuates the text. Whereas the narrative that is actually most crucial to the operations of the text never fully interpolates the "proper" narrative of desire, by the novel's end, the "improper" homosexual ends take center stage not only as failed projects of interpretation but also as failed projects of interpellation. These repeated failures of intimacy and possession pronounce their respective narratives unreadable, as they simultaneously facilitate the growth of other narratives. The fact that Miriam expires while Paul's life continues to develop negates the simultaneity Freud poses between pain and pleasure, life and death. The text pronounces Paul and Miriam's intimacy a fluke; each misinterprets the other, and Miriam becomes an instrument for Paul's growth.

Violence and the "Lapse into Temporality"

The fact that Paul might consider his body's resemblance to his father's coal-marked but youthful physique "strange" reflects the alienation he experiences from the productive values of a *proairetic* social body. In his letters, Lawrence implicitly constellates the prolonged youthfulness that characterizes this worker's active body, sociability, and a life-imbued narrative that strives against death toward immortality. In 1914, one year after the publication of *Sons and Lovers*, Lawrence wrote of a proposed lecture series with Bertrand Russell. Russell would give lectures on ethics and Lawrence on immortality. The point was to "have meetings, to establish a little society or body around a *religious belief, which leads to action*."[28] Most importantly, Lawrence deeply stresses forward movement in a constant direction, "always toward the Eternal thing: We *mustn't* lapse into temporality" (*Letters* 84). Lawrence's devotion to the "Eternal thing" resembles Paul's fanciful vision that ridding ourselves of individuality promises immortality. Immortality itself, as represented in the youthful body of the miner, depends on maintaining a set of active, *proairetic* or impersonal social values that resist exclusivity and possession. Exemplified in Paul's feeling that Miriam suffocates him, leaving his body "empty," with "no barriers between us," the text suggests that heterosexual possession cancels the possibility of both individuality and social being and, furthermore, immortality (*SL* 232). While Paul appears to suggest that the excruciating, personalized intimacy with Miriam dissolves his individuality by preserving no "barriers between us," it actually does so by constructing a false sense of individuality around the illusion of psychological depth. In contrast, the violent finale of the text explores how the breakdown of such constructions preserves the impersonal "strangeness" that might enable individuality as a function of social being.

A novel mode of friendship forms the basis of this intimate relation, which simultaneously enables social connection while upholding the "barriers" that bar a complete invasion of privacy. According to Maurice Blanchot, whose nonviolent version of friendship best illustrates the kind of relation Lawrence envisions between Baxter Dawes and Paul Morel, friendship is the relation by which we "give up trying to know those to whom we are linked by something essential."[29] We greet friends in our "estrangement," passing "by way of the recognition of the common strangeness that does not allow us to speak of our friends but only speak to them, not to make of them a topic of conversation (or essays), but the movement of understanding in which speaking to us, they reserve, even on the most familiar terms, an infinite distance, the fundamental separation on the basis of which what separates becomes relation" (*Friendship* 291). According to Blanchot, we speak *to* our friends, not *of* them, from a distanced familiarity that redefines an intimacy that once labored in the artificial task of producing life narratives. As an alternative to this hermeneutically charged project of personalized self-disclosure, this more productive intimacy to some extent characterizes Paul's relation to his father, a relation that the text maps onto Paul's connection to Baxter Dawes. However, in marked contrast to the tender spirit of Blanchot's essay, *Sons and Lovers* yokes this "peculiar feeling of intimacy" with a violence that moves the narrative toward life, not death.

Repeatedly, the novel stresses that the "painful nearness" of the two men, their "feeling of connection," depends on shared violent impulses. While Paul and Dawes were "confirmed enemies . . . there was between them that peculiar feeling of intimacy, as if they were secretly near to each other, which sometimes exists between two people although they never speak to one another. Paul often thought of Baxter Dawes, often wanted to get at him, and be friends with him. He knew that Dawes often thought about him, and that the man was drawn to him by some bond or other. And yet the two never looked at each other save in hostility" (*SL* 386). The mode of intimacy here differs markedly from that Paul has shared with women, primarily because the two men are equally intelligible to each other, as if bound by some mutual straining toward Lawrence's sublime "Eternal thing" (*SL* 84). That the two do not speak suggests that their intimacy is part of a greater nonverbal, nonhermeneutic medium, something remarkably public. As opposed to the invasive nature of Paul and Miriam's profundities, speech here functions altogether differently. As the narrative's impersonal hunger grows stronger, Paul appears more frequently within the despised domain of his father—the public house—where the trauma of his ambivalent class origins often materializes. Here, Paul attempts to create public debate, forsaking "personal" language for the more "impersonal" medium of politics. These efforts, performatively voiced to enter public discourse and disparage it, lead to his unpopularity: "He irritated the older men by his assertive manner, and his cock-suredness" (*SL* 386). Paul's sense of superiority prevents him from merging his own work into this medium. The text ironically mocks Paul's "flow of eloquence," which appears paltry in contrast to the vivacious language of the pub. This energy erupts healthily from open talk of the body and, significantly, homosexuality. Dawes openly and vociferously employs the terms "bugger" and "sod" against a "white and quivering" Paul, whose obvious effeminacy lends him spectacular notoriety (*SL* 386).

The homophobic violence of this language uncaps the energy of the novel's climax. At this point of violent rupture, Morel's silent presence in the novel asserts itself, overturning the heterosexual logic of intimacy that has quelled it:

> [Paul] Morel, in his shirt sleeves, was now alert and furious. He felt his whole body unsheath itself like a claw ... The other man became more distinct to him ... The Young man's mouth was bleeding. It was the other man's mouth he was dying to get at, and desire was anguish in its strength. He stepped quickly through the stile, and as Dawes was coming through, after him, like a flash he got a blow in over the other's mouth. He shivered with pleasure. Dawes advanced slowly, spitting. Paul was afraid ... Suddenly, from out of nowhere, came a great blow against his ear, that sent him falling helpless backwards. He heard Dawes' heavy panting, like a wild beast's. Then came a kick on his knee, giving him such agony that he got up, quite blind, leapt clean under his enemy's guard. He felt blows and kicks but they did not hurt. He hung onto the bigger man like a wild cat, till at last Dawes fell with a crash, losing his presence of mind. Paul went down with him. Pure instinct brought his hands to the man's neck, and before Dawes, in frenzy and agony, could wrench him free, he had got his fists twisted in the scarf and his knuckles dug in the throat of the other man. He was a pure instinct, without reason or feeling. His body, hard and wonderful in itself, cleaved against the struggling body of the other man. Not a muscle in him relaxed. He was quite

unconscious, only his body had taken upon itself to kill this other man. For himself he had neither feeling nor reason. He lay, pressed hard against his adversary, his body adjusting itself to its one pure purpose of choking the other man, resisting exactly at the right moment, with exactly the right amount of strength, the strength, the struggles of the other, silent, intent, unchanging, gradually pressing its knuckles deeper, feeling the struggles of the other body become wilder and more frenzied. Tighter and tighter grew his body, like a screw that is gradually increasing in pressure, till something breaks. (*SL* 409–10)

Paul's sublime physical experience follows the complete breakdown of social distinction between the two men. The passage, alternating between a direct and personalized language and an impersonal idiom of aggression, vacillates between an explicit naming of the two adversaries and a refusal to consider them as anything but concentrated essences of men. In an effort to establish the "essential" connection between Paul and his father, the text switches to Morel in naming the young man. Concurrently, Paul loses his rationality and becomes "a great instinct," at once violent and erotic, in a fantasy of same-sex fusion that even imagines an exchange of fluids: "The young man's mouth was bleeding. It was the other man's mouth he was dying to get at" (*SL* 409–10). Paul completes this blow, and desire gives way to pleasure. This pleasure is a masochistic one, in which violence erases consciousness both of class distinction and of the individual body. A kick on the knee gives Paul "such agony," but subsequent "blows and kicks . . . did not hurt" (*SL* 410). Shared instinct erases both reason and feeling; it obliterates an individualized consciousness of the body that estranges one from both communal feeling and masochistic *jouissance*.

Nonetheless, as in texts such as *Women in Love* (1920), the struggle preserves the male body itself as its centerpiece, as if the shattering effect of the violence simultaneously and paradoxically defines that body in its exterior. The violent clash erases the illusion of psychological depth in the service of profile: "His body, hard and wonderful in itself, cleaved against the struggling body of the other man" (*SL* 409). In the full presence of sexuality, Paul's body transforms from its former effeminacy, in keeping with Lawrence's more general theory of impersonality and its valuation of the exterior over internal reflexivity. This loss of social and physical consciousness establishes Paul's connection to his father's youthful vitality. Obliterating the distinction between exterior and interior, pure exteriority builds the common interior these men experience as it simultaneously honors the boundaries between these interiors. By theorizing interiority as it literally surfaces through the exterior, Lawrence articulates an elemental form of affect that, like Eliot's version of poetic emotion or H.D.'s masochism, denies individual psychology. Cleaving against each other, Dawes and Paul appear in profile, disturbing conventional measures of psychological depth.

This impersonal diffusion, which both abstracts and finely delineates Paul Morel and Baxter Dawes, magnifies the physical exteriors of the two men. This sense of exterior, much like the surfaces valued by Virginia Woolf and Gaudier-Brzeska, best registers the contradiction of an impersonality that both perpetuates the self and dissolves it. In this vein, modernist critic T. E. Hulme also observed that the physical "always endeavors to arrest you, and to make you continuously see . . . to prevent you from gliding through an abstract process" (*Speculations* 134).[30] In *Sons and Lovers*, the dialectical return to physical distinction guards against the complete and utter disintegration of self that violence produces. Ultimately, this dialectic creates a path of development that dissolves individuality in favor of a common work shared with other men. In imagining a desublimated space of work, as opposed to Freud's claim in *Group Psychology and the Analysis of the Ego* that "sublimated homosexual love for other men . . . springs from work in common," *Sons and Lovers*'s violent climax attempts to desublimate, or sexually invest and publicize, the world of work.[31] Furthermore, the violence of this social and aesthetic process secures the formal closure of subject and object, private and public, that the *Bildungsroman* demands but precisely by negating its terms that "the individual willingly limit his freedom . . . through marriage" as a means of finding "happiness" and constructing "personality" (*Way* 22). This renunciation becomes Paul's impersonal mode of following his father into the pit, of merging private attachment with the public world of work, enabling him to compensate both for the shortcomings of his own body, which hardly resembles the work-brittle body of his father, and for the solitude of his aesthetic vocation.

However, as part of this dialectical narrative movement, Paul's violent instinct returns in Freudian fashion, as does Baxter Dawes's. At the hospital, Dawes speaks to Paul "caressingly," softly calling him "lad," much in the tradition of Morel's tender addresses. Yet after a bit more conversation "they did not talk any more" because the "instinct to murder each other had returned" (*SL* 448). Again, the turbulent force that binds them most closely forbids communicative interpretation. The conversation that typically builds personality disintegrates, leaving no code other than action to elucidate it. As Paul's loss of self-consciousness in the initial struggle with Dawes indicates, their shared instinct defies reflexivity. This instinct represents, as Blanchot might suggest, "the frankness of a relation without history" (*Friendship* 292).

In the nineteenth-century novel, and in the *Bildungsroman* more particularly, intimate relationships build upon the sharing of experiences. In contrast, Paul and Baxter connect impersonally through a strange form of affect that, devoid of environmental similarities, presumes no prior or shared experience. In forging this distanced intimacy, Paul separates from historical circumstance when he enters his father's repressed communal narrative. In its attempt to collapse social hierarchies, this form of impersonality—shared by modernists such as Eliot, Pound, H.D. and, as I am arguing, Lawrence—enables the subject access to other subject positions while preserving a difference in function. As I have argued of H.D.'s *Sea Garden*, for example, poetic impersonality functions by replicating the poetic self. Here, the poems' speakers masochistically dissolve their own personalities to enter other subject positions, producing a new kind of common interior—an impersonal alteration that retains the trace of the original personality. Similarly, for Eliot the truly "new" work of art carefully modifies the "whole existing order," readjusting "the relation, proportions, [and] values of each work of art toward the whole" (*Prose* 38). This impersonal surrender of the new to the old order does not result in a confused and conglomerate mass but in a finely distinguished arrangement of works that Eliot counts as tradition. Similarly, the impersonal intelligibility that characterizes the relationship of Paul Morel and Baxter Dawes in *Sons and Lovers* provides the terms by which two modes of work—physical labor and aesthetic creation—can unselfconsciously merge together in a way that preserves the particularity of each participant while forsaking the individualizing impulse that characterizes bourgeois narratives of personal development and social aspiration. This consolidation permits an essentially public being, where what is intractable in each individual extends outward into other social relationships.

The problem with this formulation are the conditions on which it stands; Lawrence's novel counters the individualizing impulse that Giddens attributes to modernity, its cordoning off of intimate life into the private sphere, by positing violent antagonism as the equalizing agent in the relation between subject and object, in this case, Paul Morel and Baxter Dawes. That is, *Sons and Lovers*'s equalizing gesture, which attempts to close the distance that separates subject from object, ends up supporting an antagonism that reproduces authority and isolation rather than a "common life" (*CL* 395). This antagonism repeats a trauma inherent to Paul's torn class identification, his separation from his father, and his resulting inability to merge his own work into a socially conscious medium. But it's during these traumatic moments, as Paul's turbulent meeting with Dawes indicates, that he experiences his most intense ecstasy. At least momentarily, trauma engenders a new kind of impersonal intimacy, however fraught with the tensions of Paul's continually shifting attachments.

The paradox here of an antagonistic novelist closure, where the subject is utopically reconciled with social consciousness through violent discord, further extends to the novel's intimation that violence repairs or restores social fractures as it shatters the individual body. During his bout with Dawes, Paul's body grows "[t]ighter and tighter," ever more closely defined, until it reaches an orgasmic pressure point where "something breaks" (*SL* 410). This fracture lets him relax, "full of wonder and misgiving" (*SL* 410). In the same way that it fringes Dawes's caressing speech, violence produces a healing fellow feeling. Likewise, shared violent instinct indicates the essential sameness of Baxter Dawes and Paul Morel as two life narratives that briefly conjoin to disformulate the central narrative. I have argued that this juncture is consistent with Paul's, and Lawrence's, fantasy of immortality—of a narrative that, when held strongly together, replicates only by moving forward, not by doubling back. The open, exposed repetitions of this text harshly critique the proper *bildung*, which manages and masks its repetitions to build the illusion of a unique and expressive personality, at one with both itself and the world. This form of narrative, I have suggested, also elaborates an impersonal form of intimacy that, in its respect for interior boundaries, renders the other completely intelligible, a veritable prosthetic extension of the self.

However idealistic this impersonality, the closure of subject and object it celebrates, depends on a rarified knowledge that Lawrence, like H.D., authoritatively limits to a select few. Furthermore, the self-replicatory strategy of this impersonality could also be understood to extend the ego in a way that obliterates difference in the service of social dominance and authority. Even as it connects work to more public and collective forms of existence, the violence that lies at the heart of this impersonality is ethically suspect. In this problematic vein, so much of *Sons and Lovers* seems to be obsessed with Baxter as Paul's inaccurate double. Their telepathic mental processes evoke Freud's "The 'Uncanny'" and the "doubling, dividing, and interchanging of the self" that forms a stage of "unrestricted narcissism."[32] Unlike the nineteenth-century *Bildungsroman*, which adequately manages repetition, or the need to tell and retell, *Sons and Lovers* erodes the very narrative it seeks to articulate. The violent intimacy that the text deems productive condones the violence that Walter repeatedly directs toward his wife as well as Paul's psychic insensitivity to women, privileging one form of social consciousness at the price of others. That is, the text's attempt to inscribe Paul within a social consciousness, a narrative of class, through traumatic repetition elaborates a form of commonality that excludes any community with women. As a result, Paul's narrative completely disintegrates, particularly as Baxter returns to Clara, quite significantly "broken" (*SL* 453). By the end of the novel, Paul, caught up in the demonic thrust of impersonalization, can scarcely distinguish himself from the "fused ... conglomerated mass" where "[n]othing was distinct or distinguishable"

(SL 464). Separated both from the Oedipal narrative and from that of his father, temporality—Paul's specific relation to history—vanishes, and the young man finds his relation to his environment indiscernible, with "no obstruction to the void in which he found himself" (SL 464).

Perhaps this collapse represents the text's self-conscious acknowledgment of the ethical problematic of violent impersonality. Human engagement this intense ultimately annihilates all engagement, particularly in its disregard for the rules that might order and manage those connections. Consequently, the ethical and aesthetic flaws of impersonality are often spatial. That is, the fusion of boundaries Paul experiences in his union with Dawes ultimately defeats its own purpose of transcendence, immortality, and social consciousness, leaving him with no sense of meaningful space with which to gauge the boundaries of his own ego, his own personality. That is, the failure of personality is also the failure of impersonality. Narrative itself becomes immaterial, unable to cohere within such impersonal chaos.

Paul's rather sad expiration and final breakdown suggests that the novel's vision of a public consciousness that preserves some glimmer of individual strangeness is a purely utopian fantasy, unable to be sustained by the limitations of literary form. Once Dawes is "broken," Lawrence's experimental *Bildungsroman* disintegrates. This collapse reflexively acknowledges the force of a modernity that compartmentalizes personal life, creating an irresolvable antagonism between public and private dimensions of self-formation. That this synthesis can only be articulated clearly through stunningly brief moments of violence presents an insurmountable ethical tension and implies that a *proairetic* code of action can hardly carry an entire novel. Yet Paul's wish that Miriam "come publicly into full possession of [her]self" on her twenty-first birthday offers a productive paradigm that preserves the dignity of an unmappable self-possession within public being. This alternate form of intimacy, which does not require hermeneutic disclosure, instills itself in Paul's most productive and gentle relations with women. These relationships often rely on the "doing of something," whether he is talking with the girls at the factory or taking down the "splendid" hair of a "morbidly sensitive" hunchback (SL 139).

Given such intimacies, my hope is that the ethical difficulties of this novel, and of Lawrence's work more generally, do not prevent a reparative reading of it. In particular, the principle of action *Sons and Lovers* endorses registers itself separately from the interior revelations that often supply novels with profound meaning and occurs particularly when this *proairetic* mode infuses sex, problematizing its status as revelatory of the private self. Furthermore, in fusing the impersonal or transcendent with the historical or social, the novel situates Paul instinctually away from circumstance and sociohistorical conditioning as it enables him to reconnect momentarily with a narrative of social class. If Lawrence's mediation on sexuality functions as a trope for public being, then the telepathic eroticism of Baxter Dawes and Paul Morel represents a disintegrating movement toward an impersonal being. While Moretti reads the *Bildungsroman* as facilitating a culture of personality, *Sons and Lovers* can be thought of as an attempted or experimental *Bildungsroman* invested both in the dissolution of personality and in explicitly testing the limits of the form itself. The text can then be said to once again straddle the boundaries of realism and modernism, but only if we accept the view that the "distortion" of modernism, and this should include the distortion of the "personality," precludes social existence.[33] Tony Pinkney is partially correct in arguing that Lawrence's exacting and often cold prose leans toward a Poundian imagism, and thus modernism, while the novel's attempt to close private and public space works nostalgically backward toward realism but fails. Ultimately, the novel engages in this realist project but only through a modernist impersonality and narrative vision of intimacy that breaks down the boundaries between individuals while preserving their private particularity. The dissociation essential to the modernist aesthetic then becomes the very means by which the individual is utopically recast into the public sphere.

4

Problem Space

Wyndham Lewis, Mary Butts, and the Impersonal Object

Life, simply, however vivid and tangible, is too material to be anything but a mechanism, and the seagull is not far removed from the hydroplane. Whether a stone flies and copulates . . . is little matter . . . What I am proposing is activity, more deliberate and more intense, on the material we know and on our present very fallible stock . . . Let us substitute ourselves everywhere for the animal world; replace the tiger and the cormorant with some invention of our mind, so that we can intimately control this new Creation. The danger, as it would appear at present, and in our first flight of substitution and remounting, is evidently that we should become overpowered by our creation, and become as mechanical as a tremendous insect world, all our awakened reason entirely disappeared.

—Wyndham Lewis[1]

The activity of relationality must be distinguished from the unbounded sameness that in Nietzchean terms, could be seen as the goal (and origin) of all correspondences. Distinguished and protected: the peace of the undifferentiated is also a deathlike stillness, and what we have perhaps too hastily called the superstition of difference could be reformulated as a wish to preserve those frictions that preserve all relations from life-defeating fusions.

—Leo Bersani and Ulysse Dutoit[2]

The epigraphs above offer seemingly divergent accounts of the term activity, both of which are relevant to the theory of impersonality T. S. Eliot articulates in "Tradition and the Individual Talent," where he suggests that we dispense with "what is individual, what is the peculiar essence of man" in exchange for the common medium of aesthetic emotion.[3] The brand of activity Lewis advocates in this particular 1919 essay from *The Caliph's Design*, "The Physiognomy of Our Time"—ostensibly an evaluation of Marinetti's futurism and a treatise on the ideal "act of creation in art"—is impersonal in this sense: it attempts to proliferate human subjectivity into the external world to exceed "the scope of ... personal existence," such that human consciousness permeates "all forms of life" (*CD* 78, 77). Yet this "substitution and remounting" is not purely an act of domination, as it may appear in Lewis's description (*CD* 77). Rather, such intrusion is also an "act of creation" that renders its architect vulnerable to impersonal diffusion, in "danger" of losing himself to the power of his creation. While the "activity" Lewis advocates does threaten to discount relationality altogether, trading respect toward discrete existence for "a death-like stillness" or "life-defeating fusion," he also stresses the need for some form of structure or "frictions" to preserve the fundamental differences that distinguish subject from object, suggesting that the expansion of human consciousness should never be "indiscriminate, mechanical and unprogressive" (*CD* 77; *Arts* 144). Such is the ethical problematic of impersonality: the collective fusion it demands, born of abandoning the "peculiar" in the effort to narrow the distance that separates subject and object, effaces distance altogether (*Prose* 37).

This contradictory position is not uncharacteristic of the various positions Lewis would take on the question of objects at different points in his career.[4] It also reflects more generally the dynamics of a modernist impersonality motivated by contradiction, where acts of aesthetic surrender wind up reproducing structures of authority, and the desire for true individualism in art is in actuality a critique of individualism. Because he so explicitly (perhaps more so than any other modernist) engages these tensions in his prolific critical commentary on modernism, I begin here with Lewis as a means of identifying the issues at stake in a larger modernist project reflexively concerned with the object as both a discrete and a relational entity, an index both of radical otherness and of the human. Within this context, I turn to the modernist writer Mary Butts, whose work, I argue, intervenes in the quandary Lewis identifies but does not resolve, addressing the question of how to preserve the basic structure of respect that attends subject-object distinctions within an impersonal aesthetic practice prone to "death-like stillness" and "life-defeating fusions" (*Arts* 144). Writing from the 1920s up until her death in 1937, Butts, like Lewis, engaged vociferously in fictional and critical commentary that offered what Bruce Hainley has called a "big Shut Up to much of modernism's nonsense and hush-hush."[5] Typical of the self-aggrandizing alliances she frequently drew, Butts wrote in a 1927 journal entry that Eliot was "the only writer of my quality"; while acknowledging that he "dislikes me and my work," she stressed the similarity of their projects addressing the "negative side" of the Sanc-Grail, "The Waste Land."[6] While Butts had no problem advertising her exclusion from the recognizable currents of aesthetic modernism, her unceasing devotion to the world of objects plants her solidly within a modernist network that includes figures as diverse as Lewis, Oscar Wilde, Virginia Woolf, and Elizabeth Bowen.

Fueled by Nathalie Blondel's impressive biography, attention to Butts's work has been largely biographical, focusing on her critical recovery as a writer of obscure and experimental prose, a "fag-hag" and a hanger-on to rather celebrated groups of gay men (including such luminaries as Jean Cocteau), a drug addict who traveled "astrally," a bad mother, and, according to Lewis himself, a "big carroty anglish intelligentsia . . . and buxom heiress" (*MBSL* 188).[7] In 1922, Virginia Woolf rejected Mary Butts's novel *Ashe of Rings*, which she called an "indecent book about the Greeks and Downs," as unsuitable for publication by the Hogarth Press (qtd. in *MBSL* 122). After Butts had visited for tea, Woolf returned to her diary to comment on her own troubles regarding the mixed critical reception of her novel *Jacob's Room*: "I want to be quit of all this. It hangs about me like Mary Butts's scent."[8] Woolf's statement curtly underscores the troubles of Butts's professional life. Like Woolf, Marianne Moore also dismissed Butts's work as "out of harmony" with *The Dial*, most likely because she felt the magazine risked too much in publishing its explicit depictions of homosexual relationships (qtd. in *MBSL* 188). Unlike the members of Bloomsbury and other established modernist circles, Butts held no stable affiliations with sources of intellectual and financial power.

Much like Lewis, Butts quite seriously envisioned her role as a critic of a developing and often fractious modernist culture. As a testament to their connection, Butts both arrogantly identified with Lewis and rather hungrily imagined her subordination to the virile masculinity she attributed to him. In 1920, Lewis had actually asked to paint Butts, and in her diary entry of the same week, she writes that Lewis was "the first man I have met whose vitality equals, probably surpasses mine" (*MBSL* 70). As "the most male creature" she had met, she lewdly confesses with an aplomb quite typical of her self-assertions that it would be "a pleasure to be raped by him—Yes that's true" (*MBSL* 70). Butts's sexual attraction to Lewis perhaps reflects a shared reverence for the "intellectually strong" over the "intellectually weak."[9] Jane Garrity has discussed in detail Butts's particular form of xenophobic conservatism, arguing that her novels privilege a "notion of ancestral memory" constructed around "Englishness, aristocratic continuity, spirituality, and crucially, the conjunction of femininity and nature" (*Step-Daughters* 189). In this "embrace of irrationality," Garrity asserts, Butts turns to the bucolic English landscape to lament the "cultural and economic dispossession" of postwar European life, demonizing the foreigner as racially, ethnically, and sexually inferior (*Step-Daughters* 189).[10] One particular problem is Butts's anti-semitism, evident in her depiction of Paul in her story "The House Party" or Kralin in *Death of*

Felicity Taverner, a Russian Bolshevik Jew "who would sell the body of our land to the Jews."[11]

As with other modernists I discuss in this book, Butts's reactionary beliefs often accompany more progressive ones. For example, the bucolic, often dehumanized locales of Butts's prose operate as corrective, alternative landscapes to the overly privatized modernist sets she connected to cities such as London and Paris.[12] Like Lewis, she was one of Bloomsbury's "bitterest detractor[s]," but she also suggested that Lewis managed his vitality badly, "like a great voice badly produced" (*Solid* 91; qtd. in *MBSL* 70). In her scathing critique of the set (in which she includes Lewis), written one year before her death in 1937, Butts praises Lewis's "violent gift" but unsurprisingly finds the polemicist's bravado lacking in tolerance, professing "a belief in humanity which appeared to go so far and not enough."[13] While Butts does not support this statement with particular examples, she is most likely referring to the texts that, according to Tyrus Miller, cemented Lewis's status as a "fascist-leaning" enemy to "fashionable modernism": *The Apes of God* (1930), with its notorious parody of Woolf's Mrs. Dalloway; *Men Without Art* (1932), a more explicit challenge to Woolf; and, most flagrantly, *Hitler*, in which Lewis adamantly professed his admiration for the heroism of the Nazi leader as a friend to the German people (*Late* 76). In any case, she appears to be concerned more with the actual ends or consequences of Lewis's pronouncements, not necessarily the aesthetic preconceptions that led to them. Regardless of the exact source of her criticism, and despite her conservatism on some issues, we can see in Butts's fiction a deep engagement with the project of finding more reparative resolutions and ends for some of the problems that emerge from texts such as *The Caliph's Design*. At stake for Butts is the question of material placement or grounding within a modernism (and modernity) whose extreme version of activity offers no concrete points of reference for collective emotional attachment. More particularly, Butts's own version of impersonality contests the violence that theories of activity like Lewis's confer onto objects but also seeks to transform domestic spaces, conceived in many modernist tracts as static and overly personal, into sites of active and impersonal modernism.[14] In this sense, she responds to what Christopher Reed has identified as the "anti-domestic tenor of avant-garde architectural theory," which, in critiquing "the conventional function of the home as a refuge of privacy and an assertion of individual—or family—identity," conflated traditional domesticity with femininity and sentimental decoration.[15] In embracing an aesthetics of impersonality that synthesizes the form of activity Lewis advocates with the values of domestic space, Butts's prose tends to rework a set of issues—concerned with the boundaries between subject and object—that emerges much earlier in modernist discourse.

In texts such as *Armed with Madness*, Butts reclaims for the avant-garde a space that had been limited by its connection to the feminine and the "personal," affirming the connections between the intimate values of space and an aesthetic that values activity over stasis. In doing so, she intervenes within a rather lengthy modernist trajectory that links interior space to the "personal." The idea that domestic existence somehow limited one's perceptions to the parameters of "personal" or subjective experience extends beyond the purview of masculine modernists such as Lewis. Even for Virginia Woolf, as Ann Banfield argues, "the room as symbol finds it precise philosophical gloss . . . as the 'here' and 'now' from which or upon which a perspective is perceived."[16] The "room" thus inscribes personal experience. As Woolf's 1930 essay "Street Haunting: A London Adventure" asserts, one must "step out of the house" and exit the "solitude of one's own room," where "we sit surrounded by objects which perpetually express the oddity of our own temperaments and enforce the memories of our own experience" to fully enlarge one's "central oyster of perceptiveness, an enormous eye" (*Collected IV* 155, 156). I argued earlier that modernists such as Lewis cemented the meaning of personality (and the passive, idle aesthete, depleted of manly vigor) to Wilde and the "room," particularly in his mockery of the "male-invert fashion" and its governance of domestic space.[17] Furthermore, as I have suggested, texts such as *Sons and Lovers* situate aesthetic production away from the Oedipalized sphere of private domestic relations and into the public world of masculinized violence.

Given this trajectory, which plants the impersonal away from the coordinates of domestic existence, I argue here that Butts attempted to energize an impersonal, avant-garde practice organized around the intimate values of space. And while gender is certainly relevant to this argument, I do not seek to correlate this concern too stringently with Butts's role as a woman writer or with her affiliations with other women. Ultimately, Butts's troublesome gender and sexual politics reinforce the difficulty of drawing a coherent feminist or queer politics from her writing.[18] Rather, I read Butts's work in its push for an aesthetic practice that positions the object world—the coordinates of lived, intimate, space—as an empathic and necessary ground for building more communicative and enduring relations among humans, particularly as these idealized relationships confront the overly personalized and privatized affiliations she observed in more highly identifiable groups such as Bloomsbury.

In this regard, Butts's work can be best understood in reference to a variety of modernist contexts, and I begin the chapter with the premise that the applied arts and modernist theories of design—often the context for Lewis's statements about human consciousness and subjectivity—provide a crucial frame for understanding Butts's vision of the object. In the first section of this chapter, I look to the growing importance of design in modernist circles as a field of aesthetic fulfillment for men explicitly engaged in reappropriating domestic interiors from the "ladies joy" in decoration.[19] For example, in *The Decorative Art of Today*, as I suggest earlier in this book, Le Corbusier contrasts his strong design with the cluttered insincerity of the department store, whose wares hide "beneath decoration" to eclipse "flaws, blemishes, all defects" (*DAT* 54). For such a serious designer, this sort of spatial culture can only connote hysterical femininity, thus furthering the divide between decoration and design: "Decoration, decoration: yes indeed, in all departments; the department store became the 'ladies joy'" (*DAT* 55). Here, the department store represents an overly personalized stew of decorative items that supports bourgeois domesticity. The source of "ladies joy," it reinforces "personality" by moving into the room, rather than stepping out of it.

While Butts's work affronts such bourgeois domestic norms, I argue that her fiction counterintuitively emphasizes the role of a grounded or situated object life in theorizing empathic engagement, an idealized synthesis of "passion and detachment" (*DFT* 169). In contrast to the chaotic frenzy of the department store, Butts's modernism consistently addresses how to properly place objects in order to develop a form of affective attachment that preserves the discrete integrity of those objects. Ultimately, Butts advances a spatially intact form of impersonality that avoids the "life-defeating fusions" Bersani and Dutoit identify, where engagement requires a specific form of phenomenological grounding—ownership—that occurs through private and concrete attachment to objects (*Arts* 144).

The Phenomenology of the Bedroom: Feng Shui or Wallpaper?

In this section, I return to Lewis as an important modernist interlocutor whose various contradictory pronouncements and fraught professional entanglements offer a crucial framework for understanding Butts's own concerns about human/object relations. Lewis's contributions to the first edition in *Blast*, published in 1913, in particular illustrate how clearly the fields of literature and the applied arts overlapped in their considerations of space. More important, Lewis's essays from both *The Caliph's Design* and *Blast* foreground the conceptual and ethical challenges that attend impersonality as phenomenological issues. I suggest throughout this book that the basic arguments of phenomenology offer resolutions to some of the most pressing problems and contradictions that emerge from modernist versions of impersonality. In its most basic formulation, a phenomenological position, according to Jean-Paul Sartre, responds to the reflective procedures of "psychology and of psychologism" as insufficient for explaining the "essence" of "man's being in the world."[20] As Merleau-Ponty observes, such reflective discourses promote detachment, reducing the subject to nothing more than a "mere object of biological, psychological, or sociological investigation" while reinforcing the Cartesian error of detaching the subject from the rest of the world.[21] In contrast, phenomenology is "a matter of describing, not of explaining or analyzing"; it returns to "things themselves" by offering "an account of space, time and the world as we 'live' them" (*Phenomenology* viii, vii). Thus phenomenology allows us to privilege "things" themselves before their consumption, since consumption itself reflects a subject-centered model of the world. As such, a phenomenological perspective, particularly as it characterizes the work of figures such as Butts, Eliot, Woolf, and Lewis, among others, offers an alternative to a critical rhetoric that follows the logic of the market—where objects are considered primarily as commodities—understood in terms of who or what is consuming them. That is, critical and theoretical studies of objects have operated by building a rather resolute relationship between market forces, private ownership, and consumption. Furthermore, such arguments often work from the assumption that both subjects and objects struggle with their inevitable reification and the impossibility of escape from the pervasive forces of objectification through the market and the bonds of private ownership.[22]

Nonetheless, in the impersonal, phenomenologically oriented object life I am describing here, objects are freed from this pattern of consumption and restrictive ownership. Such an impersonal ethos does not reject personal ownership altogether, but rather redefines—or reorients—it more ideally as an activity that disperses rather than solidifies the personality of the owner. As I argue throughout this book, modernists promoted a version of impersonality that, whether explicitly in critical tracts or implicitly as an aesthetic or ideology informing various literary texts, diminishes the individual as a "personality" containing various psychological recesses or depths. This antipsychologism, I have suggested, also attended a distrust of the humanist "procedure of analytical reflection" (*Phenomenology* ix). As T. S. Eliot observes in "Tradition and the Individual Talent," the artist must let go of "personal" emotions to produce a "concentration" of emotion that cannot be "recollected" nor "happen consciously or of deliberation" (*Prose* 43). Such is the premise of phenomenology, where emotions, according to Sartre, are not the "resources of experience alone" (*BW* 61).

This is not to say that either phenomenology or impersonality abandons the subject in a purely empirical concern for the world of things. Merleau-Ponty's specific phenomenology rejects both the extreme subject-centered perspective that reduces the world to mere consciousness and, alternatively, a purely object-centered empiricism. Rather, as Colin Smith observes in his classic essay on the subject, phenomenology sees the "subject and his world ... as standing in a relation of mutual 'participation.'"[23] While this participation is not necessarily "deliberate" or reflective, according to Smith, the point is that the "making" of "*our* world" is a "two-way transaction" (italics in original; "Notion" 111). Merleau-Ponty affirms the importance of this mutuality when he faults "[a]nalytical reflection" because it "knows nothing of the problem of other minds, or of that of the world" (*Phenomenology* xii). It does not build a "relation to the world" or seek to transcend one's experience of the world to understand "what makes that experience possible" (*Phenomenology* xiv, xvi). One might even view Pound's call for "[d]irect treatment of the 'thing,' whether subjective or objective," as a formulation for the sort of "mutual participation" Smith identifies, in that it appears to recognize the basic intentionality of the "thing" and its difficulty ("Notion" 111).[24] That is, objects consistently exceed their materialization in human consciousness, such that, as Smith points out, there is no "absolute object, i.e. an object which presents to us all it aspects simultaneously" ("Notion" 117). This residue or "complex," to quote Pound, that which does not announce itself to the subject, constitutes the image itself; in this way, the "thing," simultaneously participating in "*our* world," reassures its integrity by constantly challenging the ability of human consciousness to fully apprehend it (*Literary* 3; "Notion" 11).

Given this relationship between objects and human consciousness, phenomenological thinking posits a "world" of reciprocal participation and meaningful apprehension in its very definition of space. In its importance for the modernism I discuss here, a phenomenological perspective maintains that certain conditions be present for space to have meaning in the first place. Merleau-Ponty contends that space itself disappears when there is "no margin" for measuring the "physical and geometrical distance which stands between" the self "and all things" (*Phenomenology* 286). From this perspective, space coheres when a "'lived' distance" preserves relation and position in the external world, separating yet binding the subject "to things which count and exist for [her]," as it "links them to each other" (*Phenomenology* 286). Thus, while Lewis's *The Caliph's Design* links creative activity to the erasure of space, Butts's writing responds precisely to this threat of erasure in its call for the preservation of space, a stylized activity that respects both distance and the mutual "participation" of all things. This activity does not merely preserve the conventional coordinates of space. As Sarah Ahmed has noted in her powerful critique of heterosexuality as a "straightening device," the "queer moments" of Merleau-Ponty's phenomenology challenge perception so that the subject does not always "see straight" and the world no longer appears "the right way up."[25] Similarly,

Butts's spatial etiquette reorients the subject away from the personality, possessive ownership, and individual psychology precisely by tending toward objects in ways that both preserve and "unstraighten" space.

Despite Lewis's position in *The Caliph's Design*, his earlier essays from *Blast* actually illustrate how a phenomenological conception of space safeguards a network of material differences. In unlikely anticipation of the contemporary interest in feng shui as self-help interior decor, Lewis's "Feng Shui and Contemporary Form" exhorts its reader to properly respect the external object. As it anticipates the advocacy of activity that will appear later in *The Caliph's Design*, Lewis's interest in the ancient Chinese art of placement derives from the activity it brings to what is otherwise still life. However, in contrast to the Lewis of *The Caliph's Design*, the author's rhetoric centers on the word "influence," which appears to describe the force the object world exerts over the psychological, subjective world, not vice versa. "Most men see," he claims, "[t]hat a mountain river or person may not 'suit'—the air of the mountain, the character of the person . . . and so influence lives" (*Blast* 138). The "influence" of the concrete object world—a "mountain river or person"—Lewis suggests, does not "suit" the psychological and ultimately weaker aspects of "character" and "air." In other words, the material world exceeds the pressure of human consciousness (*Blast* 138).

In diminishing individual agency over objects, Lewis offers a phenomenological understanding of the object in advocating an objective form of relation that "MUST be SO," not subject to psychological deliberation or will (*Blast* 138). As I argue in the introduction to this book, this form of relation is invested in equalizing asymmetries in power and authority, in so far as it privileges the placement of things beside each other, erasing the distinction between subject and object, top and bottom, active and passive. Lewis's objects do not move in response to their own internal forces; in his scheme, psychology is externalized and objects "influence" other entities in response to their meticulous placement in relation to each other (*Blast* 138). Here, objectivity, as commonly assumed, does not simply connote empirical detachment, which ultimately inhibits aesthetic development.[26]

For the Lewis writing in *Blast*, then, an object is bound in a form that "MUST be SO," yet excessive detachment incapacitates true objectivity. Consequently, writing six years later in *The Caliph's Design*, Lewis mocks the "cheese," "coal scuttle," and "saucepan" of still life painting as overly and sentimentally detached (*CD* 78). His distaste for these domestic objects, as Douglas Mao has suggested, reflects his antipathy toward Bloomsbury and, more particularly, Roger Fry's Omega Workshops, of which he had once been a member.[27] The Omega Workshops, an effort that allied itself with Bloomsbury intellectualism, sought to utilize modern production techniques in the service of more individualized, personal forms of aesthetic expression. Projects included hand-painted fabrics, furniture, and wall coverings. The workshops also nourished hopes of substituting, according to its 1913 prospectus, "wherever possible the directly expressive quality of the artist's handling for the deadness of mechanical reproduction" (qtd. in *Solid* 18). In opposition to Eliot's impersonal imperatives and those of modernists such as Le Corbusier, this aesthetic valued the work of art as a manifestation of individual artistic initiative.

Ultimately, for Lewis, the Omega Workshops displayed the wrong attitude to the "material world," an attitude that supported "the English variety of art man" involved in the pursuit of "'jolly' little objects like stuffed birds, apples, or plates, areas of decayed wall-paper" (*CD* 123). These are not professional artists, according to Lewis, but rather they exhibit only "rather jaded and amateur tastefulness" (*CD* 124).[28] This battle over the meaning of interior design as a specific kind of aesthetic territory and stage for objects reveals a precise point of contention: the link between domestic space and "the personal." For example, one year after the publication of *Blast I*, in a June 1914 issue of *The Egoist*, Gaudier-Brzeska launched a number of severe criticisms concerning Fry's Omega Workshops; praising Lewis's new Rebel Art Centre for its ability to "employ the most vigorous forms of decoration," he inveighed against the excessively sissified "prettiness" of Fry's home exhibits.[29] Four years later, Fry still seemed cowed by these accusations, adopting a defensive position that deemed his critics cold, detached, and impersonal. His 1917 article "The Artist as Decorator" purportedly seeks to democratize art by discussing the minutia of hand-painting wallpaper, as it attempts to distinguish his own work from "the dead mechanical perfection to which the house painter has devoted years of study."[30] While Fry does not mention explicitly those who attacked him in 1913, his reference to the housepainter as a figure who must conform to his master's wishes or lose his source of employment reads also as a defense of a more personalized aesthetic. Fearful of a depersonalized approach to aesthetics, Fry links the house painter's lack of creativity to his rote attention to order and authority. In Fry's world of hand-painted wallpaper and similar delicacies for the home, the artist must synthesize spirituality with the artisanry of collective guild activity in order to restore personal sensitivity to an otherwise impersonal and authoritarian aesthetic.

The Disease of Impersonality

In offering this history of modernist debate over the meaning of objects and interiors, I am attempting to identify a precise point of anxiety around which Butts, writing much later, fixes her own analysis. That is, Fry's fear of an authoritarian, depersonalized aesthetic that diminishes human agency culminates in questions of ownership and the empirical placement of objects.[31] For Butts, unlike Lewis, one possesses objects most tastefully and ethically in the "choice" of arranging and placing them (*DFT* 69). But this choice does not reify the individual or personality as the arbiter of taste. Rather, this position offers a middle ground that is especially important in negotiating the tensions between an overtly authoritarian aesthetic, in which objects "MUST be SO," and the overpersonalization of art Lewis faulted in Fry and company (*Blast* 138). Butts offers a more viable politics for rejecting sentimentality as a factor in the physical intimacy that characterizes an ethical and empathic relation to objects.

I invoke the term empathy here in reference to the distinctly modernist perspective of Wilhelm Worringer's 1908 treatise *Abstraction and Empathy*, which proves especially useful for understanding how empathy might form the basis of an aesthetic practice, particularly as the text moves the term beyond its humanist connotations in connecting it to a decentered subject. Worringer's analysis overturns what seems to be a false dichotomy between two poles of aesthetic apprehension, particularly as that binary has been supported by humanist ideals of empathy. He critiques this version of empathy as related to a platonic form of aesthetic subjectivism whereby the subject finds beauty in her ability to live herself out pantheistically in the forms around her, where "the precondition for the urge to empathy is a happy pantheistic relation of confidence between man and the phenomena of the external world."[32] This aesthetic position, Worringer argues, corresponds to a psychological or "psychic state" that is too subjective, inadequate for understanding the beauty of art that transcends the viewer's specific historical positioning in space and time (*Abstraction* 15). However, the critic complicates this manner of apprehending art by suggesting that each urge to empathy entails a corresponding abstraction of the subject. That is, the subject's desire to expand the self in ascertaining the beautiful also coincides with her self-alienation, an abstraction that dissolves the self. Worringer's repeated premise that "[a]esthetic enjoyment is objectified self-enjoyment" reflects what he sees as the modern subject's "need for self-alienation," the "urge" to liberate "oneself from individual being" (*Abstraction* 24–25).

Ultimately, then, the empathic relation to the external world Worringer critiques as overly subjective turns into an impersonal, antisubjective aesthetic position. As Worringer explains in more detail,

> [T]he process of empathy represents a self-affirmation, an affirmation of the general will to activity that is in us. We always have a need for self-activation ... In empathizing this will to activity into another object, however, we *are* in

the object. We are delivered from our individual being as long as we are absorbed into an external object, an external form . . . We feel, as it were, our individuality flow into fixed boundaries, in contrast to the boundless differentiation of the individual consciousness. In this self-objectivation lies a self-alienation. This affirmation of our individual need for activity represents, simultaneously, a curtailment of its illimitable potentialities, a negation of its ununifiable differentiations. We rest within our inner urge to activity within the limits of this objectivation. (*Abstraction* 24)

This observation especially accords with the dialectic of impersonality I outline in this book, where membership within a greater aesthetic, impersonal community demands surrender and submission of the self or personality. For Worringer, a conventionally empathic perspective is a limited perspective, resigned to the parameters of individual experience in apprehending the work of art. However, as this passage suggests, the desire for empathic "aesthetic enjoyment" does not necessarily magnify the self or the subjective experience of art. In fact, this style of "activity" accords with that Lewis outlines in *The Caliph's Design*, where "aesthetic enjoyment"—the subject's overextension into the object—results in objectification, increasing the vulnerability of becoming "overpowered by our creation" (*CD* 74).

While Lewis does not use the terms empathy or abstraction, the connection he proposes between the overexpansion of subjectivity and its consequent objectification parallels Worringer's assessment of the relationship between empathy and abstraction, which are in actuality united by the common "need for self-alienation" (*Abstraction* 23). In abstraction, however, "the intensity of the self-alienative impulse is incomparably greater and more consistent" (*Abstraction* 23). According to Worringer, the urge to abstraction developed because of man's need to "divest the things of the external world of their caprice and obscurity" to instead regard "the thing in itself" in its "necessity and regularity" (*Abstraction* 18). In other words, in abstraction, the viewer seeks to affirm the autonomy of art by wresting the art-object from its status as relative to the human world. As with Pound's version of imagism, the "thing in itself" is characterized by "crystalline beauty" and the immediate directness of what Worringer terms its "material individuality" (*Abstraction* 20). For Worringer, abstraction supports its own conception of space; it suppresses the "representation of space" because "it is precisely space which links things to one another, which imparts to them their relativity in the world picture" (*Abstraction* 22). Given this phenomenological understanding of space, in which space itself makes the relationship of things possible, it follows (and Worringer affirms this) that an empathic relation to the external world is a dimensional relationship. Rather than detaching the subject from the object, such a perspective, like Lewis's conception of feng shui, situates things in terms of their use and connection to the rest of the external world.

My purpose here is not to affirm one of these accounts of space over the other as necessarily true for modernist aesthetics but to point to how a specifically impersonal modernist conception of object life unites these "poles" of aesthetic apprehension into a more coherent aesthetic practice. As I have argued of figures such as Gaudier-Brzeska, Virginia Woolf, and now Mary Butts, the impersonal aesthetic often seeks to flatten space as Worringer understands it but is often highly conscious of the ethical dangers involved in a complete "suppression of representation of space" (*Abstraction* 22). Ideally, the modernist promotion of surface does not fully rob space of its dimension, the precise positionality of the external world. For modernists such as Butts, this spatial relationship contributes to an ideally empathic relationship to objects that does not reify the self. In using the term empathy, I am essentially reclaiming the term from the subjective humanism Worringer critiques. Particularly as it relates to modernist conceptions of object life, Worringer's dual conception of empathy as both affirming and alienating offers a way of rethinking our relationship to objects that extends beyond the question of their consumption and other forms of sentimental appropriation. For example, working from Worringer's perspective, one could argue that Ezra Pound's call for "[d]irect treatment of the 'thing' whether subjective or objective," overtly affirms a form of abstraction that is antithetical to the values of intimacy and empathy. However, within the impersonal aesthetic practice I am outlining, Pound's very concern for accuracy in perception and representation of "the thing," as its environment situates it, values the object both in its individual materiality and in its relation to other things.[33]

The pervasiveness of such issues as they inform a modernist perspective is even more apparent when read within the context of the rise of fascism in Europe and the development of a modernist collector's culture. For example, the work of Janet Flanner, the famed American expatriate and contributor to magazines such as *Harper's* and *The New Yorker*, discloses how closely the development of twentieth-century art coincided with ongoing disputes about the role of private possession in an aesthetic atmosphere that cemented artistic authority to an impersonal aesthetic. Flanner's 1957 memoir, *Men and Monuments: Profiles of Picasso, Matisse, Braque & Malraux*, documents the newly developing market for modern art, where the young artists and composers of the twentieth century, including Cocteau, Diaghilev, Stravinsky, Picasso, Derain, Braque and Matisse, "were united in a vertiginous production of modernity, of which the public—a heady, variegated mixture of fashionable Parisians, Internationals, intellectuals and practiced tourists—acted as the enthusiastic recipient."[34] In opining that the collecting frenzy had actually devalued modern art, as prices for it were in reality much lower than they had been a generation before, Flanner appears hard-pressed to imagine an alternative. Indeed, the dystopic alternative she records at the end of *Men and Monuments*—the second European war—fully divests art of ownership. Flanner's wrath targets Nazi looting of modern art collections, actualized through the "physical act of carting pillaged beauty off to the homeland" in "myriad trainloads of the classic, from bronze Apollos to stone saints" (*Men* 220). Even more pressing for Flanner is the fact that Jewish art collections had become "technically ownerless" because Jews, by Nazi decree, belonged to no state and therefore possessed no property rights (*Men* 222). Taking art as the ultimate personal possession, Flanner suggests implicitly that some modicum of a private or personal relationship to objects safeguards the value of both humans and objects.

While Flanner's concern is largely with the world of valuable art, the connection she proposes between art's loss of ownership and the failure of human empathy represents the full culmination of a problem that Butts also understood, particularly in two overlapping ethical and aesthetic concerns that guide her work: England's connection with imperialist pillage; and the privatized exclusivity of intellectual pillage. Butts faults the intellectual circles that frequently excluded her with having circumscribed aesthetic space too tightly, making it into a finely knitted web of privatized social relationships. Similarly, her prose tends to read Britain's imperialist ethos in terms of space, as wresting objects from the locations that might afford them more meaningful aesthetic and social relations. Texts such as Butts's 1928 novel *Armed with Madness* or her 1931 story "In Bloomsbury" underscore the relation that exists between imperialism and intellectual and cultural exclusivity. That is, Butt's work depicts what she sees as the genteel pretense of owning and managing culture and art as a direct outgrowth of the imperialist mentality.

Like Flanner's, Butts's texts demonstrate the necessity of acknowledging the empirical status of the object while preserving its function as an index of attachment. Her concern is not necessarily with great art but with the objects that produce lived space. Certainly, we can entertain divergent arguments for how the ownership of art objects might be different from or similar to the ownership of household objects; however, Butts does not maintain a distinction between the ownership of objects that can be classified as art and those that are nothing more than junk. Rather, she is interested in how one lives among objects. Private possession is important not as a mode of consumption but as a stylized affective activity. For example, the second novel of Butts's 1928 *Taverner Novels* series, *The Death of Felicity Taverner*, repeatedly returns to the topic of how to correctly possess things.

Butts credits Felicity Taverner, whose death is the subject of the novel's mystery, with a style of possessing objects that parallels her relations to the human world: "Her choice of objects—of possessions—was perfect, and her virtue—for she was most men's friend and very few's lover—had the same passion and detachment" (*DFT* 169). Lauding a style of ownership that blends "passion and detachment," Butts defines possession as an ethics and politics, a lifestyle. A "choice," the lives of these objects are determined by ethical agency, rational and deliberate decision making. Similarly, the Taverners, Butts writes, did "not tire of real things once they . . . got them home to play with" (*DFT* 301). In praising the family, Butts does not simply define their "real things" as relating to a presumed authenticity, against spurious imitations or copies. Rather, Butts's rendering deduces a "real thing" as an empirical surface, perceptible to touch, sight, and smell: "The polish on a horse's coat, the china-red lacquer of Adrian's car, two shots as a half-mirror, were to them surfaces as pleasant as petal or silk. Like others of our age, they had re-discovered also that the still-life, that however it may get itself painted, it is not *nature mort*, but that each haphazard arrangement can be composed of formal perfections of shape and light—plates on a table, a basket of folded linen, a sea-scape off the beach in a glass dish" (*DFT* 301). In detailing these surfaces, Butts's prose lovingly creates its own still life, placing each object in reference to a composition of "formal perfections." This formal symmetry occurs in a world where the walls of a habitation are "in their place again" when a "shining room" is "charged-up with pain." For Butts, the affective life of an interior works paradoxically; in the ideal spatial scenario, the fixed, precise, and demarcated arrangement of concrete things enables more a fluid state of engagement.

As a consequence of this interest, Butts's work engages heavily with the ethos of collecting, synthesizing the irresolution that Flanner identifies between a modernity frenzied with "collecting" in various forms and a privatized attachment to a singular art object. As an alternative to the closed sense of culture she sees in privatized intellectual coteries, and as a means of creating a meaningful space for situating avant-garde politics, Butts frequently insists that objects require specialized physical and empirical placement as a sign of respect and as a means of promoting empathic relations. In this effort, Butts's prose quite literally collects objects that range from remnants of cut and polished glass, to the Blake paintings her mother callously sold after her father's death, to the jade cup that inspires the fanatic and destructive hunt in *Armed with Madness*. In doing so, she draws no marked distinction between the value of high art and the objects that attend day to day existence, instead insistently returning to the activity of pillage that renders all such objects ownerless—as loot. For example, in *Armed with Madness*, one level of Butts's narrative campaign actually subverts veneration for the modernist art object by confusing the distinction between art and camp, or art and kitsch. However, another level of the text reveals an extreme anxiety about the kind of mobile placelessness that kitsch or camp implies.[35] The plot of *Armed with Madness*, if one might call it that, follows a race to discover the questionable source of a jade cup, "a queer glass dish" (*Armed* 132). The narrative thus escalates through variously authored acts of inventing and solidifying the background of the cup, of placing or positioning the cup in historical space. Picus, the reported headmaster of this game, has supposedly stolen the cup from his acerbic father, a collector by trade, who claims that the cup is an early church vessel, a Keltic altarpiece, which might "well have been part of a crusader's loot" (*Armed* 132). Other interpretations of the cup's origins abound: it may be the "poison-cup of a small rajah" in India, the Sanc-Grail, or nothing more than "an ash-tray in a Cairo club" (*Armed* 84, 140). Ultimately, Butts suggests that the quest to authenticate such an item is a pointless one.

In demonstrating the futility of this search, Butts calls attention to the faulty logic of collecting; the cup is inherently less valuable as a copy or replica than when it stirs the human imagination to envision it in differentiated forms. The text critiques the collector's logic of Picus's surly father, whose search for the cup's origins refuses respect for the numerous ways it chooses to show itself. Yet the old man is correct in saying that the cup is loot. And while Butts seemingly takes delight in divesting the cup of its sacred status, its protean amenability to numerous visual interpretations lends a nervous edge to her descriptions of the vessel. Connected solidly to no one and nothing, the cup's elusive personality (or lack thereof) has become a disease, both for itself and for the aesthetic community *Armed with Madness* invites its reader to examine. The characters' irreverent treatment of the cup, evident in its use as a prop in contests for power that consist of hiding it, stealing it from others, and consigning it more generally to a life of immobility, divides their community. In one way or the other, the cup's status as loot, its placelessness, creates spacelessness—an absence of meaningful community whereby the position of objects can be apprehended.

By focusing on the art of placing objects, Butts's work examines the relation between the proper placement of objects and the appropriate style of ownership. Private possession, it appears, is essential for objects to remain both soluble and intact in their boundaries. In creating a diffuse sense of boundary, Butts's etiquette of placement deprivatizes the world of objects and humans, refusing to uphold a completely demarcated sense of subject and object while avoiding the subjectivizing tendencies that emerge from *The Caliph's Design*. Butts's description of Felicity Taverner suggests that objects only become "possessions" when they are the subjects of "choice," an idealized process that builds, rather than severs, the affective relation between these objects and their collectors (*DFT* 169). Felicity's idealized synthesis of "passion and detachment" facilitates this empathic exercise of choice, of carefully claiming an object as one's own (*DFT* 169).

The suggestion that empathic connections between the human and external world only develop from some degree of attached and private ownership of objects, in which choice trumps senseless consumption, offers an alternative to the critical contention that the only solution to the inevitable commodification of objects lies in their utter deprivatization, or freedom from the bonds of possession. For Butts, an utterly deprivatized object life, which liberates both objects and social relations from structures of private ownership, often disables affective and empathic bonds. That is, Butts refuses to uphold a binary between the deprivatization of objects, their removal from exclusive private possession, and private ownership. Ultimately, Butts sees the basis for collective forms of empathy in a particular style of private ownership that dissolves the self rather than solidifies it. Butt's impersonality necessitates a specific style of empirically possessing an object, one that diffuses the self while preserving the object's discrete integrity.

Bloomsbury, or "Intelligentsia in Excelsis"[36]

Given this interest, Butts's fiction often mocks aesthetic spaces that prove even harsher environments for a healthy object life. Butts's story "In Bloomsbury" (1932) savagely exposes the facile nature of coterie politics through the story of a wealthy family whose "magnificent collection of jade" connects them to the British Museum.[37] The siblings certainly style themselves appropriately: one paints, one practices "elaborate dissipation," one has "a fashionable taste in sex," and all have received "admirable" educations. Likewise, they "talked the current psychology, dressed in the admired disorder of their world . . . had a true and just, if rather *faisandé*, understanding of the arts" (*Altar* 28). Primarily, the narrative directs its derisive scorn at the family's inability, despite its cultural power, to appropriately own the objects of its wealth. As affluent producers and consumers of culture, the family has not acquired the proper skills of objectification.

The Curtins are aptly named because their cordoning off or privatization of lived space produces an atmosphere that disables a veritable object life, despite all their efforts to appropriately acquire one. It is also no secret that "Curtin," as it is used in this story, becomes a pseudonym for Bloomsbury intellectualism made famous by Virginia, Lytton, Clive, Leonard, and others. For Butts, Bloomsbury represented a sense of identity that she linked explicitly to "personality." In her scathing critique, "Bloomsbury," written one year before her death in 1937, she directs most of her rancor toward the men of Bloomsbury, both gay and straight, showcasing both her *ressentiment* and her sense of the group as a singular and recognizable personality, built upon rather crafty forms of network and affiliation. This network included the group's American "bride," T. S. Eliot, along with Lytton Strachey and, oddly, the "serpent" that grew from the group's midst, Wyndham Lewis ("Bloomsbury" 35, 38). Butts relates to these men as a functioning "group," regardless of whether they were or not, promoting the idea that Bloomsbury is a name people recognize and have feelings about: "Bloomsbury—you hear people say today, and it's not a compliment. Applied correctly and incorrectly to a number of persons of the highest individual distinction, as a collective noun it is used to express a complicated reaction including envy and dislike" ("Bloomsbury" 32). Butts pins the rhetorical strategy of her argument on this presumed agreement between herself and the "people" she references. She then credits this audience with inventing a string of pejorative terms describing the group: "'intelligentsia in excelsis,' '. . . barren leaves,' 'N.B.G. [No Bloody Good]' . . . 'mental hermaphrodites,' 'brittle intellectuals,'" to name a few. As an "observer, some sort of witness" to a phenomenon, Butts claims that she would never be out of touch "so far as Bloomsbury *personalities* were concerned" (italics in original; "Bloomsbury" 33). This personality of Bloomsbury clearly involves its role as a group people recognize. In this way, personality, particularly in the negative context Butts ascribes to the term, becomes a key feature of group identity.

As a "group," Bloomsbury, unlike the various "isms" that cohered through abstract sets of intellectual imperatives and declarative manifestos, functioned as a group in the concrete stabilization of its identity—its personality—through its relation to domesticity, material culture, and decorative aesthetics. Nonetheless, several critical accounts suggest that Bloomsbury was not a fully identifiable entity at the time Butts was writing, even though she had no trouble identifying it in both her fiction and criticism. Jane Garrity writes that Butts's critical essay "Bloomsbury" was not accepted by publishers because the group was not well known in England.[38] Likewise, Christopher Reed argues that Bloomsbury really developed into a more cohesive "cultural force" in the 1960s, "when the nascent feminist movement recognized in Virginia Woolf some of its most pressing concerns."[39] Regardless, Garrity's work suggests that Bloomsbury was an identifiable "personality" to a niche audience of cultured *Vogue* readers, as the magazine "circulate[d] its fashionable lifestyle in the commercial market place" for emulation or copy ("Selling" 29–30). While there is no evidence to suggest that Butts was part of this audience, the group was prominent enough to inspire a venomous response that drew attention to her own marginalization as a writer.

Interestingly, Butts does not say much about the women of Bloomsbury. Indeed, her "hit list" focuses on men and characterizes the group as overtly masculine, much in contrast to Christopher Reed's thesis that Bloomsbury was critically ostracized because of its effeminacy. She links the group to the perpetuation of an English national culture, identifying the publication of Lytton Strachey's *Eminent Victorians* as the prelude to Bloomsbury's command of "reasoned" cultural production: Always good at timing, that was their moment. Intelligent enough to associate themselves with the Ballet, strong enough to force down the public throat the new painting out of France; with Mr. Clive Bell's *On Art* for theory ... They were now a ring, a magic ring, with which was gathered all that had been saved from the War" ("Bloomsbury" 33). Butts draws these men, exemplified by Bell and Strachey, as forceful, charismatic, and manipulative. Her position seems rather odd, if not paranoid and off base, considering that many of these men were known for their sexual notoriety. Duncan Grant, Maynard Keynes, and Lytton Strachey were all gay, and as Christopher Reed has argued, the reputation of the group later suffered much at the hands of a "patriarchal" and homophobic critical culture ("Bloomsbury Bashing" 58). Regardless, Butts credits this "ring" with closing itself too fully, having manipulated and exploited through unrestricted access—or, more precisely, "looted"—the few remaining cultural treasures that remained unravaged by the First World War.

In contrast to the precarious balance between physical stasis or placement and activity or movement that structures the ideally lived space, the *dramatis personae* of both "Bloomsbury" and "In Bloomsbury" create a strict environment that shrinks space, to return to Merleau-Ponty, in a way that "leaves no margin" for determining the "physical and geometrical distance which stands" between the self and "all things" (*Phenomenology* 286). If space exists only when the "the position of things becomes possible," then "In Bloomsbury" accents the tense irony of a culture that values objects in their apparent detachment yet fails to register how its own spatial etiquette denies the lives of those objects (*Phenomenology* 243). This diffuse tale centers around the disturbance that transpires when the family's long-lost cousins of indeterminate racial origin come to visit, sparking the wildest nativist fantasies the London sophisticates can produce. The narrator, who appears to be the Curtins' acquaintance, unites the siblings with their cousins while registering the irony of the Curtin museum connection and stellar collection of jade: "Ghengis Khan's men: out of Karakorum in High Asia: the Golden Horde. Jade hunters in Kurdistan; to Bloomsbury: to gentlefolk in an eighteenth-century house. How long a trail? Men to find, and men to love and make, and men to keep and love. The becoming, the *durée* of a work of art. Jade lasts: jade you cannot destroy or make or unmake. Jade is secure. Jade is loot" (*Altar* 45). Here, the narrator considers the *durée* of this beloved object, jade, to contemplate how the Curtins' obsession with their possession's legacy ironically cripples their roles as owners of this beloved green substance. The truth is that the jade will outlast the Curtins and that their attempt to appropriate its organic immortality is also an attempt to block history. That is, the Curtins' belief in their sole ownership of the jade blindly shelters their own collection to the rape and pillage that has ultimately placed it in their hands. The cousins embody the imperial violence behind the jade, which the narrator reads as the quintessential representative of the ambiguities surrounding the object. Jade is "secure" and jade is also "loot." By formulating this paradox, which aids Butts's critique of imperialism, the author reveals an extreme fascination with the empirical substance of this material, perceptible both to touch and to sight, and its social status as a work of art. But rather than divorce the work of art from the empirical, Butts tends to see its "objecthood" and its subversiveness as dependent on the very boundedness of its empirical structure. As a result, jade becomes loot in its ability to evade private ownership, even while the Curtins offer it their particular attachment. Ultimately, jade's transcendence lies in both its inorganic, or unliving, nature *and* the social network through which it is exchanged and valued.

As the quintessential modernist object, the particularly fortified yet vulnerable gemlike substance Butts features in her story solves a major modernist quandary. As an object, the jade provides the essential mediation that meaningful space needs to exist without sacrificing the value of its discrete existence. It thus unites the two poles of aesthetic apprehension Worringer identifies: abstraction, which detaches subject and object, and its converse, empathy. As loot, the jade exposes the hypocrisy of the Curtins' refinement and the frailty of the social space they attempt so delicately to cultivate. Because it evades ownership as a "thing itself," the jade's rootlessness disturbs the space the family purports to construct around it. Its material security shrinks the social space the Curtins have used it to build. The arrival of the South African cousins precipitates this spatial collapse, as they figuratively reclaim the "loot" as their property. As the narrator records the irony of the wolfish cousins' entrance into the British Museum, she wonders what it is they are going in to see: "What had they gone in to look at? They had entered like pirates who dare not swagger, who would loot if they could. Loot was their property and they would collect it. Heartened by the thought of a smash and grab raid of the British Museum, I followed them inside" (*Altar* 43). By visually reterritorializing the loot as their own, the cousins expose the irony of how the Curtins and the museum have acquired their precious objects. They further redress the code of bodily conduct demanded of them in both their visit to the museum and the Curtins' Ashways estate, exposing how the sets' particular style of ownership condemns their property to transient irresolution and aesthetic death.

The cousins dominate the Curtins' lived space because they understand their own status as objects. They present themselves as such, and the text appears both to mock the Curtins' empirically based but speculative judgments of their cousins and to suggest that the "two wolves" are indeed an empirical reality. In keeping with scientific method, the Curtins had "decided to keep notes on anything we observed and report" (*Altar* 47). The narrator's vision, however, is different; it is a kind of seeing that "completed itself, image by image," as if "a cinema, an *acualité*, infinitely prosaic." The two men "lope in like powerful animals," carrying a landscape with them, a Yeatsian "desert with wild beasts" (*Altar* 41). The next "scene," which occurs on the "steps of the British Museum," is odd because the cousins panoramically carry their own situatedness in a manner that unmasks the facade of the "scenes" of the museum. For the narrator, the primitive panoramic tableaus that occupy the museum both solidify and confuse the cousins' identities: "Down the narrow lit shaft of the Assyrian Room I saw them, looking at the lions arrowpierced and stabbed. Their eyes were on the glance backwards. For what might be coming up behind? An animal or a man. One drew the attention of the other to points about lions. Neither was greatly interested" (*Altar* 43). The narrator's viewpoint centers the cousins both within and without the spectacle of the museum itself. Her own confused questioning of what the cousins would actually want to see in the museum occurs because she assumes they are viewing replicas of their own brutish selves, enclosed in panoramic tableaus. Their feral presence completes or enlivens the museum by destabilizing its contents. On one level, their displacement occurs because they disturb the relations between spectator and spectacle. Accordingly, the irony of their visit to the museum lies in the sameness that exists between themselves and the stuffed beasts that draw their gaze.

But as evidenced by the lack of interest that each cousin ultimately shows for the Assyrian room, they never recognize their affiliation with the objects in the museum. The recomposed and restructured bodies of dead animals do not solicit enough interest to achieve the status of objects. In terms of Worringer's construction of aesthetic modernism, the cousins invalidate the museum precisely because they do not see themselves in any of its supposed objects. Just as Worringer understands interested spectatorship as simultaneously self-affirming and self-alienating, the cousins appear to recognize no relation between their concepts of self and their observation. "To enjoy aesthetically," Worringer argues, "means to enjoy myself in a sensuous object diverse from myself, to empathize myself into it" (*Abstraction* 5). Apathetically lacking all interest or pleasure, they fail to project themselves into the scenes they observe.

This lack of humanist empathy highlights the peculiar ways in which the powerful cousins, "with their tanned faces and great bones," function as objects while at the same time enlivening the story's critique of Bloomsbury (*Altar* 41). Within the museum, the cousins' disruption of the subject/object division that typically structures the relation between spectator and spectacle disparages how socioaesthetic relations construct themselves around the apparently detached state of the object world. For Butts, true objects actually solicit interest. Thus the cousins' disinterest in the Assyrian Room does much more than simply disrupt the division between subject and object, spectator and spectacle. Their apathy condemns the museum exhibit, in its isolation, to the status of a nonobject. As the narrator remarks, "inside were the mysterious treasures of the world, separate, almost sterilized but *there*" (italics in original; *Altar* 43). As long as these items remain displaced, uncannily "there," separate from the social relations that produced them, they remain nothing more than loot. In its valuation of a specifically placed, empathic object that possesses what Wyndham Lewis would call "influence," the story thus scrutinizes an imperialist culture that forms its social relations precisely by seeing objects in their social detachment (*Blast* 138).

Yet the detached, displaced "treasures" of the museum seem strangely well placed, as the narrator emphasizes, "*there*." In contrast, the cousins, whose bodies overpower the stylized space of the museum, appear monstrous within its manicured confines. The narrator's faintly erotic obsession with the corporeal aspects of the cousin's placement critiques the codes of spatial etiquette that govern a privileged life of aesthetic pleasure and consumption. The larger than life cousins overturn these rules of bodily and spatial conduct, as the question the narrator asks of them discloses her surprise at how their magnificent bodies could respond to a context so completely removed from them. In the frequent confusion, the narrator's obsessive cataloguing tends to focus on how the cousins move; they "lope in like powerful animals," travelling "on the same stride that might side-step at any moment," frequently "heavy in hand," like "visiting mountains in a delicate landscape, mountains that were even careful where they put their feet" (*Altar* 41, 42, 46). The cousins literally "impose their weight" on the Curtins' oversized egos, exposing the smirky inclusiveness of a shrunken space so delicate that the position of things cannot withstand the intrusion of strangers. The Curtins' and the narrator's objectification of the cousins takes on a life of its own to the point that the cousins, as objects, dominate whatever impulse the Curtins' possess to subjectively personalize their own lived space.

Ultimately, the cousins' challenge to spatial etiquette directly involves their bodies. Butts's prose, abundant with attempts to sabotage the mores of the intellectual elite by aligning their aspirations with those of bourgeois culture, often fastens on the body to disrupt what she considers problem space. "In Bloomsbury" points to the problem of a spatial etiquette that is too strict and that reinforces only habit. This sort of habit orders coterie life in such a way that dramatic expectations develop from the sheer boredom it produces: "No one had ever seen them enjoying themselves . . . Not very long ago it was time for something to happen to them. In reality they had all been marking time, are still marking time, until something should happen in the world; something sufficiently vital—that is to say, strange and oblique—to catch their whole attention, exercise them, use them" (*Altar* 40). In keeping with Curtin hypocrisy, the siblings transform habit into a kind of action, which further excuses the inaction of literally "marking time." Although the Curtins don't seem to understand exactly what it is they are waiting for, the cryptic event occurs upon the arrival of their cousins, whose every movement, every facial feature, expresses a hard, almost crystalline sense of action. The cousins carry "not a light" in their eyes but a "glint" (*Altar* 41). Even the reader remains unsure of the precise nature of this event, so that the Curtins actually appear to expect something more like a scene or tableaux. The cousins, "fine brutes . . . dark, lean creatures," physically enable this development (*Altar* 49). In their fierce exactitude, they are a style. The visual counterpart of Pound's imagism, they reveal a "sense of freedom from time and space limits," despite the precision of their demarcation.[40] Stripped bare yet alarmingly steeled for invasion, the cousins erotically attract the Curtins', and the narrator's, attention.

The primitive action of the cousins' bodies forces the Curtins into the submission that disrupts habit, and this is the event the Curtins really await. For example, Clarissa, the female of the group, muses over the effects of having an affair with one of them. But such an event, the text suggests, would have been too normal to have produced the appropriate change to the Curtins' habitual regime. They require a more dramatic and impersonal phenomenon, something that would physically change them, "exercise" their personalities beyond the limits of individual control (*Altar* 40). If we return to the phenomenological framework that informs this chapter, such an "exercise" would enable them to exist beyond the world of habit. Merleau-Ponty links the acquisition of habit directly to the body, where breaking and creating habits entail certain arrangements and rearrangement of the corporeal schema and, further, of space (*Phenomenology* 142). A condition of movement, the "motor significance" of "[h]abit expresses our power of dilating our being-in-the-world," the power with which we move (*Phenomenology* 143).[41] From this perspective, the Curtins may be seen to await the arrival of an active object, which resists their efforts to "hunt" or objectify it but in turn is able to impersonally "exercise" them by shrinking their dilated being. That is, to change their habits, something must disrupt and rearrange the physical spaces of their bodies or, as Merleau-Ponty puts it, change their "existence by appropriating fresh instruments" for apprehending the external world (*Phenomenology* 143).

(Im)personal Hygiene

Butts's fixation on the remaking and rearranging of bodies extends throughout her work and comprises a crucial strand of her particular version of aesthetic impersonality as it encodes an ethics of living in space. In the final mock-explosive episode of "In Bloomsbury," Fabian, one of the Curtin siblings, dramatically inveighs that the cousins are "[p]arasites on us, and a disgusting prey on society" (*Altar* 57). While a parasite generally robs another body of its energy, erases its vigor, and depletes its health, the cousins of "In Bloomsbury" animate the Curtins' rather lackluster imaginations. Such a parasite, be it an alternate form of the self or a long-lost cousin, disrupts habit and invests a narrative with action as it robs individuals of agency. A parasitic relationship is also an impersonal one, since it disturbs a notion of individuality and singular personality. For Butts, action depends on the rearrangement of the corporeal schema and of physical space more generally. Along with loot, Butts also links action, as exemplified in movement—be it carting, pillaging, or more positively, placing or loving—to her concern for the seriality of objects. In speaking of seriality, I do not simply refer to mass-produced objects, though Butts, like many modernists, was concerned with copies, particularly bad copies. We frequently associate a series with recurrence, with reproduction, with the same. I have argued in this book that impersonality—particularly as it works as a theory of invasion, self-replication, and bodily rearrangement—often produces a sameness that results from a collapse of spatial demarcation. This dissolution of physical and formal boundaries is clearly important, in that it often produces the commonality that allows empathy to develop. However, this spatial diffusion is also a threat. Butts's obsessive interest in series of items appears to stem not only from her distrust of copies but also from her interest in them. In attempting to move beyond individuality in terms of character and occurrence, her work reaffirms seriality as it simultaneously emphasizes the discrete integrity of the object.

However much Butts appears to render suspect the classical trappings of plot by confusing the reader and her characters about what "really" happens in the story, she does tend to create plot according to the model Peter Brooks identifies in *Reading for the Plot: Design and Intention in Narrative*. Following Tzvetan Todorov, Brooks claims that plot "is constituted in the tension of two formal categories, difference and resemblance."[42] In Butts's story, the serial appearance of objects, in this case gloves, creates the plot; their simultaneous similarity and difference organize the space of the story. As Brooks observes, this "same-but-different" narrative presents temporal form according to an "implicitly spatial model" (*Reading* 91). That is, in offering a "spatial model" of narrative form, Butts's fiction explores two related literary and aesthetic quandaries that characterized modernist theories of both impersonality and empathy. The first concerns the difficulty of carefully nourishing an empathic life with soluble boundaries without sacrificing the value of the object's discrete and independent being. The second, metacritically broached in Butts's fiction, in which objects constitute narrative itself, involves the challenge of constructing narrative around object life. This problematic addresses the question of how a communicative object with "influence," lacking the boundaries that ensure complete insular security, might maintain the sticking points that structure narrative development and organization.

In its placement of objects, Butts's "With and Without Buttons" foregrounds these issues in narrative development, intricately observing the minute distinctions that frustrate any attempt to fully copy another event. Here, two sisters attempt to trick their cynical neighbor Trenchard by feigning the presence of a ghost and waking the "female power" of the old house they share with him (*Altar* 23). "With every door and every window open" to the world and to the earth, the house is "a female power asleep," waiting for the sisters to exercise or stimulate it into action (*Altar* 23). The sisters' revenge against the dismissive cynicism Trenchard aims at their own, less conventional belief systems, his "faith of disbelief as inaccurate as excess," consists in strategically "placing" the contents of a box of old gloves within Trenchard's part of the cottage, which is separated from theirs by a common wall. The sisters, who speak frequently from the mutual viewpoint of an impersonal "we," relate the success of their ploy to its apparent action and its ability to function as a series. While one sister in the story controls its narration, in the beginning it is not clear as to which one she is. Consistent with an impersonal style of narration that reduces the potency of the individualized "character," the pronouns "us" and "we" take center stage as the story unfolds: "It was trying to get out anyhow, but if he had not irritated us and made us want to show off, we would not have made ourselves serviceable to it. And it was we who came off lightly" (*Altar* 22).

The "we" here, which reads as if the narrator literally suffers from multiple personality disorder, resembles a royal we whose power lies in the fact that it is not an "I." Indeed, as the story progresses, the sisters appear unable to operate independently, and one takes offense at the other when she does. Moreover, the sisters remain unnamed and hardly separable. Butts disables their personal identities as a means of enhancing their impersonal power, which develops through their deindividuation.

The same "we" applies to the trick they want to play on Trenchard. When the narrator asks what the trick will be, the other sister answers that it does not matter: "Because before we begin we'll *do* something. Anything. A last year's leaf for a start, so long as it can go into a series—on his blotter or his pillow. We're always in and out. We'll put them there and get asked round for the evening and start when we see one, and that's where our village story begins. All that he has to get out of us is that there is a story, and that wet leaves of whatever it is we choose are found about. Signatures, you know" (italics in original; *Altar* 24). Interestingly, the sisters imagine the series as related to a specific kind of placement of the objects they use to enact what they later describe as their "ill-doing" (*Altar* 23). This impersonal "doing" fuels narrative structure, initiating a series of events that defies the original intentionality or agency of this action.[43] The sisters also relate the series of occurrences they build specifically to their narrative, or their ability to produce a story and jointly author it through their "signatures" (*Altar* 24). That is, the placement of objects becomes a metaphor for narrative itself. The objects catalyze action, guiding the narrative's sequence and timing. The organization of this plan is thus important to the sisters, who ascertain that their narrative will collapse if each occurrence in the series of events is exactly identical. The story then explores the major problematic that attends both narrative and impersonality more generally: What happens to narrative when its objects are the same? How does narrative maintain its organization within an impersonal structure that deindividuates character and event? Fearing narrative collapse, the particular force of the sisters' deception depends on how well they stage events that are similar enough to be called recurrences.

The objects required to create the ghostly and impersonal recurrences parallel the sisters themselves. Slightly altered versions of each other, they are essentially the same, yet faintly different. The gloves that provide the ruse of the tale are by no means artworks, but they copy themselves in such a way as to facilitate precision of placement as part of a serial action that organizes space. The content of these particular gloves is the same: "[a]ll one size . . . and for one pair of hands." The exteriors of the gloves, however, warrant the story its title; "With and Without Buttons," some "have all the buttons and some have none and some have some" (*Altar* 25). Each glove is an inaccurate reflection of the next. They are not simply copies of each other, which would make them impossible to place, but designed slightly differently to enable the "placement" that builds narrative. Butts's narrative strategy maximizes placement as a code of action to energize domestic life, bringing it out of the confines of the private and personal into the collective, interdimensional, and interobjective world, simultaneously securing the kind of boundedness that meaningful space needs to exist.

To reiterate, I have argued thus far that space is meaningful when its structure preserves the forms of attachment necessary for keeping it intact. Space coheres when objects can clearly enunciate their locations but not when these positions completely forbid movement. An impersonal sense of space, as I have attempted to define it, tempers the full transfusion of boundaries that the utter deprivatization and depersonalization of space entails: the loss of exclusively attached object relations. The object is neither habitually attached to a subject that has lost its ability to apprehend it as a discrete entity, nor is it resolutely detached. For modernism, this particular version of space offers an ethical midpoint between an utterly detached "ironically anti-social subject position" and Wyndham Lewis's authoritative injunction that humans prosthetically replicate themselves into the external world (*Modernisms* 3). More generally, by synthesizing fixity and movement, this impersonal version of space presents a way of thinking about affective attachments that does not reify the objects of those attachments. Such attachments are symbiotic in nature, especially because objects mutually act upon each other. While it may be difficult to characterize this relationship as an ethics, since it appears, as with Lewis's version of feng shui, to limit human agency, it only limits this agency to the extent that it emerges from coherent psychological recesses of self and personality. Instead, in Butts's work, and in many of the other modernist texts I discuss in this book, agency and ethical action arise from the surface, where the object is counterintuitively "understood" as a sensible, empirical outside. In Butts's particular version of impersonality, objects exert agency over humans, as opposed to more conventional forms of ownership where humans express their personalities through the objects they acquire.

Given this change in the source of agency, in "With and Without Buttons," the sisters are correct in interpreting the privileged objects of their game as a "choice of stimulants" (*Altar* 25). As a stimulant, the object actually generates and negotiates the appearance of other objects. For this reason, after the sisters "feed [Trenchard] a glove," they begin to realize that "the gloves will feed themselves" (*Altar* 27). The observation is syntactically ambiguous. It both reaffirms the stereotypical role of women as caregivers and "feeders" while exposing the limits of those actions. As objects, the gloves defy human intentionality after they have been given life, "wound up," through the deliberate and careful placement of the first glove (*Altar* 27). The figurative notion that "the gloves will feed themselves" contrasts amusingly with Fabian Curtin's pernicious assertion that his South African cousins are parasites. Whereas the Curtins ironically and blindly suggest that their cousins both literally and figuratively enlarge themselves through access to English sophistication, the gloves form a natural, though inorganic extension of the body. The gloves are not exterior to the body, like a parasite, but part and parcel of a "normal" corporeal schema. They do not feed off the body or deplete it; rather, the glove completes the acceptable, idealized body. By the time the action of the story really begins to accelerate, or "feed" itself, the gloves that the sisters had originally flatly "placed" transform into multidimensional objects, "open like a hand" (*Altar* 33). Such animation becomes essential to their active roles as objects.

More particularly, "With and Without Buttons" rather indelicately makes it clear that Butts's phantom limb objects compensate for the sexual inadequacies of the female body, or the lack of power that comes with sex. As the sisters point out, they could "have made [Trenchard] make love, to either or to both of us, any day of the week." Because they "wanted to have power over him, the power women sometimes want to have over men, the pure not erotic power, whose point is that it shall have nothing to do with sex," the sisters cannot accomplish their goal with only their bodies, to "suggest him into an experience" (*Altar* 24). Sex is plainly not an effective lure; what is required is a demonic attachment, a ghostly body that is at once a veritable body yet detached and strangely recomposed. In much of her work, including *Armed with Madness*, Butts suggests that women move beyond their own bodies and beyond their sexuality to occupy a higher, more empathic, and ultimately more objective ground. The gloves of "With and Without Buttons" prove strange vessels for this type of empathy, particularly since the sisters are less than empathic in the ruse they devise for their captive, Trenchard.

More accurately, the gloves that literally move Butts's story highlight the conceptual paradox inherent in this conception of the object. However discretely placed, the gloves harbor an extremely diffuse, animate, and expansive power that, detached from a verifiable human hand, remains estranged from a unified self or ego. These items threaten a normative and gendered organization of space, as represented by the wall that separates the sisters' part of the cottage from Trenchard's. The glove, which both shapes and is shaped by the body, cements Butts's ideology of ethical living with bodily reinscription. In "With and Without Buttons," this reinscription surfaces as a smell that threatens a way of life, an other that cannot be reduced to an object. The strong odor of the gloves breaks down the artificially erected boundary that exists between Trenchard and the sisters as a solvent that dissolves the tight security of Trenchard's "simple faith," which the text deems pseudorational and masculine (*Altar* 22). For Trenchard, the empirical reality of the gloves' smell, which reminds him of something he had smelled once "in Africa . . . [b]ad skins," becomes the most offensive aspect of their appearance (*Altar* 31). He repeatedly encounters the odor's potency and desperately asks one of the sisters if she will retrieve the perfume she wears to mask it: "What's that lovely scent you wear . . . I want to smell it. Get that" (*Altar* 36). But when the Parisian *parfum* appears, the stench triumphs—"sweetness, like a lady-like animal, of old kid gloves" (*Altar* 36). In terms of Trenchard's personal experience, the smell then evokes the female body and Africa, what for him must be the most untidy, unhygienic female body of all, fiercely assaulting his European safety of immaculately pressed white linen shirts. While Trenchard's rejection of the gloves forms Butts's subtle critique of how English colonial ideology affects its valuation of the object, Trenchard's response to the smell also highlights his inability to empathize with the objects that surround him. This critique builds on smell to impersonally reimagine and incorporate a truly foreign, dynamic body into her text—one that lacks hygiene and whose origin, like the Curtins' cousins, is figuratively animal. Whereas the sisters' invasive control of the gloves suggests that they overidentify with these objects, Trenchard's willful alienation from them represents a gross detachment that drives him to his own insanity.

By focusing on the strange secretions of objects as impersonal forces that impinge upon the senses, Butts's modernism reimagines the person by emphasizing the permeability of both human and inanimate boundaries. In "With or Without Buttons," this movement across boundaries is depicted in the sisters' forceful attempt to alter Trenchard's acceptable range of imagoes. However, the sisters do not fully understand their prank, which, supernaturally speaking, has taken on a life of its own that surpasses their intentions. The final blow it delivers to Trenchard does not involve a glove but a piece of "dark green cotton, dirty and torn," which literally attacks him, invading and staining his tongue and his mouth with its strange secretions (*Altar* 37). After the strange remnant is "dragged off" by the sisters, one is left to surmise that the unsightly fabric is actually part of an old woman's undergarment, a petticoat. This petticoat, belonging to one dead Miss Blacken, has become a rather ubiquitous feature of village superstition, and the sisters use the story to fuel Trenchard's obsession. Significantly, the violation of space Trenchard experiences when this small female delicacy wraps itself tightly around his head is not visual but olfactory claustrophobia. "It was winding itself tight," he says. "But, oh God, it was the smell of it" (*Altar* 38). Trenchard responds to a shrinkage of lived space where smell creates its own claustrophobia. In the special powers it holds over space, Butts elevates this tattered piece of fabric to the status of the object *par excellence*. Not only is this object saturated with political and human meaning, but its very objecthood offers a strange paradox to both the reader and the characters of "With and Without Buttons." It is important that both must work to identify the scrap of cloth as part of Miss Blacken's petticoat. The object is difficult to place, but everything about it suggests that it is perfectly placed, with exceeding care, in its placelessness. This relationship can be viewed phenomenologically as reflecting the sort of mutual participation I noted earlier, where Trenchard's ability to smell the object can be understood as the object's specific reply, or payback, to Trenchard's objectification of it. Merleau-Ponty points out that sense perception operates as a specific kind of language, which is "why it can literally be said that our senses question things and that things reply to them" (*Phenomenology* 319). Referencing Cezanne, who declared that a picture actually contains a landscape's smell, Merleau-Ponty also suggests that the specific sensory responses a thing evokes, through the arrangement of color, for example, often signifies "by itself all the responses which would be elicited through an examination by the remaining senses" (*Phenomenology* 319). Thus the gloves and the petticoat remnant are complete in their objecthood because their visual appearance relates exactly to how the remaining senses will apprehend them. This sort of object is fixed and finite in its exactitude, yet, as the story suggests, eerily out of place. The gloves produce shock and fright out of their unexpected appearances, just as the strange, unsightly relic smothers Trenchard with its invasive smell.

"Au Salon"

One place where we'd rather have tea
(Thus far hath modernity brought us)
"Tea" (Damn you!)
Have tea, damn the Ceasers

—Ezra Pound[44]

The power Butts confers on forgotten objects further dignifies the unlovable or scrapped object, the Bachelardian refuse in the corner.[45] Throughout her work, Butts maps the distinction she makes between the polish of the salon and the junkyard onto her assessment of modernist literary culture. Her critique of expatriate Paris is especially evident in *Armed with Madness*: "If Paris is a lovely salon displayed for conversation, London is a lumber-room to be foraged for junk, rubbish, white elephants, treasure" (*Armed* 114). Butts's irritation coincides with Ezra Pound's, whose acidic poem denigrating salon life titles this section. For Pound, the salon has even failed to master the arts of lovely conversation. It is a place for consumption, or petty gossip, slander, and tea. Among other things, Pound's poem seeks to overturn the cultural objectification of aesthetic life altogether, descrying the commodification of poetry as cultural capital for social trade and imperialistic pillage like tea. In contrast, Butts tends to embrace a kitsch sensibility of junkiness that, however much a product of her own economic and professional *ressentiment*, disparages Parisian salon culture as pretentiously displayed rather than ideally placed.

Butts's 1932 story "From Altar to Chimney Piece" contains her most emblazoned fictional attack on Parisian salon culture. According to Janet Lyon, the salon was "private" and "class-marked," a "pre-cursor to the public coffee house"; it "provided a forum for the enactment of ideal speech situations" at the same time that it "firmly controlled the directions speech might take."[46] In the case of Butts's story, the author's criticism targets not the "enactment of ideal speech situations" but the controlled enactment of ideal spatial situations. The text indicts what it sees as a modernist establishment based on inherited financial security and social prestige whose unfeeling authoritarian control of both lived and literary space renders that space meaningless. The story, which Butts originally began as the "Gertrude Stein Song," appropriately finds it subject in "Gertrude Stein and her house" and the various webs of sociability it facilitates (qtd. in *MBSL* 304). A nexus for the various affiliations that characterized expatriate modernist culture, it attracted such renowned friends as Hemingway and Picasso while demanding a fierce loyalty for its legendary proprietor.[47] The narrative itself follows a middle-aged English war veteran whose obsession with a young American girl of questionable origin leads him to Stein, fictionally disguised as Miss Van Norden. Vincent, a bourgeois hanger-on with a lingering nostalgia for "high European life," follows his young American Cherry to Miss Van Norden's salon with some uneasiness, conscious that the girl will evaluate the success of his stay there to determine whether she will marry him (*Altar* 252). On one level, Vincent, like other characters in the story, is the target of Butts's derisive pen. However, Butts privileges him through his ability to observe and reflect upon the odd formality of Miss Van Norden's "tea" (*Altar* 252). After entering the salon, Vincent notices the visitors in "circulation" at a rather immaculately governed pace: "Exceedingly slowly they went, a flowing stream, turning their heads from left to right to look up at the celebrated collection of pictures, or down on to the tables, at books and manuscripts and *objets d'art*. With pauses and repetitions, jerks and restarts, but always round and round the same way, counter-clockwise; so that, unless you caught someone up—and that you felt was something you should not do—you hardly met anyone who was there" (*Altar* 252). Butts's depiction of the room's tight order and self-conscious construction denies it the status of space. If Stein's salon, as Lyon has suggested, sought to cultivate "a collective visual aesthetic rooted in the act of scrutinizing [her] large collection of controversial anti-representational post-Impressionistic paintings," then Butts's story declares Stein's project a failure ("JBH" 35). According to Butts's critical eye, the "seeing" solicited by Stein's celebrated collection of pictures is ritualistic and rote, unimaginative and conditioned by socioaesthetic training and tedious decorum. Butts describes an aesthetic code of behavior governed so strictly, a space so shrunken, that whatever action it creates is only valuable in its repetition.

Oddly enough, the passage at hand reminds one of Stein's famous practice of seating painters in front of their own paintings so as to force some kind of self-recognition.[48] The paintings do produce self-recognition in the fact that they elicit social insularity and paranoia. The visitors' revolution around the tables yields no attachments, only sights of their counterparts' backs; Butts exposes the salon, ostensibly frequented as a room for looking, as it cultivates a paranoid fear of looking—at other people. In stark contrast to the house in "With and Without Buttons," which opens itself to the world, this illustrious chamber possesses objects that do not perform their proper function. Rather than impersonally expanding the self beyond its subjective limitations to encourage collective looking and empathic spectatorship in Worringer's sense, the items on display here lack sufficiently critical recipients. The look elicited by these paintings, much like the museum in "In Bloomsbury," does not free the self from its confines. In other words, Stein's salon is a place that forbids empathy. The room refuses attachment, and Vincent commits an egregious *faux pas* when he attempts to speak to Cherry from *across* the long table and, even more shockingly, "when he anchored himself with a bun and more tea in a dim corner" as a placed stranger, and observer (*Altar* 252). Aware of the indelicacy of such an act, Vincent attempts to appear absorbed in the Fragonard opposite him. Given Stein's pride in her illustrious and inventive patterns of seating, Vincent's self-appointed action of seating himself violates the taboos that secure the anonymity and neatness of what is, otherwise, a void. While Stein sits as well, she serves the appointed function of regulating the movement, directing it all too authoritatively.

Conclusion: Object Lessons

Vincent's action is too familiar, invasive, because he tactlessly locates himself as a point in space that others must notice and negotiate, even if he does only sit in the corner. That is, from the viewpoint of the salon set, he values himself as highly as the art object, which comprises the only other fixed points of attraction in the room. Most importantly, his perverse movement depreciates the value of the room, since seating oneself is often the first step in inhabiting a room, or transforming it into lived space. In Butts's stories the absence of lived space, characterized by a detachment that denies the objects on display any connection to the human world, evidences failure of both intimacy and empathy. Butts thus identifies the emptiness of a form of observation that is both affectively detached and disinterested. More specifically, she critiques an aesthetic decorum that establishes a false binary between aesthetics and the intimate values of domestic space and the corresponding belief that such an arrangement is productive of some advanced degree of sociability. Surely, the "security" of Stein's collection prevents it from promoting the objective relations that would produce empathy. The assortment of hallowed paintings are placed too rigidly and, according to Butts, solidify only Stein's own great personality. It does not promote empathy, which results from an engaged form of perception that respectfully affirms the existence of the object and simultaneously places it.

Certainly, Butts was not the only modernist to have denounced Stein's space on these grounds. Stein's publisher, Robert McAlmon, affixed Stein's "great personality" to her ability to "afford to entertain freely" and found it "interesting to surmise" what women such as Stein and Mabel Dodge "would have been without inherited security."[49] My own reading of Butts's work emphasizes her attempts to synthesize the diverse meanings of security and action, place and placelessness, to produce a theory of meaningful socioaesthetic space. This impersonal spatial ideal consecrates the object but, contrary to Bourdieu's interpretation of this process, does so by refusing to detach it from surrounding human life.[50] Ultimately, this empathic impersonality requires an acute sense of interior connection that is available only through the animism of objects. While animism typically suggests that humans confer life or vitality onto objects in the mirror of themselves, as in Lewis's command that we "substitute ourselves everywhere for the animal world," these works refuse to model the external world according to the abstract boundaries of the human (*CD* 74). This animation of objects does not anthropomorphize them but impersonally reconfigures the self according to their parameters.

As with Lewis, for Butts, the object's empirical appearance is a key component of its ability to influence the human scene—its reorientation of space. Empirical perception amounts to a form of engagement that respectfully affirms the existence of the object and simultaneously places it. This specific modernist ethics of apprehending the external world departs from much of what contemporary critical and queer theories have touted as radical or progressive, particularly regarding the claim that objects must lack grounding to avoid their inevitable reification. In contrast, writers such as Butts, and even Lewis, emphasize the lessons that can be learned from the visible appearance of objects. These lessons include the idea that objects, like humans, possess interiors that they communicate through a phenomenological grounding *beside* each other in a lived arrangement or scene. As with the concentrated sense of impersonal poetic emotion Eliot theorizes in "Tradition and the Individual Talent," this sense of profile or breadth decenters the subject as the repository of a hidden psychology lodged within its secret recesses or, to return to Sarah Ahmed, "unstraightens" our perceived notions about space and the way we inhabit it. This impersonal ethics of empathy offers an opening into the external world that extends beyond individual psychology, subjectivity, and personality. As a result, Butts's work allows us to view a concept that has traditionally been claimed for humanism from a posthumanist perspective that decenters the subject. Whereas a humanist version of empathic exchange tends to see it as a transfer of subjectivity, Butts's literal profile of the object-world suggests that empathy is more a matter of surfaces—"as pleasant as petal or silk"—not heart-wrenching or agonizing or self-involving (*DFT* 301). Empathy is not merely a matter of sentiment or psychological involvement, nor does it result from an attempt to possess or infiltrate the external world in "life-defeating fusion" (*Arts* 144). Instead, Butts constantly negotiates the ethical and spatial distances that protect the integrity of the object without disregarding private possession altogether. As an alternative to the exclusivity of private ownership, her work advocates an impersonal mode of private possession, where the relationships between subjects and objects are primarily social, attached rather than detached, arising counterintuitively through the precise placement of each object in its relation to its surrounding world. This version of modernism both affiliates itself with and departs from the harsher modernist ideals of Pound and Lewis. A more reflexive and ethically self-conscious version of Pound's imagism, Butts's impersonal modernism affirms the proximity of subject and object, dispelling fixed identity in favor of a more soluble sense of self.

As I have argued, this more soluble self cannot be represented in terms of an interior that exists in opposition to an exterior. Rather, this impersonal sense of selfhood is linked to empathy as a way of seeing, a form of visual apprehension and perspective that registers surfaces: "the polish on a horse's coat" and the "china red-lacquer" of a car (*Armed* 301). Along with Virginia Woolf, T. S. Eliot, Gaudier-Brzeska, and Wyndham Lewis, Butts participates in the making of an impersonal modernism that, in its attention to the surface of things, visualizes interiority. Merleau-Ponty's understanding of depth as "a juxtaposition of points, making it comparable to breadth" illustrates further how this version of impersonality depends on a specific relation to objects that flattens subject/object distinctions (*Phenomenology* 255). The "juxtaposition" here refers to a specific mode of seeing, which also serves as an ethical means of negotiating the distance between oneself and the external world. This relationship is impersonal, for, "to treat depth as breadth viewed in profile . . . the subject must leave his place, abandon his point of view on the world, and think himself into a sort of ubiquity" (*Phenomenology* 255). For Butts and, as I argue in the following chapter, Elizabeth Bowen, the object world enables this sort of relation, resolving the problem of an intrusive politics of activity that inhibits the development of meaningful space, both literally and narratively speaking. In the ideal impersonal spatial relation, mutual communication or telepathy emerges from the physical object when it both expands and disciplines space. That is, space must somehow acquire a distinct organization to communicate itself into existence, but that organization cannot merely bend to the dictates of human subjectivity. For example, Lewis's proposal to actively extend the human subject into space ultimately reinforces a Cartesian logic of authority and domination, of a top and bottom, in which the "subject is nothing but what it thinks it is" (*Phenomenology* 198). In contrast, the impersonal aesthetic I identify here extends the subject by means of the object in a way that does not merely amplify individual subjectivity but transforms the subject into more than "what it thinks it is." This particular kind of identification depends on the organization of aesthetic space, tempering the violence of complete and utter deprivatization with a situated attachment that enables connections with others. In the next chapter on Elizabeth Bowen, however, we shall see what happens to narrative when that space breaks down and the subject's "ubiquity" becomes too extreme, having overidentified with the forgotten objects in the corner.

5

A "Solicitude for Things"

Elizabeth Bowen and the *Bildungsroman*

> We defend ourselves from the rooms, the scenes, the objects that make for hallucination, that make the senses start up and fasten upon a ghost. We desert those who desert us; we cannot afford to suffer; we must live how we can.
>
> —Elizabeth Bowen[1]

> He, she, Portia, three Quaynes, had lived, packed close in one house through the winter cold, accepting, not merely choosing each other. They had all three worked at their parts of the same necessary pattern. They had grasped the same door handles, listened to the strokes of the same clocks. Behind the doors at Windsor Terrace, they had heard each other's voices, like the continuous murmur inside the whorls of a shell. She had breathed smoke from their lungs in every room she went into, and seen their names on letters each time she went through the hall. When she went out, she was asked how her brother and sister were. To the outside world, she smelled of Thomas and Anna.
>
> —Elizabeth Bowen

Elizabeth Bowen's 1938 novel *The Death of the Heart* defines what it means to "live" as a matter of impersonal acceptance, not personal choice. This kind of living, where the material architecture of the house—its "door handles" and "clocks"—sabotages the desire for self-possession and containment, makes more "real" the phenomena that cannot be contained or formalized in these structures: "voices," "smoke," and "smells" (*Death* 192). Objects continually exceed their materialization, creating residues that deny humans the comfort of subordinating them to their own consciousnesses. One wants to smell of oneself, not of other people. Living thus becomes a stance, a mode of affective survival that necessitates a vigilant defense against remembering. Objects then pose a particular threat to this posture; indices of affective attachment, they "make for hallucination" that threatens emotional safety (*Death* 191).

As the epigraphs suggest, domestic space itself produces this sort of affective restlessness in Bowen's fiction, creating an atmosphere that Bowen herself would later characterize as "unfamiliar."[2] Indeed, *The Death of the Heart* harshly exposes the modern fantasy of domestic comfort and familiarity, based as it is on both the privatization of domestic space and the expansive version of personality it supports. However, for Bowen, as with her contemporary Mary Butts, this discomfort endows lived space with its ethical significance, such that the material coordinates of quotidian life pose a challenge to both the organization of personality and social hierarchy. This confrontation arises as objects, given their hallucinatory residues, redefine the world of feeling. Objects "make for hallucination" because they threaten the safety of what is taken as the objective, empirical real, making present an "absence" (*Death* 190).[3] This relationship is both impersonal and phenomenological, as Bowen's work, like other texts I have discussed in this study, confirms the connection between modernist aesthetic practice and phenomenological accounts of space. In his famous account of hallucination, Merleau-Ponty writes that "[h]allucination causes the real to disintegrate before our eyes, and puts a quasi-reality in its place," bringing "us back to the pre-logical basis of our knowledge."[4] Bowen complicates the philosopher's assessment that the "pre-logical" substance of hallucination is "quasi-reality"; admittedly, the most logical, rational way to "live" in the world is to avoid hallucination, which means that one comes to terms with "absence" through a failure to remember that "blots people out" (*Death* 190). However, the comfort of this acceptance, as Bowen suggests, does not allow one to feel. What does is the verifiable, logical presence of the object, which makes such absence impossible. Consequently, rather than drawing the world of hallucination as necessarily prelogical in contrast to the world of the real, Bowen's text constructs a dialectical relationship between the empirical certainty of the object and the essential prelogical "knowledge" of hallucination. The world as experienced through objects makes possible the world of feeling, of grief in particular.

Nonetheless, for the characters of *The Death of the Heart* and other Bowen novels such as *The House in Paris*, the possibility of giving way to such acute perception produces serious anxiety. This anxiety, I suggest, figures into Bowen's critique of a culturally approved, ethically disengaged desire for self-possession—or personality—that aims to build domestic familiarity through the bourgeois accretion of things.[5] I argue further that as it probes the relation between personality and things, *The Death of the Heart* defines itself as a *Bildungsroman* critically invested in examining its own operation. The novel, like Bowen's earlier works, including *Friends and Relations* (1931), *The Hotel* (1928), *The Last September* (1929), and *The House in Paris* (1935), participates in what Jed Esty has identified as "modernism's rewiring of the novel of development."[6] Indeed, the basic failure to enter adulthood that Esty attributes to Lois Farquar, the protagonist of *The Last September*, also signals the inability to take ownership of one's personality as a sign of adult social and cultural authority. Consequently, the primary tension in Bowen's plots often emerges from this drama of self-possession. Given the claim that the traditional *Bildungsroman* is a genre of "progress . . . of male self-possession," it is fair to say that Bowen's impersonal "rewiring" of the form embeds its protagonists in relations characterized by acts and states of dispossession ("Virgins" 257). This concern with dispossession in particular plants Bowen's critique of the development plot within the particular history of impersonality I have outlined in this book. But unlike Eliot, for whom the loss of personality augments authority and expertise, the characters of Bowen's fiction lack the privilege of owning a personality in the first place; having been dispossessed by others, they are the abandoned, the orphaned, and the displaced. Youth is not an exalted state but is instead the product of some kind of adulterous, indecorous, or even unspeakable affair. This extreme illegitimacy characterizes a development that has not merely been stalled or delayed but seriously deformed by a too early entry into adulthood, where spatial displacement accompanies and exacerbates these deformed paths of development.

My reading of Bowen's fiction, then, attempts to triangulate three essential characteristics of her work: her experiments with the novel of development, impersonality, and her concern for spatiality—or more specifically, the roles and lives of objects as they organize domestic space. That is, if the *Bildungsroman* narrates the drama of personality, how one comes into possession of oneself, then it is also intimately connected to the question of how and what one possesses; like personality, objects are subject to possession and conversely, dispossession. Given these connections, Bowen utilizes the world of objects in her fiction to launch her critique of personality and its prevalence in the novel of development. In doing so, she participates within a larger modernist genealogy, represented especially by Lewis, Butts, and Lawrence, as well as Eliot and Woolf, equally concerned with the asymmetries that develop between subject and object, human and external world. For Bowen, such imbalances occur particularly through a promotion of personality that subjugates the object to the world of the subject. My interest here is in the ethical radicalism of Bowen's writing as it looks toward an impersonal organization of space in hopes of creating a more empathic, less cruel, material setting. Within this progressively impersonal vision, she does not so much personify or anthropomorphize the objects that set the domestic stage but incorporates them within her fictional fabric to dispel the notion of individual subjectivity, personality, and character.

These objects do not materialize realistically *against* the inner worlds of these fictional characters; rather, their hallucinatory residues open these worlds as they extend beyond the individual personality.

It is through this frame that Bowen's work can best be incorporated into the history of modernist thought. In general, Bowen's contributions to the modernist literary period remain unexplored in most criticism of her work, which is especially difficult to periodize since she continued writing after 1945 up until her death in 1973. While the past two decades have demonstrated a renewed critical interest in Bowen's oeuvre, many critics continue to read Bowen's interest in space and place literally rather than theoretically, claiming her as a regionalist, Anglo-Irish novelist or in some cases relegating her fiction to a conservative literary canon where she is revered as either a novelist of manners lamenting the fated Irish ascendancy, a middlebrow version of Henry James or Virginia Woolf, or a lost Victorian in the mode of E. M. Forster. Her apparent political conservatism has led critics to position her work against the arguably more radical aims of modernism, especially regarding her relation to the international milieu of London or Paris. Maud Ellmann, for example, insistently stresses the author's disconnection from modernism, particularly its more identifiable circles, arguing that Bowen tended to avoid "movements and manifestoes," especially feminism.[7] Characterizing Bowen as a "realist" writer stifled by the modernist necessity to narrate "inner life," Ellmann argues that Bowen (in contrast to Virginia Woolf) opts for the "world of cars and cocktail-shakers, typewriters and telephones . . . the gadgetry of modernity" (*Shadow* 5). While Ellmann's analysis highlights the importance of objects in Bowen's fiction, the distinction she draws between Bowen's realism and Woolf's more subjective modernist universe reduces modernism to a particularly sophisticated version of subjectivist narcissism that disregards the object world, where the subjectivity ascribed to "inner life" must either override the claims of the outside world or simply be at odds with it.[8]

Ellmann's assessment to some degree follows the logic of Peter Nicholls's famous claim that modernists valued the subjective over the objective in a dissociated authorial stance that privileged "*separateness* from the social world."[9] Taking this interpretation of modernism, it is possible to argue that Bowen's empirical interest in objects plants her outside of an aesthetic practice whose basic failure is its disengagement with the external world, valuing individual subjectivity at the expense of objectivity, the actual conditions of life. Yet critics such as Douglas Mao have complicated this line of argument by emphasizing the "peculiarly" modernist "feeling of regard for the physical object as object—as not-self, as not-subject," characterized further by the desire to apprehend the object as a discrete "fragment of Being, as solidity, as otherness in its most resilient opacity."[10] I suggest here that Bowen shares this "feeling" but also complicates it, particularly as the "solidity" of objects in her fiction works to expose the instabilities of self, character, and personality (*Solid* 4). Bowen's fiction indeed stages a specifically modernist drama between the material fabric of lived space and the threat of its subordination to a more mobile, intrusive form of human consciousness.[11] However, texts such as *The Death of the Heart* ultimately endow objects with agency of their own to examine how they function as both discrete *and* relational entities. In this ethical vision, objects—neither detached from nor sentimentally attached to the encroachments of human emotion—become the impersonal agents of human feeling, engendering a space for empathic engagement and exchange.

Personality and the *Bildungsroman*

The mutations that distinguish *The Death of the Heart's* unconventional narrative structure, along with its prolonged attention to the ethics of living among objects, characterizes what I am calling an impersonal novelistic form. This impersonality informs Bowen's inquiry into the conventional *Bildungsroman*, which accords in many ways with the challenge contemporary feminist critics have offered to the form's investment in linear development, progress, and a sense of coherent identity available only to men.[12] While my own argument often coheres with this sort of feminist inquiry, especially since *The Death of the Heart's* protagonist is an orphaned, adolescent girl, I am less interested in launching an overtly feminist critique of the *Bildungsroman* as I am in identifying a specific historical shift represented in the modernist appropriation of the form. Indeed, I have somewhat coincidentally devoted two chapters of this book to the modernist *Bildungsroman* as a particularly impersonal form of the novel, a focus that reflects the centrality of the novel of development to an impersonal aesthetic. As perhaps the most identifiable novelistic form, the *Bildungsroman* models successful development through the construction of personality. It follows that modernist experiments with the form would question this institutionalization of personality, which occurs precisely through the novel. Consequently, in my own reframing of the novel of development, I am most interested in how the modernist *Bildungsroman*, as exemplified by *The Death of the Heart* and other texts such as *Sons and Lovers*, dismantles subjectivity and personality rather than creating it.

In *The Death of the Heart*, Bowen both critiques and redraws the conventional *Bildungsroman*, along with the bourgeois fantasy of domestic familiarity it supports, where the subject learns to exist happily and peacefully within the demands of socialization. More particularly, the novel's concern for the status and place of things, their relation to public and private dimensions of self-formation, space, and spatiality, along with the ethical and engaged actions of living and feeling, works into a rather complicated critical apparatus. In its significance to my own argument, Franco Moretti's well-known account of the *Bildungsroman* as an inherently "*weak*" form, ultimately discarded in the twentieth century, provides a crucial foundation for understanding how the *Bildungsroman* might indeed operate in the twentieth century but as a significantly altered, experimental form constructed around a self-conscious examination of its own normalizing operations.[13] Organized to elude "whatever may endanger the Ego's equilibrium," the *Bildungsroman*, according to Moretti, is invested in the "free and open construction of personality"—one's distinctiveness "as an individual unique and different from others" (*Way* 12, 17, 40). This aspect of personality gives way to an additional characteristic of the term, the impossibility of ever "expressing fully" one's personality. As a result, "personality remains a consistently unsatisfied idol," preferring "never to have to bend for anything" (*Way* 40). The contradiction of a harmonious personality that is by nature at odds with its own expression appears to fuel the disdain for personality we see in modernist texts by figures such as Lewis, who, as I have argued, link the fictive promises of democratic modernity to people's "wish to express their personality."[14] Lewis detests the public expression of personality, harshly rebuking the myth that such expression is a reflection of freedom, when in reality it is nothing more than "a pattern imposed . . . by means of education and the hypnotism of cinema, wireless, and press" (*Art* 148). Echoing this sentiment, Moretti observes that as the *Bildungsroman* seeks to balance the "external and internal . . . the 'best and most intimate' part of the soul and the 'public aspect of existence,'" the goal is not the freedom but the "stabilization" of the individual and his relation to the social world as "maturity" (*Way* 30, 26). Thus the conventional closure of the *Bildungsroman*, in which the subject becomes "normal" by "perceiving the social norms as one's own," requires that the subject "willingly limit his freedom . . . through marriage" and the "happiness" that accompanies it (*Way* 16, 22).

The happiness born of stable personality is intimately connected to the way one lives in domestic space. That is, as the end result of its development, the personality is able to function in the larger world by virtue of its domestication in the home. "Modern personality," claims Moretti, "lodges at the centre of everyday life," most notably, the comfort of the domestic setting, which one constructs through relation to possessions or things (*Way* 40). Using *Wilhelm Meister* and *Pride and Prejudice* as examples, Moretti contends that the *Bildungsroman* essentially narrates an "aesthetic education," in which personality builds a home for itself primarily through the acquisition of things and where the "harmonious objects *par excellence* . . . are precisely homes" (*Way* 36, 39, 37). This model presupposes a particular temporal narrative logic based on a continual acquisition of external relationships as one encounters the world outside the home. Nonetheless, the incubator of personality is the home, and things function here as the manifestation of human personality or interiority.[15]

It is useful here to examine briefly the Marxist foundations of this argument and its importance for my own. As Pierre Bourdieu claims in *Distinction*, "personality" is "at stake . . . in the capacity to appropriate an object of quality."[16] In other words, the quality of the possession determines the strength of its owner's attachment to it and thus the potency of her personality. Bourdieu's definition of personality as dependent on *how* one appropriates objects emphasizes both the difficulty and importance of theorizing a form of an attachment to the object world that does not sentimentally amplify the personality, as in the model Moretti identifies. Like Bourdieu, Marx explicitly uses the term "personality" to signify the outcome of private ownership as a means of forging one's place in the world of more public aspirations. "Exclusive ownership," Marx argues, allows the owner "both to preserve his personality and to distinguish himself from other men, as well as relate to them."[17] Key here is the idea that personality, produced through private ownership of objects, is an essential tool for establishing bourgeois social relations, in building the synthesis of bourgeois aspiration and acceptance of social norms that sustains the successful *Bildung*. Consequently, if the successful *Bildung* requires that the hero acquire a "personality" and establish social connections, then it also demands that its subject procure and take up the appropriate relation to its possessions. In this sense, appropriate ownership enables the comfortable domestic existence that will create harmony as the hero enters the bigger world.

"Living," or Feeling

My goal here is not to initiate a Marxist analysis of Bowen's work but to underscore the pervasive link between personality and objects in the novel of development. The relation between the appropriate ownership of objects and the successful *Bildung* appears most concretely in nineteenth-century examples of the form such as George Eliot's *The Mill on the Floss*, itself a critique of the *Bildungsroman*, where the most palpable sign of public disgrace is having to sell one's furniture.[18] What is nostalgically lost through this dispossession is the familiarity and comfort of home. In its particularly modernist take on this model, *The Death of the Heart* details a domain whose style of domesticity both disperses the personality and inhibits true aesthetic experience. It does not produce a sentimental record of loss, as with a text like *The Mill on the Floss*; rather, its protagonist, Portia Quayne, suffers from an alienation and rootlessness that is the only existing condition of her life. In this sense, *The Death of the Heart* both adheres to the trajectory of the conventional *Bildungsroman* and illustrates its deformation, overtly questioning the assumptions that the *Bildungsroman* takes for granted. For example, what is the purpose of building a *Bildungsroman* that renders such domestic familiarity impossible? Furthermore, what role should the home play in a *Bildungsroman* that only emphasizes the vulnerability of social connections?

The narrative of *The Death of the Heart* follows the 16-year-old, orphaned Portia Quayne, who has been sent to live in the home of her half-brother Thomas, some twenty years older than she, and his stylish wife, Anna, an interior decorator, as the fulfillment of her father's dying wishes that she experience a "taste" of "*normal, cheerful* family life" for a year (italics in original; *Death* 13). The child of her father's adultery, "of an aberration . . . of a panic . . . of an old chap's pitiful sexuality," Portia is already at odds with the function of the bourgeois home and the arrangement of objects it supports (*Death* 323). The irony of Anna's profession, one ostensibly designed to increase the livability and aesthetic comfort of an interior, is reflected in the emotional restraint of her own household design. Anna is not warm, maternal, or particularly nurturing, and neither is her home, which, "queasy and cold," blocks the growth of the expansive personality Moretti identifies (*Death* 221). The "speckless" house is completely depersonalized, containing "no point where feeling could thicken," "no place where shadows lodged" (*Death* 50). No occupant of Windsor Terrace—at least from Major Brutt's perspective, one of its "unheard of" and unwelcomed callers—dares to tweak "a thing . . . from its flat, unfeeling position" (*Death* 313). Objects in this home are arranged impersonally to distract and distill feeling, to keep visitors and history at bay while intensifying the solitude of an environment characterized by an enforced radical privacy where "[c]allers were unheard of . . . They had been eliminated; they simply did not occur . . . Their privacy was surrounded by an electric fence" (*Death* 109). Nonetheless, some visitors manage to enter the carefully crafted scene. These include Portia's treacherously consuming love object, the 24-year-old Eddie, a rat-like prey on middle-class society; Matchett, the quite voluble housekeeper; St. Quentin, Anna's novelist friend; and finally, Major Brutt, a hapless World War I veteran and pal of Anna's ex-lover, Robert Pidgeon.

Such enforced privacy prevents Portia from forming the external relationships that fuel the successful *Bildung*, further delaying the cultivation of her character. Particularly in regard to the formal development of her character, the early portions of the novel explicitly thematize the novel as an exploration and critique of the typical *Bildung*. In a conversation between Anna, St. Quentin, and Portia, Anna, complaining that she "hate[s]" her own "lax character," satirically suggests that her own *Bildung* has left her unhappy and has thus been unsuccessful (*Death* 31). St. Quentin, as if in witty literary parody, continues the conversation with even more sharp and ironic insight into this vulnerability: "'I'm afraid we can't do much about your character now. It must have set—I know mine has. Portia's so lucky; hers is still being formed' . . . Anna bit off a yawn and said: 'She may become anything'" (*Death* 31). Much like Lois's in *The Last September*, Portia's lack of form and direction suggests that she does not cohere to the proper timeline of bourgeois aspiration. While St. Quentin suggests that Portia is "lucky," the young girl actually suffers rather severely from this lack of guidance and direction. Lax characters like Portia, who "may become anything," never really "set," or find an acceptable position within an appropriate cultural milieu. As a further indication of this formlessness, Portia sits silently during this conversation, adding to her companions' anxiety regarding her presence alongside their own fixedness. Similarly, in school, where she "was not a success," the girl frustrates her teachers by failing, in a situation reminiscent of Forster's *Howards End*, "to concentrate" (*Death* 64). Not having learned that "one must learn," she is vacant, inattentive, and incommunicative, a developmental failure, to say the least (*Death* 64).

The sterile and ghostly spaces Anna has created at Windsor Terrace reinforce this communicative silence, unwelcoming for the proper incubation of a developed, recognizable character. Instead, Portia's probing and mute discernment renders her almost inhuman; she is likened to a "snake, or a rabbit," a "wild creature," a "bird already stunned," and "a kitten that expects to be drowned" (*Death* 55, 377, 47). These frequent comparisons, the kitten being the most amenable to domestication, plant Portia outside of the domestic sphere Anna has created; as such, there is no familiar bridge between the girl's interiority and the domestic interior. Portia's consequent spatial alienation leads to the more formal alienation she experiences as an apt "character" in the novel itself, where her quiet anonymity reflects the inability to demarcate herself as a complete character, or personality. This rather impersonal lack of concentrated selfhood, or personality, certainly exacerbates her invisibility, leaving her all the more inappropriate as a subject for the *Bildungsroman* and even more threatening to the Quaynes. Her diffusion couples paradoxically with her smallness in a house where she is always a stranger. Consequently, the novel is a *Bildungsroman* about a quest for a home that is not a home and, by order of her illegitimate inheritance, a place where this much longed for "atmosphere of familiarity" never materializes (*Way* 24). If anything, an atmosphere of "strangeness" characterizes

Portia's entry into an impeccably furnished house where "rooms were set for strangers' intimacy, or else for exhausted solitary retreat" and "everyone has learnt to be lonely" (*Death* 50, 179).

Through this problem with familiarity, Bowen's fiction self-consciously works to dismantle this form of interiority as it merges through objects into the concept of personality. Rather than create the expansive personality demanded in conventional narratives of character formation, Bowen's interiors actually dissolve personality or delineated literary character by dispersing the self into the external world. This function of the "home" and its role in development is immediately announced as a theme in *The Death of the Heart*. The house itself constantly sabotages Anna's preference for a detachment that would stave off intruders or, at least, maintain the set roles she has designed for them. But such detachment is ultimately impossible. The question of how people must "live" is too urgent: "Wherever we unconsciously feel," remarks the narrator in regard to Portia, "we live" (*Death* 180). The intention of Anna's detachment is ostensibly to obstruct this feeling act of living, yet the world of objects in the text ultimately compels her in a different direction. In Windsor Terrace, "living" encodes the stakes of emotional survival, where domestic space and the objects it contains must be manipulated to protect against the possibility of hallucination. When Anna remarks to her friend St. Quentin that Portia has come to "live with us," his reply extends the definition of the term: "Live? I thought she was only staying?" (*Death* 21). To "live" represents an index of permanency here, and on one level, this usage seems fairly standard in Bowen's fiction. For example, in *The House in Paris*, the word "living" also becomes part of critical rhetoric, chronicling the difficulty of a world that has denied its youthful protagonists any set points of reference, most precisely their mothers.[19]

In both *The Death of the Heart* and *The House in Paris*, the inability to live anywhere catalyzes the literal dissolution of character. Having character here means to exhibit a kind of interiority that can essentially live itself out comfortably in the things around it or concretize itself in the guise of a coherent personality. In contrast to this model, Bowen's fiction creates literary worlds that impede this objectification of personality and thus calls attention to the instability of character itself, as it is exacerbated by the difficulties of living.[20] As they "make for hallucination," the residues and secretions of Windsor Terrace's material infrastructure augment this difficulty (*Death* 191). In a passage taken from her diary, Portia describes, in her childlike yet acutely observant idiom, her experience of coming back to the house after buying a stamp: "I felt still odder than I generally do, and the house was still more like always than usual. It always gets more in the afternoon. When Thomas comes in he looks as though he was smelling something he thought he might not be let eat. This house makes a smell of feeling" (*Death* 140). The deliberately confusing syntax of these lines plays on the word still, drawing attention to both the stasis of the house and its active role in human lives. The house "actively" makes a smell of feeling. Feeling can now be "sensed" but only through the mediation of the house itself. Unlike things that can be seen, a smell cannot be objectified or quantified. As with Portia's claim that "she smelled of Thomas and Anna," the "smell of feeling," remotely perceptible, characterizes the vulnerability of the network it flimsily binds (*Death* 190).

Given the threat these sorts of residues present to character, it makes sense that Anna ultimately sustains or "sets" her character by guarding it from the agency objects exert in emotionally dissecting humans. Matchett, the stern, rather Jamesian housekeeper and Portia's only confidante, offers a foreboding description of the furniture and its uncanny ability to permeate human emotional boundaries:

> Furniture's knowing all right. Not much gets past the things in a room . . . If Mr. and Mrs. Thomas are what you say, nervous, no doubt they are nervous of what's not said. I would not be the one to blame them: they live the best way they can. Unnatural living runs in a family, and the furniture knows it, you be sure. Good furniture knows what's what . . . Oh, furniture like we've got is too much for some that would rather not have a past. If I just had to look at it and have it looking at me, I'd go jumpy, I daresay. But when it's your work it can't do anything to you. Why, that furniture—I've been at it for years and years with the soft cloth. I know it like my own face. (*Death* 101)

Matchett's probing analysis here points to her ethical centrality to the novel. She does not merely personify the furniture but rather lengthily analyzes its role in a particular style of living, of emotional habitation. By concealing the interior world of people who are absent, blotted out, the furniture records, watches, and remembers in a paranoid atmosphere artfully designed to ensure complete privacy. Portia, unlike Anna and Thomas, begins to understand that one need not fear the hallucinatory potential of such objects and their emotional residues. Rather, she learns to reroute this cultivated emotional detachment into an impersonal form of relation to objects that occurs at the risk of suffering, characterized by respect, vulnerability, openness, and connection—love: "Only in a house where one has learnt to be lonely does one have this solicitude for things. One's relation to them, the daily seeing or touching, begins to become love, and to lay one open to pain" (*Death* 179). As Portia appears to understand, the object world might potentially transcend Anna's design for it. Rather than block feeling, as Anna would have it, the object world becomes a route to feeling.

Hotel Habits, or the "Lengths" of Possession

"She'll bitch up our good house."

—Mary Butts[21]

It is a wary business, walking about a strange house you know you are to know well. Only cats and dogs with their more expressive bodies enact the tension we share with them at such times. The you inside gathers up defensively; something is stealing upon you every moment; you will never be quite the same again. These new unsmiling lights, reflections and objects are to become your memories, riveted to you closer than friends or lovers, going with you, even, into the grave; worse, they may become dear and fasten like so many leeches on your heart.

—Elizabeth Bowen

Portia's more radical perspective accords with this moment of narrative insight from *The House in Paris*. Like "leeches on your heart," the world of objects parasitically channels the affective traumas and the joys of day-to-day living. The agency the narrative grants to these objects reroutes the direction of the classical *Bildungsroman* as Moretti defines it; rather than engorging the ego through the effective control or ownership of objects within the domestic sphere, this model disseminates interiority into the world at large. Portia most concretely exemplifies this process in her overtly impersonal attachment to hotels, rather than a singular home, as the emotional loci of self-development. Based on the model of the *Bildungsroman* I have elaborated, Portia's strange "familiarity" with hotels leads to her deviation from the outlines of the traditional, successful *Bildung*, where the subject synthesizes private and public aspects of existence by finding a space of belonging in both the home and the "big" world. Hotels have come to represent her domestic experience and, in doing so, have determined her specific mode of relation to objects. From a modern or cosmopolitan perspective, the hotel could be understood as a glamorous, bohemian locale where the aesthetically inclined could make themselves at home in the world. But one is also reminded of the general misery that transpires in the hotel rooms of modernist novels, particularly for the financially insecure. In the case of Jean Rhys's down and out women, for example, the hotel exacerbates their loss of placement, nourishing their alcoholism, financial dependency, and general malaise. Given their financial position, these heroines often become items of exchange among men, who may visit them without risk to their own character within the anonymity of the hotel room.[22]

In *The Death of the Heart*, Portia appears to register this aspect of hotel living, suggesting that life in hotels operates according to a principle of exchange, where exclusive attachment yields to "people always coming and going," and where objects are either lost, left behind, or exchanged (*Death* 57). As Portia remarks to Major Brutt, "people look as though they'd always be there and the next moment you've no idea where they've gone" (*Death* 57). This kind of traffic breeds in Portia a strangely impersonal relation to things. At school, Portia's teacher first reprimands her for attempting to read a letter clandestinely in class and then for failing to put her bag in the cloakroom. Miss Paullie's displeasure has nothing to do with whether Portia is missing her mathematics lesson but with the fact that she catches Portia reading "a letter under the table" (*Death* 67). As practiced by both Anna and Portia, furtive and "unprescribed reading," part of the "typical *Bildungsroman* plot" Jerome Buckley has famously identified, is a major narrative vehicle in the novel (*Season* 17). The letter in question, which Portia has received after an encounter with Eddie, moves across various scenes and locations until Matchett, in a rather drawn-out "tucking-in" ceremony, catches Portia hiding it under her pillow (*Death* 105). The problem for Matchett is not the existence of the letter but Portia's placement of it, which implies paranoia and secrecy: "That's no place for letters at your age—it's not nice" (*Death* 105). This need for secrecy belies a private world that cannot translate itself openly into the Quaynes's attempt to redeem Portia from her improper development.

Portia's unwitting advertisement of what she conceals follows her throughout the novel. In the same style of paranoia that characterizes her clandestine reading of the letter, Portia also tends to attach herself permanently to her private belongings. Miss Paullie, the head of the school for "delicate girls" Portia attends, warns her against such proclivities: "To carry your bag about with you indoors is a hotel habit, you know." For Miss Paullie, hotel habits expose an ill-breeding that disregards what should remain private and, furthermore, signify an unnatural and paranoid attachment to belongings: "Why did you not leave your bag in the cloakroom? Nobody will take it here, you know?" (*Death* 67). Portia's curious attachment to her bag reveals her overall failure to understand the art of private possession. Like the diary, this item appears at the beginning of the novel and moves through various scenes. Though Anna has expertly selected the bag as part of her chic, age-appropriate wardrobe, Portia's friend Lilian still manages to observe that "[y]ou carry it in such a queer way" (*Death* 64). The exchange is humorous, as Portia professes her fear of leaving it somewhere and then asks Lilian to show her how she carries hers. Of course, Portia fears forgetting the bag because of its contents. It is not a solid object but one that holds or contains other objects, most notably the letter Portia draws from its recesses. Yet this function of hiding and containing makes the bag conspicuous and problematic for both Miss Paullie and Anna, who make it clear that there are certain protocols for possessing tastefully rather than conspicuously, for living properly with and among things.

Portia's stylistic failure to properly possess her property according to bourgeois expectations parallels the failure of her socialization. If the *Bildungsroman* seeks to synthesize individual aspiration with socialization as a means of building personality, then Portia's paranoid style of possession functions as a deliberate exploration and critique of this model. Portia's unsteady relation with the things in her life elaborates an ethics of possession and spatiality based on the disequilibrium of the ego—its inability to concretize itself as a personality through domestic experience. Again, this disconnection acts as a radical critique of a modernity that embeds interiority within a domestic sphere with distinct rules for private possession. For example, in diagnosing Portia's "hotel habits," Miss Paullie refers to the young woman's violation of a standard social etiquette supported by this very function of modernity, a breach first instituted by the public nature of her father's adultery and later her own failure to understand the distinction between public and private, impersonal and personal acts of possession. But more so than Miss Paullie, Anna most shrewdly recognizes Portia's failure to fulfill this prescription: "She is so unnaturally callous about objects—she treats any hat, for instance, like an old envelope. Nothing that's hers ever seems, if you know what I mean, to belong to her, which makes it meaningless to give her any present, unless it's something to eat, and she doesn't always like that. It may be because they always lived in hotels" (*Death* 6). What troubles Anna most is Portia's impersonal relation to things; because she does not appear to own anything, Portia's life in hotels has taught her to reverence things improperly. This lack of shared reverence for the same things facilitates Anna's desperate inability to inculcate Portia with the proper rules of social behavior and contributes to Portia's threatening presence in Anna's home. Portia appears omniscient and all-seeing, primarily because they simply cannot "get" her personality. Once again, Portia's apparent lack of personality, the solubility of her character, follows her failure, in Bourdieu's sense, to suitably consecrate the objects of her surroundings.

Portia's "callousness" toward objects, her oddly soluble yet detached relation to them, attends the overly public, impersonal aspects of her existence that will ultimately dissolve her own character. Through this impersonality, Bowen redraws the trajectory of the *Bildungsroman* while quite controversially critiquing private ownership as a mode of relation and symbol of "personality." The text does not merely repudiate these social relations, as it does not dispute the importance of private ownership altogether, but restructures them in an effective and subtle critique of form. By reinvesting the object as a mode of relation, Bowen does not deflate the project of the *Bildungsroman* altogether but attempts to alter its values. Hence the book opens not with direct communication between Anna and Portia but with discussion of the most important object in the novel: Portia's diary. In the opening scene of the novel, Anna admits to her friend St. Quentin that she has read Portia's diary. Because Portia is unable to successfully privatize it in her singular possession, the diary is another object in the novel that she is unable to possess properly. "You were mad ever to touch the thing," remarks St. Quentin, suggesting that this object, with its particular linguistic excesses, threatens the safety of Anna's detachment (*Death* 4). And it does. The plot of the novel reflects the quiet intensity of Anna's clandestine reading, as its finale leads to Portia's eventual discovery of this act and the "empathetic damage" that ensues.[23] Anna reads Portia's aesthetically displeasing diary—"[o]ne of those wretched black books one buys for about a shilling with moiré outsides"—with an overwrought neurosis, not only as a concrete object that manifests the interior of its writer, but also as a route to her own interior (*Death* 7). Stuffed carelessly into Portia's escritoire with all kinds of papers that Anna and Thomas would generally "throw away," the diary both attracts and repulses the interior decorator (*Death* 6–7). This precious bit of messiness within Anna's polished and varnished house invites invasion. Anna surrenders to this invitation, assailing Portia's privacy as a masochistic means of defending her own manner of protected living. Reading Portia's diary allows Anna to establish intimacy with the book as an object and furthers her own self-objectification, channeling the pain she accesses vicariously through her ritualistic compulsion to read it. After such literary sessions, she feels pained and "disagreeable" about her life (*Death* 401). Indeed, the diary propels such a bout of paranoia that reading it develops into a form of self-critical, if not self-annihilating, reflection. The diary, and every frantically taut situation Anna's reading of it spawns, is the "apogee of bad taste" for a people who "detest intimacies" (*Death* 405–6).

From a phenomenological perspective, the diary is the most important object in the text. Not only does it threaten the kind of prelogical, hallucinatory deception that will dissolve the fixity of Anna's character, but the dynamics of inside and outside it manifests complicate its role as an object. The book is an example of what French phenomenologist Gaston Bachelard terms "hybrid objects" or "subject objects."[24] In his anti-Cartesian study of intimate space, *The Poetics of Space*, Bachelard writes that such objects, for example a chest of drawers, have a "quality of intimacy" because they are "very evident witnesses of the *need for secrecy*, of an intuitive sense of hiding places" (italics in original; *Poetics* 78, 81). Interestingly, Anna must produce a narrative of how she came upon the diary in the first place, which she retrieves from another hybrid object in the text, a little *escritoire* that she included in her decoration of Portia's room. Significantly, the desk has "drawers that lock, and quite a big flap to write on," which "locks too" (*Death* 6). Not only is Anna astounded by and drawn to the overflowing messiness of the *escritoire*, but she is most painfully disturbed when she finds that it is not locked. In this case, Portia fails to understand the proper protocols for possessing objects. Anna has her own desk that locks, which she organizes and guards diligently. Thus, while the *escritoire* overtly betrays a "*need for secrecy,*" it appears that certain hiding places are acceptable only when properly maintained, whereas others, under desks and pillows, for example, are not.

The key here is not to broadcast what one conceals, which is why, aside from his inexplicable sadism, St. Quentin later informs Portia of Anna's covert reading. If the diary ironically makes public Portia's "*need for secrecy,*" then the question is "from whom?" (*Poetics* 81). Of course, Anna originally draws attention to the diary as an impermeable object by referring to its "wretched, black" outside (*Death* 7). Nonetheless, the "from whom," Anna herself, is the focus here, for Anna does not learn so much about Portia in reading the diary as she does about herself; Portia's diary is not a means for Anna to access another interior but to create her own. The text offers no indication that Anna possessed one before the diary, as it appears to have dissolved in the past, unable to enter the networks of human communicative exchange. Toward the end of the novel, Anna attempts to justify her reading to Thomas: "Her diary's very good—you see, she has got us taped. Could I not go on with a book all about ourselves? I don't say it has changed the course of my life, but it's given me a rather more disagreeable feeling about being alive—or at least, about being me" (*Death* 399). Anna's suggestion that the diary is a tape, or "archive," implies that it serves not as a subjective account but as an objective record or accumulation of events in the Quayne household.[25] Though the diary is constantly the subject of conversation, the reader acquires little knowledge of its contents, thus reinforcing its status as an objective "thing," a surface or outside as Anna originally describes it. Consequently, Anna relates to the diary as a visual record, a cinematic device that sees or witnesses life in Windsor Terrace. As an agent that fixes or catches the Quaynes, the diary blurs the boundaries between the interior dimensions of psychic life and an objective style of recording. This function of the diary also peaks Eddie's interest. In one of the first private and most excruciating "love" scenes between Portia and Eddie, Eddie wheedles Portia into allowing him to take the diary. He then makes her promise not to write about him, claiming that "I hate writing: I hate art . . . I won't have you choosing words about me" (*Death* 136–37). Given this description, the diary, as subject/object, corresponds to a specific narrative style that affords Portia, at least to some extent, the power of authoring others. Objective, it records and visually sees. At the same time, Portia subjectively "chooses" the words that make for this seeing.

Consistent with the dynamics of impersonality I have identified in this book, the diary, as an impersonal subject object, phenomenologically reroutes interiority onto the surfaces of things, flattening the dimensions of interior and exterior. The diary's significant status in the novel, as well as its role in propelling the narrative itself, further reinforces the connection between phenomenology and impersonality I have attempted to illustrate at various points in this book. Especially as Anna apprehends it, the book represents the problem of a "reinforced geometrism" that, according to Bachelard, supports the "dialectics of outside and inside" (*Poetics* 214). A real experience of intimacy and imagination, the philosopher suggests, is impersonal, where the flattening of space dissolves the barriers that separate inside from outside. Ultimately, this liberatory movement away from geometric space "allows us to explore the being of man considered as the being of a *surface*" (*Poetics* 222). In keeping with this analysis, if Anna were able to move beyond a geometric consciousness of the diary in particular and of space more generally, she would not have to "read" the diary in the first place. That is, her need to distinguish the diary's interior from its exterior as a means of learning about herself denies the diary's more radical possibilities as an impersonal object. Anna's specific consciousness of space means that she is unable to actualize St. Quentin's suggestion that she "see things from [Portia's] position," or empathize with Portia—not through reading depths but in seeing a surface (*Death* 330). Rather than truly see, Anna simply questions St. Quentin's recommendation: "Even supposing one wanted to for a moment, how is one to know how anyone else feels?" (*Death* 404). Anna's question is ironic, considering her own excursions into the boundaries of Portia's private life. Bound completely within her own narcissism, Anna fails to understand that the answer to her question lies in the diary itself.

As a means of linguistic "peeping," the diary affords Anna a sense of vision, but she cannot fully embrace the dualism it represents. That is, she relates to the diary personally, not impersonally; because she reads only about herself, she is not able to transcend her limited perspective. Anna is able to open the diary, but she fails to give up her own bounded perspective as a way of inhabiting its interior, of empathizing with its contents. Anna's obsession with the narratives the diary contains—her own, in particular—deepens her personalized relation to the diary. To return to Wilhelm Worringer's *Abstraction and Empathy*, which I discussed in the preceding chapter, "empathy" describes a particular kind of aesthetic practice characterized by a personalized mode of apprehending the object. Such an engagement reifies the self as it seeks to live itself out in the external through a "relationship of confidence."[26] Worringer is highly critical of this humanist-inspired aesthetic position, but Anna's reading of the diary is even more problematic. The "relationship of confidence" Worringer identifies as the goal of an empathic engagement with the object is replaced with neurosis and paranoia, resulting in an inability to feel. This kind of affective relation does not simply project the personality onto the object; it exploits the object to access a personality and a narrative (*Abstraction* 15). Consequently, Anna is capable of neither empathy nor abstraction, which, according to Worringer, references the impersonal "need for self-alienation" present in "all aesthetic experience" (*Abstraction* 23). As a result, she is affectively stunted and, despite her professional interest in managing things, is unable to establish any clear relationship with the world outside herself. In contrast, Portia exemplifies a more radical perspective. To take Worringer's terms, her own abstraction in the text, the lack of set personality and ego that reinforces her omniscience, allows her to relate empathically to objects in a way that does not solidify her own personality. Portia is most able to feel but often to her own detriment. Only Portia, to reference Merleau-Ponty, "leave[s] [her] place, abandon[s] [her] point of view on the world" to "think [her]self into a sort of ubiquity." This type of displacement, argues the philosopher, is the means by which "breadth is immediately equivalent to depth" (*Phenomenology* 255).

As I have argued, this sort of phenomenological relationship, in which the immediacy of surfaces is valued over the "depths" that attend psychology and hermeneutic analysis more generally, is a major characteristic of the modernist impersonality I am outlining—Eliot's version of poetic emotion particularly, as I posit in the introduction. This impersonality, in which "profile" trumps depth, characterizes Portia's relation to humans and objects (*Phenomenology* 255). During her visit to Waikiki, the very noisy and bustling residence of Anna's former governess Mrs. Heccomb where Anna spent much of her childhood, Portia attests that "here I do see how everyone feels" (*Death* 249). This quiet omniscience, or "scared lurking," where Portia stares "like a kitten that expects to be drowned," augments her faceless, probing discernment, which is further objectified in her diary, a record of visually witnessed feeling (*Death* 47). Much like the letter Portia reads beneath her desk, the diary broadcasts its own duty to conceal in a house where everything is artfully designed to deny an interior.

Despite Anna's inability to empathize, or see, the world around her, the objects of Windsor Terrace at least offer the possibility of the impersonal intimacy I am attempting to outline. The text suggests that a place, whatever unfamiliar atmosphere it attempts to generate, can always generate intimacy, particularly if feeling is present. "Wherever we unconsciously feel," says the narrator in regard to Portia's hotel life, "we live" (*Death* 180).

The intimacy that at least momentarily arises between Anna and Portia is essentially of the same type that characterizes that of Paul Morel and his father in *Sons and Lovers*; it builds itself unconsciously to suit the fine demands of Anna's disdain for intimate revelations of the self. This sort of intimacy does not preserve the self but extends it, exchanging "depth" for "profile." The object world is the medium that bridges this connection, so that when Portia intrudes upon Anna and Eddie having tea, nothing is actually said, but "between Portia and Anna extended the still life of the tea tray" (*Death* 333). However indirect, the still life of the tea tray excludes Eddie, actively "extending" only those who live with it, for whom an unspoken understanding characterizes their relationship. The tea tray, and the mode of connection it enables, defines what it means to live relative to its own placement.

At the same time, the prominence of the tea tray in this scene discloses the absence of direct communication between humans. Situated within such a communicative strain, both Portia and Anna take their places unconsciously among a network of objects. By extending itself between Portia and Anna, the tea tray actively inducts the two women into its own world of objectivity—of breadth rather than depth—as it abstracts the two women away from their personalized existence. Only in this mode, however edited, can Anna, who the text claims was not considered "properly upper class," communicate with Portia about her own past, which she seems conveniently to have forgotten (*Death* 186). Significantly, this awkward exchange occurs by way of another object, a picture Portia saw of a "little suffering Anna"—who "looked like a cripple between her cascades of hair"—in her room at Waikiki. Portia's visit, where she is seemingly socialized according to the "spontaneous" and "highest voltage" nature of "free living," occupies the center section of the novel, titled "The Flesh" (*Death* 222). Rather than respond to Portia's fixation with reminiscence, Anna defensively asks questions: "'There's a picture of you there, in my room.' 'A photograph?' 'No, a picture holding a kitten.' Anna put her hand to her head. 'Kitten?' she said. 'What do you mean, Portia?'" (*Death* 334). Anna is at once quick to turn the tables on this exchange, denying the intersubjective mediation that develops from the mutual seeing of an object. True to her general feelings about intimacy, she both evades and is attracted to the questions that might produce a narrative of the past. Ironically, as if answering to some unconscious desire to know herself or her past, Anna, not Portia, asks the questions whose answers the older woman seems to have conveniently forgotten. When Portia returns from Waikiki, Anna, consistent with her preference to "not have a past," shuts down Portia's narrative of her stay (*Death* 101).

Waikiki, with its noise; its often rude, familial banter; and its frantic breakfast rituals, counters Windsor Terrace and its "speckless" mode of living (*Death* 304). The place explicitly encourages a very different relation to objects, where people maintain rather indelicate but almost always "happy relationship[s] with the things in the room" (*Death* 246). Mrs. Heccomb's "sexy" and rather snappishly opinionated stepdaughter Daphne, with whom Eddie not so surreptitiously holds hands at the movies, "never simply touched objects, she slapped down her hands on them" (*Death* 177). This physicality contrasts starkly with the self-conscious sobriety and sterile delicacy of Windsor Terrace. Significantly, Portia returns from Waikiki to a Windsor Terrace that glistens with Matchett's "thorough" spring cleaning. The mirrors are so clean that their "jet-sharp reflections hurt the eye" as each "polished object stood roundly in the unseeing air" (*Death* 302, 301). Unlike the emotional frankness of Mrs. Heccomb, Daphne, and Waikiki, everything in this house is designed to deflect feeling. At Waikiki, however, feeling is not smelled but seen. This seeing represents the same objective style of recording that characterizes Portia's diary. To see "how everyone feels" means that she empathizes impersonally by attending to the surface of things in an acute style of perception that does not magnify her own personality or intrude upon the depths of other beings (*Death* 249).

Of course, Anna finds this perceptiveness highly disconcerting. Consequently, whatever empathy the chalk drawing or the tea tray creates between the two women regresses into mutual anxiety. By the end of the scene, Portia feels "blotted out from the room, as little present in it as these two others truly felt her to be" (*Death* 337). Rather than learn from Portia's ability to see, people like Anna, the narrator suggests, fix their senses "on what is possessable" (*Death* 191). Throughout the narrative, the term "possess" adopts multiple meanings and permutations. On one hand, the impersonal transfusion between Anna and Portia transpires when the object world of the tea tray possesses the human world. In this context, "possession" means that the tea tray inhabits or invades another entity as a prosthetic extension of itself. This impersonal overture fuses the objective and subjective worlds, providing a common medium for the transfer of feeling that allows one to see things from the position of others. What we see here is a kind of "possession" that disavows the defensive posturing of personal and private ownership. On the other hand, to fix on what is "possessable" means to retreat or detach from the feeling world into the world of objects as mere accessories, like the handbag that receives so much attention in the text, designed to pacify suffering by eradicating both selfhood and the past. Possessing an object in this manner means to deny it as a route to feeling or empathy, to guard against hallucination by locking it down or intruding upon it, which is most likely why Portia's diary, which evades possession, vexes Anna so intensely. Both forms of possession facilitate a relation to things that denies any cohesive expression of selfhood. While one relation facilitates detachment in the guise of extreme privacy, the other "lays one open to pain," enabling the intersubjective exchange of empathy (*Death* 179).

Bowen's distinction here suggests that objects can always potentially elude attempts to possess them. Furthermore, the text indicates that submission to the objects we defend ourselves against often forms our only route to feeling. Portia's attraction to Anna's picture and Anna's corresponding detachment from the past retrieves the impersonal from a purely aesthetic sphere and reroutes it into Portia's need for emotional connection and engagement within domestic space. In emphasizing this intimate relationship, *The Death of the Heart* defines the object in terms of its ability to produce empathic connections that actively define the interior dimensions of human life. Connections to objects unfetter the world of human interiority, of emotion, empathy, and feeling. This empathy contrasts with the pejorative version Worringer elaborates, where the critic faults the European viewer who too confidently empathizes himself into art, or the sensuous forms around one, as if it reflects his own life. Rather, this form of empathy aligns itself with an abstracted existence characterized by an impulse to self-alienation. For Portia, this self-alienation often comprises her most productive and confident relationship with objects, such that, in *The Death of the Heart*, empathy does not oppose abstraction but complements it. In the ideal empathic exchange, the subject does not contribute something extra or "supplementary" to the object as Worringer suggests. Rather, the object dissects, opens up the subject, abstracting her into its own objective world. The object itself, not the subject, facilitates the "relationship of confidence between man and the external world" that Worringer quite negatively attributes to empathy (*Abstraction* 45). Yet Portia, constantly unseen and vigilantly all seeing, often fails to develop this confidence, particularly in relation to the world the Quaynes have provided.

Ultimately, both Bowen's novel and Moretti's ruminations on the *Bildungsroman* suggest that the confident domestication of aesthetic experience relies on the private possession of things as means of amplifying the personality. However, as Anna's obsession with the diary suggests, this relation is never secure; objects can always potentially elude attempts to possess or control them. Consequently, the text indicates that submission to the objects we defend ourselves against often forms our only route to feeling. *The Death of the Heart* presents the object ideally in terms of its ability to produce the sorts of connections and engagements that actively define the interior dimensions of human life as opposed to the conventional *Bildungsroman*, where objects serve as a utilitarian route to social distinction and personality. Connections to objects unfetter the world of human interiority, of emotion, empathy, and feeling, qualities that are often at odds with the more cohesive ideal of personality. Unfortunately for Portia, many of her most productive relationships with objects occur at the price of a self-alienation in which she is unable to establish confidence with the larger world of social expectations.

Because of this distrust, Portia's *bildung* does not succeed. To return to both Moretti's and Bowen's explicit terminology, Portia never achieves the level of familiarity or confidence with the small world required to integrate bourgeois domestic experience into a "personality." In contrast, the more radical relationships Portia inhabits with the things in her life dissolve the personality. This ethical distrust of personality parallels the doubts about "character" Bowen articulates in *Pictures and Conversations*, that artificial outline that gives the natural "amorphousness" of human beings "shape," the "desideratum: hence the overlordship of characters in novels who have it, over the desirous reader who has it not" (*Pictures* 59). We can extrapolate that this "shape" appears only in a make believe world where individual aspirations directly synthesize with bourgeois sensibility, and where the personality enlarges itself in its ability to appropriate the world around it. In contrast, Portia's portable property further reconfigures the classical *Bildungsroman* by attaching itself to a person, not a locale. More at home in the depersonalized space of the hotel, portable property trivializes the ego-invested life of the "small world" by refusing to domesticate or privatize aesthetic experience, which explains why Portia's behavior menaces the Quaynes so intensely. At school, Portia's teacher ensures her that she can be secure in her right to ownership, that no one will take her bag or her letter, and that she does not have to carry such items guardedly on her person. But Anna's compulsive reading of Portia's diary exposes the hypocrisy of this belief in security. Portia's "hotel habit" of carrying her possessions with her publicly discloses just how inhospitable the Quaynes's "small world" is.

"Things Hidden in a Corner"

Portia's portable property is surprisingly unportable. She hoards impersonal letters and papers, what Anna calls "begging letters" or "quack talks about health," the equivalent of junk mail (*Death* 6). These are letters that could be addressed to anyone, the kind that Anna and Thomas would normally throw away. Likewise, Portia owns hundreds of miniature hand-carved bears from Switzerland, which she has temporarily placed in "arrangements" on her mantelpiece (*Death* 27). Fearing that they collect dust, Anna disregards them as problematic distractions from the ease and cleanliness of the bedroom she has so carefully designed. While Matchett attempts to defend Portia's "bears' party" as her "arrangements" or "Miss Portia's hobbies," the situation is, according to Anna, "shocking" (*Death* 27, 6). Portia's taste in decoration is surprisingly unmodern, yet it details a very modern spatial predicament that reveals much about what she needs from space. Bachelard devotes a chapter of *The Poetics of Space* to such miniatures, which, he argues, illustrate a particular style of establishing intimacy with the external world. The miniature, he argues, represents for the dreamer a distanced vantage point that symbolizes for her a nest or a home: "Distance disperses nothing but, on the contrary, composes a miniature of a country in which we should like to live. In distant miniatures, disparate things become reconciled. They then offer themselves for our "possession," while denying the distance that created them. We possess from afar, and how peacefully" (*Poetics* 172). In this kind of relationship, which also offers a rather interesting example of Worringer's "abstraction," the subject becomes immobile, "confined," or reduced through its identification with a thing of miniature proportions (*Poetics* 172). Given this model of identification, Portia's attachment to her "hundreds" of bears is impersonal; though she is actually able to "possess" the bears, such ownership does not engorge the personality but instead alters, even shrinks, its parameters. In this way, Portia can idealize the bears as an inviting society and space of habitation. By offering these items friendship, she gives each object, to borrow from Bachelard, "more poetic space than it has objectivity" (*Poetics* 202). In other words, Portia's idealization of the bears expands intimate space as it disperses her own ego. In Bachelard's terms, poetic space refers to a diffuse space where subject and object intertwine. In *The Death of the Heart*, this kind of space presents an alternative to the domestication of aesthetic experience demanded by the conventional *Bildung*. However, whereas the conventional *Bildungsroman* domesticates aesthetic experience as part of the ideal growth and solidification of the ego and personality, the poetic space Portia creates dissolves the self in a more subtle fusion with the surrounding environment—the world at large. While both positions entail a synthesis between private and public, inner and outer worlds, they ultimately achieve different ends: the externalization of the personality and, conversely, its diminishment.

To some extent, Portia's identification with things in miniature, this impersonal shrinking of herself, is less than ideal, engendering its own set of problems. In keeping with the odd contradictions of Portia's portable property, her identification with this society in miniature guides her steps into a bounded tininess that solidifies the immobility or fixedness she has never been able to experience in her life of public displacement.

Paradoxically, her portable miniature property teaches her to inhabit space in a way that reconciles the disparate elements of her existence: the claustrophobic narrowness of habitation and the immensity of freedom as learned from her nomadic hotel life. However, as the rather dismal ending of the novel indicates, this relation toward things deviates too seriously from the norms of bourgeois legitimacy, affording her no right to a verifiable public existence.

Nonetheless, this impersonal style of possession, in which distance disperses the personality, redraws the conventional *Bildungsroman* by altering the values it places on spatiality, ownership, and domestic comfort. To return to Bachelard, Portia's identification with objects resembles that of small children who hide in corners; those who are "prepared to go beyond the spider, the lady-bug and the mouse, to a point of identification with things forgotten in a corner" meditate on the neglected, the abandoned, the "insignificant," the "poor dead little things" that create a past (*Poetics* 142). These things, for Anna and Thomas Quayne, are not worth owning and thus become, like Portia, dispossessed, "drifting objects"—junk or trash, piles of paper, detritus (*Death* 390). This object position is too foreign for the tight order of Windsor Terrace, which ejects her fiercely from its boundaries and sends her tumbling back to the unbounded expansiveness of hotel life. Seriously dismayed by St. Quentin's revelation regarding Anna's reading of her diary, Portia, plagued by the excessive mobility that characterizes many of Bowen's other characters, crosses London in a series of taxi rides, including one with Eddie where she ends up in his rather squalid flat. The interior, "in keeping with the bleakness of college rooms—the unadult taste, the lack of feeling bred by large stark objects, tables and cupboards, that one does not possess," offers little comfort, and neither does Eddie (*Death* 264). In distress, she then seeks out her unfashionable and unwitting friend Major Brutt, whom the Quaynes would like to scrap much like herself (*Death* 365). Major Brutt's abode, the Karachi Hotel, where the "public rooms are lofty and large in a diluted way," is an odd space of comfort for Portia (*Death* 374). It does offer familiarity, a way to relive the only life of love she has known. These rooms hold "extensive vacuity, nothing so nobly positive as space" (*Death* 374). Space, in its very definition, makes way for an intimate life that cannot transpire in the Karachi hotel.

As illustrated in the movement from the private space of Windsor Terrace to the vacuous immensity of the Karachi Hotel, the deformation of space, or "the means whereby the positions of things become possible," underlines the failure of Portia's *Bildung* as a phenomenological predicament (*Phenomenology* 243). As Merleau-Ponty observes, "[s]pace is not the setting . . . in which things are arranged" but what makes the arrangement of things possible, "the universal power enabling them to be connected" (*Phenomenology* 243). In her room, Portia may be able to form her hundreds of miniature bears into "arrangements" (*Death* 27). She may also be able to leave her *escritoire* unlocked and disorderly, because the meaning of space itself presumes a degree of discretion and privacy, of boundary. In the Karachi Hotel, however, nothing is private, and the "thinness of these bedroom partitions make love or talk indiscreet" (*Death* 375). The extreme solubility of such an environment, a counterpoint to the acute privacy of Windsor Terrace, offers neither room nor time for things to position themselves and thus denies the possibility of space. Portia appears detached, "like some drifting object that has been lodged for a moment . . . but must be dislodged again and go on twirling down the implacable stream" (*Death* 390). Making herself at home in the hotel room, "she seemed at once to shelter, to plant here and to obliterate herself—most of all the last" (*Death* 388). Portia's annihilation of her own body further catalyzes the breakdown of spatial sensibility and positioning and, finally, the disintegration of whatever "personality" she possesses as a character. To develop into a real literary character, to "take shape," as Bowen puts it, Portia must actually live somewhere (*Pictures* 59). However, Portia, an orphan girl who has never possessed anything so significant as a home, cannot satisfy her *bildung*'s demand that she position herself within a space of familiarity, that she synthesize the competing dimensions of her own private development with the public demands of personality and socialization. Since anyone could have stayed in any of Portia's hotel rooms, she can never build a private and unique attachment to her surroundings. Consequently, at the end of the novel, Matchett arrives to rescue Portia from the hotel with little regard for discretion: "Ignoring the bell, because this place was public, she pushed on the brass knob with an air of authority" (*Death* 418). Like Paul Morel at the end of Lawrence's *Sons and Lovers*, Portia has taken on an overtly impersonal, public identity, which, devoid of personality, can no longer be claimed as her own. She will not return to a home but to the mobile world of the taxi and the surrogate parent, Matchett. In making this excessively mobile identification, she loses all the boundedness that makes her recognizable. That is, her impersonal amorphousness renders her so far from a complete character that she holds only the status of a narrative experiment.

 This self-conscious exploration and commentary on narrative links Bowen's work, like Lawrence's, to that of other modernists, as the conflicts embedded in *The Death of the Heart* reflect the antagonism between the private dimensions of Portia's self-formation—of the subjective, inner world Ellmann posits as an identifying feature of modernist texts—and her ability to express them within in a public, "realist," narrative governed by bourgeois aspirations. It is also here where Bowen's text acts as a failed *Bildungsroman* through a dystopic ending that negatively gestures at an ideal world where private particularity and eccentricity finds some sort of compatibility with the values of socialization. That is, Portia's failure of habitation amounts to the literal failure of her narrative. This collapse is consequently a critique of personality as such and its necessity as a literary end. For Portia, personality, the ideal synthesis of private aspiration with public presentation, is in reality a discord that damns her to homelessness and the comfort of small things, quite literally very small things. In detailing these minute, often portable and impersonal attachments—which, for Portia, are an essential part of self-formation and the emotional habitation of space—*The Death of the Heart* spends considerable amounts of time distinguishing the affective solubility of productive boundary setting—of an ethical impersonality—from both detached, ego-intensive modes of personal ownership and an equally detached and deracinated anonymity. Bowen's narrative eye does not simply gravitate toward consciousness as such, in the obsession with characters' inner worlds that Ellmann attributes to Woolf's fiction, nor does it position the material world defensively against an engulfing consciousness. Yet Portia's failure as a personality also signals the breakdown of this end, and the experimental factor of Bowen's novel lies in the way it gestures at such a project as an ideal that clearly cannot be sustained by the present limitations of literary form. However, in what is perhaps its most controversial and radical claim, Bowen's text announces the possibility of a more fluid medium that disables a realist/modernist binary Ellmann's analysis posits by retaining some category, however qualified, of personal and private ownership. This sense of ownership, however, does not refer to Portia's possession of objects but to the friendship she gives them, as it restores the dignity of the object and endows it with the sense of belonging that Portia does not possess at the end of the novel. Through this ethic of impersonal attachment, Bowen offers a model that, like the classical *Bildungsroman*, synthesizes private and public dimensions of self-formation. However, in a direct political affront to that model, this version does not invest itself in the construction of the individual personality but rather recasts it to discover novel modes of building relations within all dimensions of the object world.

Conclusion

Emotion after *The Death of the Heart*

"Oh, one forgets, you know. One can always patch oneself up."
". . . Is this being grown up?"

—Elizabeth Bowen[1]

"Something has gone inside me. My heart, I think."

—Elizabeth Bowen

In *The House in Paris*, the youthful protagonist, Henrietta, recounts her older sister's response to losing her heart. Despite the failed love affair, the girl goes on to marry someone else and, as Henrietta attests, "[o]n no other occasion did she speak of her heart."[2] In this case, marriage, meaning maturity, marks the death of the heart. Henrietta, however, seems unable to fully register this claim, confused as she is about the ontological status of hearts: "Henrietta knew of the heart as an organ; she privately saw it covered in red plush and believed that it could not break, though it might tear" (*House* 58, 47). *The Death of the Heart* moves this uncertainty perceptibly further. Like objects, hearts are continually broken. Indeed, alarmed by Portia's determined questioning of her own history, Matchett remarks, "Why do *you* want to start breaking your heart?" (italics in original; *Death* 99). The assumption here is not only that all adult hearts are already broken but also that engaging one's heart in such matters is useless and impractical. While Matchett implies that Portia's heart is still subject to her own possession, she must eventually lose it, or she will not survive her own development.

Adulthood, as it finalizes the death of the heart, thus accounts for the novel's title; the mature individual will ultimately learn to "patch oneself up" as a means of coming "in league" with "the world" (*Death* 385). Consequently, Irene, Portia's mother, dies at an early age, not only because she cries too much but also because of her heart. Portia's schooling intensifies this problematic heredity, as Irene "would not have dared cross the threshold of this room" (*Death* 68). Irene cannot exist as a character within

Miss Paullie's school for delicate girls since its purpose is proper bourgeois development. That is, there is ultimately no heart in properly bourgeois maturity. There is also no heart in personality. If, in the *Bildungsroman*, the hero acquires personality by taking up the appropriate relation to possessions, this entry into adulthood marks a loss, a dispossession. The heart is the object, much like the junk mail Portia collects, for which the novel of development has no use. In this case, publically sanctioned aspects of self-development trump private ones in the name of personality.

Beyond the evident nature of its publication date, 1938, I conclude this book with the *Death of the Heart* because of the texts I have addressed it most reflexively elaborates an ethics of impersonality. Ultimately, however, Bowen's novel metacritically suggests that the impersonal value system it prizes in Portia's character, based on an empathic relationship to things that respects the boundaries between subject and object, cannot survive the intrusions of conventional narrative form. In fact, Portia's impersonality goes awry, and her own organizational relationship to the world folds. Such is the more general problem of modernist impersonality I have outlined here, an aesthetic that seeks to manage the distance between subject and object by emptying them of content, forging an affective but antipsychological form of exteriority, where "experiences are not 'recollected'" and "emotion" is neither "conscious" nor "express[ed]."[3] In this relationship, the subject does not psychologically project herself onto the object. Rather, to borrow from Jacqueline Rose's analysis of Mary Butts and Elizabeth Bowen, the subject invests the object "with power" in a way that "is the opposite of investing [it] with meaning."[4] Without hermeneutic dimension and content, space flattens and organization diminishes. The "consequence" of this arrangement, Rose observes, "is disturbing . . . anything becomes possible as soon as you believe that objects have a life of their own" (*ON* 98).

On one hand, objects in this scenario are likely to get lost, as in the fates of Portia in *The Death of the Heart* and Paul Morel in *Sons and Lovers*. These texts, as with H.D.'s *Sea Garden*, Virginia Woolf's "Street Haunting: A London Adventure," and Mary Butts's stories in *From Altar to Chimney Piece*, deliberately explore the problems that result from impersonality as a progressive yet powerful tool of psychological and spatial reorientation. On the other hand, however, the spatial scenario Rose identifies illustrates the phenomenological position I have outlined in this book. As an aesthetic, impersonality diminishes the authority of the subject by reorienting space beyond its subjective organization, beyond its connection—to borrow once more from T. E. Hulme—to that "bastard thing Personality, and all the bunkum that follows from it."[5] From a phenomenological perspective, the personality against which Hulme and other modernists rallied is organized around the "geometrism" from which Bachelard urges us to free ourselves—the conventional Cartesian relationship between "inside and outside," subject and object, mind and body—as a means of experiencing the "finesses of . . . intimacy."[6] Both Bachelard and Merleau-Ponty have illustrated how this geometrism supports a subjectively oriented space. The latter in particular faults language, particularly prepositions such as "against," "on," "under," or "beside," which describe the spatial or temporal location of the object relative to the subject.[7] Such words reinforce "anthropological association[s]," which privilege the space one's body occupies, one's "bodily space," over "objective spatiality" (*Phenomenology* 101). However, the philosopher also observes that reorienting space beyond "anthropological association" would give the body no meaning of its own, because the body's particular content would be "subsumed" under the "form" of "objective spatiality" (*Phenomenology* 102).

Given this theoretical model, we can see what happens to characters in novels such as *Sons and Lovers* and *The Death of the Heart* when an impersonal, "objective spatiality" claims too much in the way of literary form and content. While Lawrence, in *Sons of Lovers*, deflates the idea of a humanist subject open to hermeneutic interpretation, the temporal and spatial alienation Paul Morel experiences at the novel's end promises no viable alternative to this dilemma. Similarly, in *The Death of the Heart*, Portia's literal disembodiment leaves her with no veritable placement in either social or narrative space. These texts then deliberately explore the problem of an impersonality that goes too far, ultimately obliterating organization and form. As I have suggested, however, phenomenology provides both a model for this problem and its solution. Merleau-Ponty suggests that subjectively and objectively oriented space need not oppose each other; objective space can manifest the meaning of a more subjectively oriented space much in the way form manifests the meaning of content. Form need not merely eclipse content as in the way the impersonal form of the novels I have discussed in the book efface their major characters. Rather, content supplies form with meaning, such that "bodily space"—or subjectively oriented space—and objective space form a "practical system." Indeed, the individual object "*come[s] to light*" against the "background" of external or objective space (italics in original; *Phenomenology* 102). Without the form-giving characteristic of space, the object or body would not be intelligible. At the same time, without the body, or subjective space, there would be no space.

Merleau-Ponty's account of space as it makes the other intelligible through a flattened "point-horizon structure" allows us to theorize impersonality in its most positive, reparative sense (*Phenomenology* 102). That is, through the philosopher's particular conception of the relation between content and form—bodily or subjective space and external or objective space—we can return to the beginning of this book and Eliot's objection to "individual talent." As I have argued, Eliot theorizes the relationship between the individual and tradition, or content and form, as a spatial phenomenon. The "new work of art" alters the "existing monuments" and "so the relations, proportions, and values of each work of art toward the whole are readjusted" (*Prose* 38). According to the spatial and temporal logic of Eliot's impersonality, individual works of art are objects, or "monuments." Such monuments take on significance by virtue of their order, or tradition. This "ideal order" does not simply represent an authoritarian hypochondria engendered by the fear of an engulfing and messy emotionality, nor is it merely a call for the erasure of the individual at the hands of tradition. Rather, we might consider these oft-quoted lines from "Tradition and the Individual Talent" as an antihumanist, phenomenological discourse on the relation between content and form, the individual and tradition. As a dialectical structure that presumes an objectively oriented space, Eliot's impersonality does not seek to erase the individual but instead offers one its protection. The organization it demands guards against the perils of impersonality that may go too far, obliterating the content of the other in its quest for universality of form.

According to the interpretation I am proposing, as a theoretical model, the meaning of impersonality exceeds its connection to acts of authority, which ultimately orient space anthropologically around a top and a bottom, a dominant and passive agent. This version of impersonality allows us to move beyond the grammar of the preposition, where positionality is understood in relation to the dominance of the subject. While many of the authors and texts I discuss in this book dissolve "oriented-space" only to reinstitute this spatial structure of power, impersonality, in its most ethical form, offers the potential of making the other intelligible beyond the scope of shared, personal experience or bodily, subjective space. Not only does the ideal impersonality reaffirm the presence of this other, but it also offers protection, such that the heart does not die in the path of personal development.

This relationship is, in keeping with most of the logic surrounding impersonality, contradictory. That is, how does an aesthetic of exteriority, which seeks to empty the subject of its depth, or hermeneutical content, preserve its heart? Rei Terada's important work *Feeling in Theory: Emotion after the "Death of the Subject"* offers an answer to these questions, challenging the charge that poststructuralist thought, which posits the death of the subject, also entails the death of feeling. She argues instead that the whole history of emotion is in effect responsible for fracturing the subject. The question is not whether emotions "are proof of the human subject" or whether they exist after the "death of the subject" but how they "entail . . . this death."[8] Certainly, modernists were thinking about this function of emotion long before the "post-structuralist dissatisfaction with the subject" (*Feeling* 4). For modernists such as Woolf, Eliot, Gaudier-Brzeska, H.D., Butts, Lawrence, and Bowen, emotion "*requires* the death of the subject" (my italics; *Feeling* 4). Woolf, for example, in "On Not Knowing Greek," praises the immediate, "lightning-quick, sneering," and "violent" nature of classical emotions.[9] In an impersonal synthesis, similar to that Eliot proposes between form and content in "Tradition and the Individual Talent," emotions exist amid a literal chorus of "undifferentiated voices" at the same time that they become "tightly bound" in individual figures (*CR* 29, 26). Ultimately, this analysis of classical emotion propels Woolf's critique of a modernity that has lost its heart:

> For [the Greeks] there were no Beauties of Hardy, Beauties of Meredith, Sayings from George Eliot. The writer had to think more of the whole and less of the detail. Naturally, living in the open, it was not the lip or the eye that struck them, but the carriage of the body and the proportions of its parts. Thus when we quote and extract we do the Greeks more damage than we do the English. There is bareness and abruptness in their literature which grates upon a taste accustomed to the intricacies of printed books. We have to stretch our minds to grasp a whole devoid of the prettiness of detail or the emphasis of eloquence. Accustomed to look directly and largely rather than minutely and aslant, it was safe for them to step into the thick of emotions which blind and bewilder an age like our own. In the vast catastrophe of the European war our emotions had to be broken up for us, and put at an angle from us, before we could allow ourselves to feel them in poetry or fiction. The only poets who spoke to the purpose spoke in the sidelong, satiric manner of Wilfred Owen and Siegfried Sassoon. It was not possible for them to be direct without being clumsy; or to speak simply of emotion without being sentimental. But the Greeks could say, as if for the first time, 'Yet being dead they have not died.' They could say, 'If to die nobly is the chief part of excellence, to us out of all men Fortune gave this lot; for hastening to set a crown of freedom on Greece we lie possessed of praise that grows not old.' They could march straight up, with their eyes open; and thus fearlessly approached, emotions stand still and suffer themselves to be looked at. (*CR* 34)

Woolf suggests here that in the wake of the First World War, our relations to emotions changed. Too wounded to approach emotions head on, the modern subject understands emotions as they are "broken up," as matters of hermeneutic inquiry to be examined "minutely and aslant." The contradictions of this security, where avoidance and detachment unite with sentimental attentiveness to detail and privileges content over form, expression and interpretation over being, have created both a literature and a modern subject that is no longer able to feel. While Woolf emphasizes the violent, explosive nature of classical emotion in earlier portions of the essay, she does not indicate that this version of emotion is less empathic, less capable of healing and nurture. Indeed, "it is to the Greeks that we turn when we are sick of the vagueness, of the confusion of Christianity and its consolations, of our own age" (*CR* 38). In contrast to our confusion, the Greeks feel "safe" as they "step into the thick of emotions which blind and bewilder an age like our own" (*CR* 34).

Significantly, detachment does not characterize this "impersonal literature," where one does not avoid emotions but "step[s] into them" (*CR* 23, 34). Emotions are not passive objects to be "recollected" and "express[ed]," to return to Eliot, nor do they happen "consciously or of deliberation" (*Prose* 43). Rather, they actively "stand still and suffer themselves to be looked at" (*CR* 34). This understanding of emotion as visible surface, as object, definitively effaces the subject as the repository of individual emotion. Such an impersonal exteriority, which positions emotion beyond psychology, allowed modernists, however problematically, to address the shallow promises of a depersonalized modernity that posited the "personality" as proof of democratic progress and self-advancement. It also surfaces as a critique of the contradictory individualistic response to the deracinating forms of mobility that emerge in a modernity torn by war, a reaction that nostalgically valued the fixed self and personality at the expense of true affective and emotional bonds. That is, impersonality does not actualize a "fall" into "fluid indeterminacy" and "featureless[ness]" as critics have claimed.[10] Rather, as Woolf's "On Not Knowing Greek" suggests, impersonality describes a highly organized aesthetic practice and ethos that promotes collectivity of feeling in its focus on the immediate and exterior presence of emotion. In terms of its contemporary inheritance, impersonality not only enables us to imagine emotion beyond the death of the subject; it also offers avenues for forming collective political attachments that deflate social asymmetry and move beyond the straight, "anthropological associations" of the humanist subject (*Phenomenology* 101). As an alternative to identity politics, this model preserves the particular organization of difference as it imagines community beyond the claims of personal identity and experience.

Notes

Introduction

1. See Wyndham Lewis, *The Art of Being Ruled* (Santa Rosa: Black Sparrow Press, 1989), 148, hereafter referred to as *Art*.
2. See Edward Comentale, *Modernism, Cultural Production, and the British Avant-Garde* (Cambridge: Cambridge UP, 2004), 9, hereafter abbreviated as *MCP*. Comentale identifies this double bind as it appears in the journal edited by Lewis, *Blast* (1913), a "defensive aesthetic manifesto, a pre-war nationalist's creed, and a bold economic critique" (9). He further argues that Lewis mourns the loss of a true aesthetic individualism in exchange for the vulgar and cheap one that parades in the name of individual creation. As an alternative, Comentale continues, Lewis imagines the individual as "forged" through the mass, privileging "chemists, mechanics, and hairdressers because they use their skills to order and define otherwise unruly material" (10). Similarly, for Lewis the true artist is able to mold and organize the physical excesses of the world around him.
3. I take this quotation from Lewis's essay "The Non-Impersonality of Science" in *The Art of Being Ruled*, where Lewis critiques the "delusion of impersonality," noting the difference between false presentations of the concept and the real thing: "A simple belief in the 'detachment' and 'objectivity' of science, the anxiety of a disillusioned person to escape from his self and merge his personality in *things*; verging often on the worship of *things*—of the non-human, feelingless, and thoughtless" (34–35). In a swift rhetorical move at the end of the essay, Lewis connects this delusion to more organized political ideologies, which he evaluates as follows: "I am not a communist; if anything, I favour some form of *fascism* rather than communism. Nevertheless, when two principles are opposed, and one of these is that of English liberalism, in most cases I should find myself on the other side, I expect" (35).
4. See Sharon Cameron, *Impersonality: Seven Essays* (Chicago: U of Chicago P, 2007), 12, hereafter referred to as *Impersonality*.
5. I will return repeatedly to Eliot's famous assessment of impersonality in "Tradition and the Individual Talent": "What happens is a continual surrender of himself as he is at the moment to something more valuable. The progress of an artist is a continual self-sacrifice, a continual extinction of personality." See *Selected Prose of T. S. Eliot* (New York: Harcourt, 1975), 40, hereafter abbreviated as *Prose*.
6. In "Tradition and the Individual Talent," Eliot immediately dismisses tradition as a purely chronological exchange, rescuing it from the charge of being

entirely repetitive or imitative, with no place for "novelty": "Yet if only the form of tradition, of handing down, consisted in following the ways of the immediate generation before us in a blind or timid adherence to its successes, 'tradition' should be positively be discouraged" (*Prose* 38).

7. See Maud Ellmann, *The Poetics of Impersonality: T. S. Eliot and Ezra Pound* (Cambridge: Harvard UP, 1987), 5, hereafter referred to as *Poetics*.
8. "The Love Song of J. Alfred Prufrock" appears in T. S. Eliot's *Selected Poems* (New York: Harvest, 1930), 15, hereafter referred to as "Prufrock."
9. See Dean's essay "T. S. Eliot: Famous Clairvoyante," in *Gender, Sexuality and Desire in T. S. Eliot*, ed. Cassandra Laity and Nancy K. Gish (Cambridge: Cambridge UP, 2004) 45, 51, 43–65, hereafter referred to as "T. S. Eliot."
10. See Judith Brown, *Glamour in Six Dimensions: Modernism and the Radiance of Form* (Ithaca: Cornell UP, 2009), 8, hereafter referred to as *Glamour*.
11. See Daniel Albright, *Personality and Impersonality: Lawrence, Woolf, and Mann* (Chicago: U of Chicago P, 1978), 31, hereafter referred to as *Personality*. Albright's implicit claim in this book carries over to his reading of genre in relation to modernist impersonality. Whereas poetry rightfully claims its role in modernism as impersonal and objective, the logic behind Albright's argument is that prose can never do the same, which is why this book looks beyond poetry to the novels of Mary Butts, D. H. Lawrence, and Elizabeth Bowen in examining the dynamics of impersonality.
12. See Michael Levenson, *A Genealogy of Modernism: A Study of English Literary Doctrine, 1908–1922* (Cambridge: Cambridge UP, 1984), 133, hereafter referred to as *Genealogy*.
13. Aside from "The Contemporary Man 'Expresses His Personality,'" examples of Lewis's explicit concern with "personality" and "impersonality" from *The Art of Being Ruled* include "The Non-Impersonality of Science" and "The Piecemealing of the Personality" along with other essays, such as "What the Anonymity of Science Covers" and "People's Happiness Found in Type-Life."
14. See Jameson's *A Singular Modernity: Essay on the Ontology of the Present* (New York: Verso, 2002), 54. Jameson identifies the individual as a key feature in the "classical celebration of modernity," which promotes individuality as an "illicit representation of consciousness as such" (54). Jameson's maxim, and what appears to be that of both Eliot and Lewis, is that "the narrative of modernity cannot be organized" around such categories of consciousness, subjectivity, and individualism (55). In mounting a tradition that is not organized around subjectivity, Eliot further subverts the rhetoric of humanism by fracturing the very ideal of modernity that grounds Jameson's critique: one that builds subjectivity around an imagined and nostalgic relation to the past.
15. See M. Merleau-Ponty, *The Phenomenology of Perception*, trans. Colin Smith (London: Routledge, 1962), 101, hereafter referred to as *Phenomenology*.
16. See T. E. Hulme, *Speculations: Essays on Humanism and the Philosophy of Art*, ed. Herbert Read (London: Routledge, 1965), 61, 5, hereafter referred to as *Speculations*.

17. See Scott Herring, *Queering the Underworld: Slumming, Literature, and the Undoing of Lesbian and Gay History* (Chicago: U of Chicago P, 2007), 22. Herring's explicit use of the word "queer" as it relates to modernist texts by Djuna Barnes, Jane Addams, and Willa Cather reinforces my own understanding of impersonality as it problematizes conventional forms of reading, interiority, and visibility.
18. See Tim Dean, *Beyond Sexuality* (Chicago: U of Chicago P, 2000), 155, hereafter referred to as *Beyond*. See also Gabriel Rotello's *Sexual Ecology: AIDS and the Destiny of Gay Men* (New York: Plume, 1998). Dean appropriates Rotello's notion of relationality as ecosystem to describe the symbolic order as composed of "different networks of signifiers that enmesh us as we move around" (154). This ecological perspective enables Dean's critique of the ways in which the symbolic order has been understood as a "purely linguistic register" (155). Similarly, Sarah Ahmed's *Queer Phenomenology: Orientations, Objects, Others* (Durham: Duke UP, 2006), following Merleau-Ponty's *The Phenomenology of Perception*, links the vertical to a "straighten[ed]" form or perception that overcomes the "queer effect" of objects that appear "off center" or "slantwise" (66).
19. See Eve Sedgwick, *Touching Feeling: Affect, Pedagogy, Performativity* (Durham: Duke UP, 2003), 9.
20. See Colleen Lamos, *Deviant Modernism: Sexual and Textual Errancy in T. S. Eliot, James Joyce and Marcel Proust* (Cambridge: Cambridge UP, 1998), 5, hereafter referred to as *Errancy*. Lamos argues in particular of Eliot's essay on Tennyson's *In Memoriam* that despite Eliot's apparent "antipathy" toward "inversion," he also embraced as "non-pathological forms of male love" where the "zeal to write originates in a yearning toward imitative identification with the elder poet, and even, in the desire for possessive appropriation, to take hold of, and overcome him" (34). The same relationship could perhaps apply to Eliot's call for the extinction of the personality in "Tradition and the Individual Talent."
21. This interrogation is the point of Heather Love's *Feeling Backward: Loss and the Politics of Queer History* (Cambridge: Harvard UP, 2007), which trades the idea of an expressive emotional subject from whom "feeling flows" for "structures of feeling," defined by Raymond Williams as a "practical consciousness of a present kind, in a living and interrelating continuity" (quoted on 11).
22. See Martin Jay, "Modernism and the Spectre of Psychologism," *Modernism/Modernity* 3.2 (1996): 93, 98, hereafter abbreviated as "MSP."
23. See Charles Altieri, "Theorizing Emotions in Eliot's Poetry and Poetics," in *Gender, Sexuality, and Desire in T. S. Eliot*, ed. Cassandra Laity and Nancy K. Gish (Cambridge: Cambridge UP, 2004), 151, hereafter referred to as "Theorizing."
24. See Pound's essay, "Affirmations: IV. As for Imagism," *The New Age* 16 (1915): 350; quoted by Ellmann, 168.
25. According to Pound's *A Memoir of Gaudier-Brzeska* (New York: New Directions, 1970), a vortex is something "through which, and into which, ideas are constantly rushing" (92). Even more famously, Pound calls the vortex a

"radiant node or cluster" (92), or "art before it has spread itself into flacidity, into elaboration and secondary applications" (88).
26. Yeats's "A Packet for Ezra Pound" was written as the preface for his elaborate treatise on the mystical, *A Vision* (New York: Macmillan, 1937), hereafter referred to as "Packet." "A General Introduction for My Work" and "Magic" appear in *Essays and Introductions* (London: Macmillan, 1961), pages 509–26 and 28–52, respectively.
27. See Christopher Reed's introduction to *Not at Home: The Suppression of Domesticity in Modern Art and Architecture* (London: Thames and Hudson, 1996), 9.
28. Mary Butts, *The Death of Felicity Taverner*, in *The Taverner Novels* (Kingston, NY: McPherson, 1992), 169.

Chapter 1

1. See Simmel's essay "The Stranger" in *The Sociology of Georg Simmel*, trans. and ed. Kurt H. Woolf (New York: Free Press, 1950), 402, hereafter referred to as *Sociology*.
2. See *Selected Prose of T. S. Eliot* (New York: Harcourt, 1975), 38, hereafter abbreviated as *Prose*.
3. See "Types of Social Relationships by Degrees of Reciprocal Knowledge of Their Participants" in *The Sociology of Georg Simmel*, 321.
4. See Wyndham Lewis, *The Art of Being Ruled* (Santa Rosa, CA: Black Sparrow Press, 1989), 148, hereafter referred to as *Art*.
5. See T. E. Hulme, *Speculations: Essays on Humanism and the Philosophy of Art*, ed. Herbert Read (London: Routledge, 1965), 33, hereafter referred to as *Speculations*.
6. See Warren Susman, "'Personality' and the Making of Twentieth-Century Culture," in *New Directions in American Intellectual History*, ed. John Higham and Paul K Conkin (London: Johns Hopkins UP, 1979), 218. The piece originally appeared in Susman's *Culture as History: The Transformation of American Society in the Twentieth-Century* (New York: Pantheon, 1984).
7. See Samuel Smiles, *Self-Help* (London: IEA Health and Welfare Unit, 1996). The precursor to the contemporary self-help genre, *Self-Help* advocated thrift and hard work in the self-realization of Britain's working and lower-middle class.
8. See Sharon Cameron, *Impersonality: Seven Essays* (Chicago: U of Chicago P, 2007), viii, hereafter referred to as *Impersonality*.
9. See Simmel's essay "Secrecy" in *The Sociology of Georg Simmel*, 330–344.
10. For more about Miss Beauchamp, see Morton Prince, *The Dissociation of Personality* (New York: Longmans, Green, 1910), hereafter referred to as *Dissociation*. Interestingly, Prince relates the peculiarities of Miss Beauchamp's fragile personality to her "delicacy of sentiment," an index of how impersonality might inscribe the sentimental. See also Prince's *Clinical and Experimental Studies in Personality* (Boston: Independent Press, 1929).

11. See F. W. H. Myers, *Human Personality and Its Survival of Bodily Death* (Charlottesville, VA: Hampton Roads, 2001), 47, italics in original, hereafter abbreviated as *HP*. Richard Noakes explains how "psychical research" came to be distinguished from other scientific practices as a pseudoscience, specifically because of its interest in the paranormal, mesmerism, and spiritualism, in "The Historiography of Psychical Research," in *Journal of the Society for Psychical Research* 72.89 (April 2008): 65–85. Regarding Myers's influence on modernists, Carolyn Burke has noted Mina Loy's preoccupation with the researcher's work in *Becoming Modern: The Life of Mina Loy* (Berkeley: U of California P, 1996). As Burke suggests, Myers's interest in clairvoyance, the subliminal self, and its "consolation on spiritual matters" spoke to many modernists, even more so than Freud. Yeats also had been influenced by the Society of Psychical Research, of which Myers was an official. Tim Armstrong, in *Modernism, Technology and the Body* (Cambridge: Cambridge UP, 1998), credits Myers with originating the automatic writing that would later become fashionable among modernist sets, both in *Human Personality* and in his earlier articles from 1885, "Automatic Writing" and "Multiple Personality." As Armstrong observes, automism for Myers is the writing of a subliminal self that is "potentially separable from the body," in other words, prosthetic (188). *Modernism, Technology and the Body* will be hereafter abbreviated *MTB*.
12. See Ian Hacking, *Rewriting the Soul: Multiple Personality and the Sciences of Memory* (Princeton: Princeton UP, 1995), hereafter referred to as *Rewriting*.
13. "The 'Homo' the Child of the 'Suffragette,'" and "The Feminine Conception of Freedom" appear in *The Art of Being Ruled*, 218–20, 239–43.
14. See Wyndham Lewis, *Blast* (Santa Rosa: Black Sparrow Press, 1997), 141, hereafter referred to as *Blast*.
15. One important text, Louis Berman, *The Glands Regulating Personality: A Study of the Glands of Internal Secretion in Relation to the Types of Human Nature* (New York: Macmillan, 1922), links human personality to the functions of the internal organs. In the text, Berman identifies certain complexes of communications between glands and internal secretions as responsible for specific personality types. Dr. Berman even goes so far as to interpret obesity as a manifestation of personality, along with rigorous definitions of femininity, masculinity, and sexuality. He further links types of personality to the prominence of various internal secretions that give rise to certain physiological features. Humorously enough, Oscar Wilde plays a prominent role in Berman's catalogue of facial types and as an example of genius. His "thymocentric" personality and face coincide with his considerable stature, his "great corpulence," his "high complexion," and "flesh and plump hands." Also remarked upon are his "large breasts" and the "exceptional size of his head" (251).
16. Ed Cohen, *Talk on the Wilde Side* (New York: Routledge, 1993) also suggests that the meaning of "personality" in Britain developed in direct relation to Wilde's notoriety. Speaking of the libel proceedings in *Wilde v. Queensberry*, he argues that "the newspapers effectively reproduced the possibility for designating Wilde a kind of sexual actor without referring to the specificity of his

sexual acts, and thereby crystallized a new constellation of sexual meanings predicated upon 'personality' and not practices" (131).
17. See Oscar Wilde, *Decorative Art in America* (New York: Brentano's, 1906).
18. See Oscar Wilde, "The Soul of Man Under Socialism" in *Plays, Prose Writings and Poems* (London: Everyman, 1996) 18, hereafter abbreviated as *Plays*.
19. I refer to these works as they appear in *Plays, Prose Writings and Poems*.
20. See *Modernism, Technology, and the Body*, 3, 100. See also Hal Foster, "Prosthetic Gods," *Modernism/Modernity* 4.2 (April 1997): 5–38. In this special issue of the journal devoted to Wyndham Lewis, Foster's essay cites the influence of Mark Seltzer's work on the double logic of prosthesis as "extension and/or constriction of the body" in both *Bodies and Machines* (New York: Routledge, 1992) and *Serial Killers: Death and Life in America's Wound Culture* (New York: Routledge, 1998) ("Prosthetic Gods" 5).
21. Especially in novels such as *Tarr* (Santa Rosa: Black Sparrow Press, 1996), Lewis tends to pair a fiercely objective narrative voice with depictions of his characters as mechanized objects, where the simple act of rolling a cigarette becomes a technological redefinition of the self. Jessica Burstein's excellent article "Waspish Segments: Lewis, Prosthesis, Fascism," in *Modernism/Modernity* 4.2, discusses these connections, grounding Lewis's prosthetic thinking within the novel literary displays of mutilated bodies occasioned by World War I. Like Armstrong, Burstein argues that the new "prosthetic body . . . succeeds where the previous body failed" (142). In doing so, the prosthetic body both shifts the scale of the standard-type body, as Burstein's analysis of Lewis's novel *Hitler* suggests, and offers a unifying, fascistic vision of a transformed, extended body that functions on another plane altogether. Aside from the evident reputation of her subject Wyndham Lewis, Burstein's article offers little explanation of why this prosthetic logic is inherently conservative or authoritarian.
22. See Le Corbusier, *The Decorative Art of Today*, trans. James I. Dunnett (Cambridge: MIT Press, 1987), xxii, italics in original, hereafter abbreviated as *DAT*. See also Le Corbusier's two volumes *Le Modulor I* and *II* (Basel, Switzerland: Birkhauser Architecture, 2004), published first in 1950 and 1955. Using various illustrations, the books present the system of proportion Le Corbusier devised from 1942–1948, designed both to bridge the metric system and the Anglo-Saxon foot-inch system and to develop a scale of proportion between the ideal man and his architectural environment. Le Corbusier's famous illustration *Modular Man*, following Vitruvius and Leonardo, locates the six-foot tall man as the source of this scale.
23. See Paul Peppis, "'Surrounded by a Multitude of Other Blasts:' Vorticism and the Great War," *Modernism/Modernity* 4.2 (April 1997): 62.
24. See Ezra Pound, *A Memoir of Gaudier-Brzeska* (New York: New Directions, 1970), 29, hereafter referred to as *Memoir*.
25. See Hugh Kenner, *The Pound Era* (Berkeley: U of California P, 1971).

26. See *A Memoir of Gaudier-Brzeska*, 50. Pound also wrote, "A kindly journalist 'hopes' that it does not look like me. It does not. It is infinitely more hieratic. It has infinitely more of strength and dignity than my face will ever possess" (49).
27. See Virginia Woolf, "Street Haunting: A London Adventure," in *Collected Essays: Volume IV* (London: Chatto and Windus, 1967), 155, hereafter referred to as *Collected IV*.
28. It can also be said that as the stranger, Woolf's narrative voice conforms to the conventions of slumming literature Scott Herring identifies in his important study of queer modernist urbanism, *Queering the Underworld: Slumming, Literature, and the Undoing of Lesbian and Gay History* (Chicago: U of Chicago P, 2007). "Street Haunting" questions forms of social and spatial intelligibility; the eye must leave its comfort zone to embrace the "[u]nderworld unknowing" that occurs when spatial codes are reoriented, making "rotten a will-to-knowledge" (*Queering* 23).
29. In *Solid Objects: Modernism and the Test of Production* (Princeton: Princeton UP, 1998), Douglas Mao, focusing specifically on Woolf's *Between the Acts*, identifies a modernism both obsessed with objects and the "'violence' of making" these objects (88). The novel, Mao argues, foregrounds the "aggression" that accompanies acts of human invention (86). More particularly, Woolf's interest in airplanes exemplifies what Mao characterizes as Modernism's concern "with the troubling *extensiveness* of human power and with the likeness between their own operations on their materials and the apparently limitless transformations effected by technology" (italics in original; 11).
30. See chapter 3, "Phenomenology," of Sartre's *Basic Writings*, ed. Stephen Priest (London: Routledge, 2001), 73.
31. See M. Merleau-Ponty, *The Phenomenology of Perception*, trans. Colin Smith (London: Routledge, 1962), 198, hereafter referred to as *Phenomenology*.

Chapter 2

1. See H.D., *Notes on Thought and Vision and The Wise Sappho* (San Francisco: City Lights, 1982), 59; hereafter referred to as *Notes* and *Wise*.
2. See Ezra Pound, *ABC of Reading* (New York: New Directions, 1960), 11, hereafter abbreviated as *ABC*.
3. See *Selected Prose of T. S. Eliot* (New York: Harcourt, 1975), 40, 38, hereafter abbreviated as *Prose*.
4. See H.D., "The Mask and the Movietone," in *Close Up: Cinema and Modernism*, ed. James Donald, Anne Friedberg, and Laura Marcus (London: Cassell, 1999), 115–16, hereafter referred to as "Mask." The essay is the third of a series of essays called *The Cinema and the Classics*, which H.D. wrote for the journal in 1927.
5. See Walter Benjamin, "Art in the Age of Mechanical Reproduction," in *Illuminations*, ed. Hannah Arendt (New York: Schocken, 1968), 231. While Benjamin speaks of a different genre of film, his preoccupations with the "cult of the movie star" are similar to H.D.'s concerns about the welding of voice

and image. The difference is that H.D.'s utopian version of an impersonal cinematic apparatus dissolves the relation Benjamin sees between cinema and personality. For Benjamin, the "separable, transportable" aspects of the film image contribute to cinema's "spell of the personality," whereas H.D. sees these very characteristics as essential for maintaining the integrity of the unwelded image (231). See also Christina Walter, "From Image to Screen: H.D. and the Visual Origins of Modernist Impersonality," *Textual Practice* 22.2 (June 2008): 291–313. Walter comments more extensively on H.D.'s film criticism, arguing that H.D. imagines an ideal spectator—distinct from the average moviegoer—who views the "filmic image" not as a "transparent mirror of reality," but as a "mediated creation and projection." The result is a state of hypnosis that allows the spectator access to the "unconscious mindbody systems that produced that state" (303).

6. Lawrence Rainey's *Institutions of Modernism: Literary Elites and Public Culture* (New Haven: Yale UP, 1999) has challenged feminist critics of the 1980s for their role in fabricating a version of H.D. who conforms to their ideals. While this intervention is laudable, Rainey ultimately offers little positive change for H.D. scholarship, particularly in his denouncement of her as a mere "coterie poet," a "distinctly modernist fable," whose dependence on her lover Bryher's lifelong patronage of "endless bounty" contributed to the "vacuity" of her poems (148–49). Offering strictly numerical evidence concerning H.D.'s "miniscule corpus of non-fiction," Rainey, oddly contending that one must have produced large quantities of literary criticism to rightly be considered a modernist, further claims that H.D. vigorously refrained from interactions with a wider public and showed little impetus to "engage in dialogue with contemporaries" (54).

7. See Cassandra Laity, *H.D. and the Victorian Fin de Siècle* (Cambridge: Cambridge UP, 1996), ix, hereafter abbreviated as *HDVF*. See also Eileen Gregory, "Rose Cut in Rock: Sappho and H.D.'s Sea Garden," in *Signets: Reading H.D.*, ed. Rachel Blau Duplesis and Susan Stanford Friedman (Madison: U of Wisconsin P, 1991), 129–54. For Gregory, H.D.'s "familiarization" of her chosen muse, Sappho, positions the modernist poet in opposition to masculine authority by affirming her interest in "women's community and erotic connections" (132).

8. To return to Maud Ellmann's observations in *The Poetics of Impersonality: T. S. Eliot and Ezra Pound* (Cambridge: Harvard UP, 1987), a book that established Eliot and Pound as the conservative spokesmen for the doctrine, the outcome of impersonality was always a conservative "ethics of personality" that served to reinforce the authority of the poet and forge a reactionary link to tradition.

9. See Sharon Cameron, *Impersonality: Seven Essays* (Chicago: U of Chicago P, 2007), 145, hereafter referred to as *Impersonality*.

10. See Daniel Tiffany, *Radio Corpse: Imagism and the Cryptaesthetic of Ezra Pound* (Cambridge: Harvard UP, 1995), 11, hereafter referred to as *Radio*. Furthermore, in *A Memoir of Gaudier-Brzeska* (New York: New Directions, 1970), Pound defines the image as a "radiant node or cluster . . . from which, and

through which, and into which, ideas are constantly rushing" (92). This vortex also corresponds to the process which is particular to the imagist poem: "In a poem of this sort one is trying to record the precise instant when a thing outward and objective transforms itself, or darts into a thing inward and subjective" (89).
11. In "From Image to Screen: H.D. and the Visual Origins of Modernist Impersonality," Christina Walter has argued similarly that the emphasis of H.D.'s "image-driven impersonal aesthetic" is on the "material body," particularly as it participates in early twentieth-century discourses of physiological and optical sciences (291). She credits H.D. with modeling a "broader, visually-shaped style of modernist impersonality" that does not simply dismiss personality, but rather attempts "to understand subjectivity in terms of bodily contingency" (293).
12. See H.D., *Collected Poems*, ed. Louis L. Martz (New York: New Directions, 1983), 5, hereafter abbreviated as *CP*.
13. See Susan Stanford Friedman, *Penelope's Web: Gender, Modernity, H.D.'s Fiction* (Cambridge: Cambridge UP, 2008), 34. Friedman distinguishes the impersonality of H.D.'s poetry and the personal nature of her prose. This contrast, she argues, "privileges poetry over prose, the end over the means to an end, her 'real self' over her 'personal self,' clairvoyance over sensibility, and art over therapy" (34). However correct Stanford Friedman is in identifying some of the programmatic differences between H.D.'s poetry and prose, my own reading of H. D's poetry departs from this account, arguing that the poem itself dialectically deconstitutes and reconstitutes the personal self.
14. In *The Sublime of Intense Sociability* (London: Bucknell UP, 2000), Shawn Alfrey identifies this poem as describing "the site of a minority discourse, where people must navigate the burden of past and present in a geography worked over by foreign influences," where the speaker figures herself as "part of the native resistance" such forces "would expel" (96–97).
15. Jonathan Culler, *The Pursuit of Signs: Semiotics, Literature, Deconstruction* (Ithaca: Cornell UP, 1981), 139, hereafter referred to as *Pursuit*.
16. See Erin G. Carlston, *Thinking Fascism: Sapphic Modernism and Fascist Modernity* (Stanford: Stanford UP, 1998), 9, hereafter referred to as *Thinking*.
17. Merleau-Ponty's *The Phenomenology of Perception*, trans. Colin Smith (London: Routledge, 1962), hereafter referred to as *Phenomenology*, defines meaningful space as maintaining a sense of order "whereby the position of things becomes possible" (243). I return to this definition of space throughout the book in discussing a central modernist anxiety about impersonality as a spatial phenomenon, which surrounds the precarious dialectic it sees between the dissolution and reconstitution of space.
18. In using the phrase "mutual parasitism," I invoke Mina Loy's "Feminist Manifesto." See *Lost Lunar Baedeker: Poems of Mina Loy*, ed. Roger Conover (New York: Farrar, Straus and Giroux, 1997), 154. According to Loy, "[m]en & women are enemies, with the enmity of the exploited for the parasite, the parasite for the exploited—at present they are at the mercy of the advantage

that each can take of the others sexual dependence—. The only point at which the interests of the sexes merge—is the sexual embrace" (154). Interestingly, H.D.'s description of the ideal relations between "reasoning men and women" in *Notes on Thought and Vision* offers a more anaesthetized and arguably impersonal counterpart to Loy's parasitism.
19. See Pound's introduction to and translation of Remy de Gourmont's *The Natural Philosophy of Love* (London: Quartet Books, 1992), xi, hereafter referred to as *Natural*.
20. I borrow the term "prosthetic modernism" from Tim Armstrong's *Modernism: Technology and the Body* (Cambridge: Cambridge UP, 1998), 77, which I also discuss in Chapter 1.
21. See Betsy L. Nies, *Eugenic Fantasies: Racial Ideology in the Literature and Popular Culture of 1920s* (New York: Routledge, 2002), 67, which explores H.D.'s "troubled, ambivalent relation to eugenics" but does little to theorize the larger socioaesthetic assumptions embedded in such thought. Nies notes H.D.'s discomfort with the eugenicist embrace of the Nordic "classical body as an icon of perfection that had survived the ravages of time," standing "above the teeming immigrant masses whose bodies were depicted in the popular press as misshapen and deformed, small and swarthy, unlike the Nordic who rose above the crowd" (77–78). Nies's description of this particular trend in statuary underscores the ambivalence of H.D.'s poem. H.D.'s explicit politics were of course antifascist, as Georgina Taylor argues in *H.D. and the Public Sphere of Modernist Women Writers, 1913–1946* (Oxford: Oxford UP, 2001).
22. See *Phenomenology*, 171.
23. See Victor Smirnoff, "The Masochistic Contract," in *Essential Papers on Masochism*, ed. Mary Ann Fitzpatrick Hanly (New York: NYU Press, 1995), 66, hereafter referred to as "Masochistic," an anthology offering a comprehensive history of developments in the study of masochism, beginning with Freud.
24. In his analysis of Freud in *Masochism in Sex and Society* (New York: Black Cat, 1962), originally published in 1941 as *Masochism in Modern Man*, Theodor Reik addresses the "paradox of masochism" as a spatial fracturing of the personality arising from the simultaneous attempt to both assuage and pursue pain. For Reik, masochism actualizes a split in the personality as people "consciously desire to avoid pain and at the same time strive for it unconsciously" (4).
25. See Sigmund Freud, *Three Essays on the Theory of Sexuality*, trans. James Strachey (New York: Basic Books, 1962), 35. See also "Instincts and Their Vicissitudes," *SE* 14 (1915): 111–140, where Freud defines masochism spatially as related to the movements of the ego. In arguing that masochism is actually sadism turned around on the subject's own ego, Freud suggests that sadism transforms into masochism when the subject returns to the narcissistic object as a means of incorporating an extraneous ego. This process does not occur outside the scopophilic process of looking, in which the subject's own body is the object of this gaze. This essential splitting in space forms the heart of Freud's theory of masochism.

26. In *Male Subjectivity at the Margins* (New York: Routledge, 1992), Kaja Silverman argues that masochism has been read in particular as an "accepted—indeed a requisite—of 'normal' female subjectivity," further supporting the logic that the male masochist cannot possibly identify with masculinity (189). Thus, Silverman's reading of Freud's *Three Essays on the Theory of Sexuality*, as well as "The Economic Problem of Masochism" and "A Child Is Being Beaten," contends that masochism is only pathological in the male, whereas it is acceptable for the woman because it already positions her as its sufferer.
27. See Gilles Deleuze, *Coldness and Cruelty* (New York: Zone, 1991), 20, hereafter abbreviated as *CC*.
28. See, for example, "H.D.'s Romantic Landscapes: The Sexual Politics of the Garden," in *Signets: Reading H.D.*, where Cassandra Laity writes that "H.D.'s enchantresses and female questers frequently decline in the sensuous trap of consuming male desire" (112).
29. My point here is not to dismiss H.D.'s interest in other women or her bisexuality. Rather, a term such as "Sapphic," as employed by Laura Doan and Jane Garrity in their introduction to *Sapphic Modernities: Sexuality, Women, and English Culture* (New York: Palgrave, 2006), better describes H.D.'s relation to sexuality. Representative of the "profound shifts—in terms of visibility, intelligibility, and accessibility—that occurred as a result of the growing public of sapphism in modern Anglophone cultures between the two World Wars," the "multiple meanings of term," the two assert, distance "us from more rigid contemporary categories of identity" (2, 3).
30. See T. S. Eliot, "The Love Song of J. Alfred Prufrock," in *Selected Poems* (New York: Harcourt, 1930), 11.
31. This discomfort stems from what Leo Bersani, in *The Freudian Body: Psychoanalysis and Art* (New York: Columbia UP, 1986), describes as psychoanalysis's contribution to the "mythologizing of the human as a readable organization" (83). H.D.'s poetry indicates her uneasiness over the prospect of a mappable self but likewise cannot imagine a self that is completely unreadable. This is also the subject of her memoir *Tribute to Freud* (New York: Pearson, 1956). In this text, H.D. struggles with the project of subsuming her intensely personal responses to Freud's personality and genius within the impersonal rubric of analysis.
32. H.D.'s destabilization of the hetero/homo binary characterizes an impersonal poetics that attempts to move, in Tim Dean's words, "beyond sexuality," much in the same way that it also moves beyond sensuality (Smirnoff). Such a movement, according to Dean in *Beyond Sexuality* (Chicago: U of Chicago P, 2000), provides a solution to the primary challenge facing queer theory, which involves "the consequences of defining oneself and one's politics against norms as such" (226). Dean asserts that moving "beyond sexuality" entails a nonpsychological understanding of sexuality that disarticulates it from "identity, from the self and from personhood" (272).
33. See Pound, *Gaudier-Brzeska*, 89.

34. While the poems of H.D.'s *Sea Garden* are not conventionally "narrative," they do, as I will argue similarly of D. H. Lawrence's *Sons and Lovers*, destabilize conventional aspects of form in ways that challenge heternormative paradigms of literary structure designed, as Judith Roof argues in *Come as You Are: Sexuality and Narrative* (New York: Columbia UP, 1996), to reassure readers with a sense of meaning and stability.

Chapter 3

1. See D. H. Lawrence, *Collected Letters, Vol 1* (New York: Viking, 1962), 395, hereafter abbreviated as *CL*.
2. See Daniel Albright, *Personality and Impersonality: Lawrence, Woolf, and Mann* (Chicago: U of Chicago P, 1978), 3, hereafter referred to as *Personality*.
3. Albright argues that "personality" exists on three levels for Lawrence: "first, the ego, the public self, the fixed shell, a mask which once was a valid self-expression but which, like anything rigid, has become a deformity . . . it is a fatal condition because it is unresponsive to the urgencies of self-development. The second level of personality is the body, what Paul Morel in *Sons and Lovers* calls protoplasm; . . . the third level of personality, the ultimate, original self, is, as we have seen, neither shaped nor shapeless; it can be described with equal validity as diamond or electricity, embryo or the soul after death" (*Personality* 29).
4. See Kate Millett, *Sexual Politics* (Chicago: U of Illinois P, 2000), originally published in 1970. Millett argues quite famously that Lawrence's "*Lady Chatterley's Lover* is a quasi-religious tract recounting the salvation of one modern woman . . . through the offices of the author's personal cult, 'the mystery of the phallus'" (238). Twelve years later, Hillary Simpson, in *D. H. Lawrence and Feminism* (London: Croon Helm, 1982), would both revise and sustain Millett's censure of Lawrence, arguing in particular of *Sons and Lovers* that its "real blow to feminism . . . lies in Lawrence's failure to connect the personal world of individual development to the larger material forces which have a part in shaping it" (37). As I suggest alternately here, Lawrence's "blow to feminism" lies in his critique of the "personal world of individual development" as incompatible with the larger world of "material forces."
5. See also Terry Eagleton, *Literary Theory*, 2nd ed. (Oxford: Blackwell, 1983), hereafter referred to as *Literary*. While Eagleton explicitly addresses *Sons and Lovers* as a "concrete literary example" of the "problem of the relation between society and the unconscious," his analysis of the novel is dominated by its focus on class politics. Indeed, Eagleton rightly argues that a "psychoanalytic reading of the novel . . . need not be an alternative to a social interpretation of it," adding that these questions might also lead us to considerations of form and narrative organization. Nonetheless, the argument is characterized by an overtly ideological and rather one-sided focus on class that foregrounds the text's rejection of Morel and both Paul's and Lawrence's desire to "extricate" themselves from the working class (153–54).

6. See Tony Pinkney, *D. H. Lawrence and Modernism* (Iowa City: U of Iowa P, 1990), 111, hereafter abbreviated as *DHL*.
7. See Judith Roof, *Come as You Are: Sexuality and Narrative* (New York: Columbia UP, 1996), hereafter referred to as *Come*; and Joseph Allen Boone, *Libidinal Currents* (Chicago: U of Chicago P, 1998), hereafter referred to as *Libidinal*. Roof in particular interrogates the notion of a "chronological, linear, unidirectional time that positions the end as the cumulative notion of completed knowledge" (7). This narrative pattern, she argues, is connected to an Oedipal desire for "mastery" that is overtly heterosexual.
8. See Susan Stanford Friedman, *Penelope's Web: Gender, Modernity, H.D.'s Fiction* (Cambridge: Cambridge UP, 2008), which I also note in Chapter 2 of this book. Friedman argues that H.D.'s poetry blocks direct autobiographical referents and thus, unlike her prose, privileges "her 'real self' over her 'personal self,' clairvoyance over sensibility, and art over therapy" (34).
9. See Franco Moretti, *The Way of the World: The Bildungsroman in European Culture* (London: Verso, 1987) 8, 12, hereafter referred to as *Way*. I return to Moretti's model of the *Bildungsroman* in Chapter 5, which addresses Elizabeth Bowen's *The Death of the Heart* as a particularly modernist alteration of the traditional *Bildungsroman*.
10. See Douglas Mao, *Solid Objects: Modernism and the Test of Production* (Princeton: Princeton UP, 1998), 21, hereafter referred to as *Solid*.
11. See my discussion of Wyndham Lewis in Chapter 4, who more aggressively advocates the "violence of making," particularly as it involves the active domination of both objects and humans.
12. See Lawrence's *Fantasia of the Unconscious and Psychoanalysis of the Unconscious* (London: William Heinemann, 1961), 77, hereafter referred to as *Fantasia*.
13. See "Tradition and the Individual Talent," in *Selected Prose of T. S. Eliot* (New York: Harcourt, 1975), 43, hereafter abbreviated as *Prose*.
14. See in particular Jonathan Dollimore's claim in *Death, Desire, and Loss in Western Culture* (New York: Routledge, 1998) that for Lawrence, "redemption lies . . . in a radical individualism and political authoritarianism" in which he seeks to "replace a humanist philosophy of collective social praxis with an aesthetics of energy" that might quell the "dwindling" of energies in the modern world (259).
15. See D. H. Lawrence, *Aaron's Rod* (New York: Viking, 1962), 73, originally published in 1922, hereafter abbreviated as *AR*.
16. See Anthony Giddens, *The Consequences of Modernity* (Stanford: Stanford UP, 1990), which provides an implicit gauge for measuring modernism's argument with the "social situations of modernity" (120).
17. In Chapter 1, I attempt to distinguish impersonality from depersonalization by discussing the work of sociologist Georg Simmel. According to Simmel in *The Sociology of Georg Simmel*, trans. and ed. Kurt H. Woolf (New York: Free Press, 1950), depersonalization results in the "leveling down of the person by the social technological mechanism" (409). For Simmel, depersonalization is

itself a set of psychological conditions, whereby the personality falsely parades as individuality.
18. See D. H. Lawrence, *Sons and Lovers* (New York: Penguin, 1994), 117, hereafter abbreviated as *SL*.
19. Giddens argues in *The Consequences of Modernity* that modernity relegates the concept of trust to relations between individuals, where the "work involved means *a mutual process of self-disclosure*" (italics in original; 121). This kind of trust is best exemplified in what Giddens terms the "ethos of romantic love," which he implicitly characterizes as heterosexual. Giddens quotes Lawrence Stone, whose term "affective individualism," describes the "notion that there is only one person in the world with whom one can unite at all levels" (121). This investment in the "personality of that person" follows a scheme of idealization that calls for the full expression of exaggerated personal emotions. This "affective individualism" resembles what I later term a hermeneutic mode of intimacy, whereby, to use Giddens' words, personal trust develops through the exchange of one's self-discovery and the "*mutuality of self-disclosure*" (italics in original; 122).
20. See Leo Bersani, *The Freudian Body: Psychoanalysis and Art* (New York: Columbia UP, 1986), 86.
21. See Brooks's account of the "Freudian masterplot" and its relation to narrative in *Reading for the Plot: Design and Intention in Narrative* (Cambridge: Harvard UP, 1992), 97, hereafter referred to as *Reading*. Joseph Allen Boone in particular questions Brooks's privileging of a "psychological paradigm" that views "all novelistic structures as repetitions of the transhistorical masterplot" (*Libidinal* 34). Judith Roof also critiques Brooks's Freudian account of narrative as participating in an "orgasmic ideology of narrative" that presumes necessary connections between "coming, death, reproduction, and the end" (*Come* 20). For my own purposes, Brooks's understanding of the relation between narrative and Freudian repetition—however implicated in heterosexual ideology—is still useful as a model for comprehending the workings of narrative and can be linked, in Lawrence at least, to the unraveling of the connection between narrative and heterosexuality as much as it can to the construction of it.
22. See Sigmund Freud, *Beyond the Pleasure Principle*, ed. James Strachey (New York: Norton, 1961), 19, hereafter abbreviated as *BPP*.
23. See Sigmund Freud, *The Ego and the Id* (New York: Norton, 1960), 26. Here, Freud argues that the most important identification of childhood is "with the father" in the child's "own personal prehistory," triangulating the Oedipus complex due to "the constitutional bisexuality of each individual" (26). Aside from her breast, Freud offers no explanation for why the mother must become the boy's sole object cathexis. Freud further claims that when the boy must give up his mother as an object-cathexis, the identification with his father may intensify. The odd variability of Freud's thesis here presents the Oedipus complex, and the child's attachment to his mother, as a process of socialization that results from social or domestic separation from the father. Significantly, Lawrence seems to "approve" this model in Paul's triangulation with his mother and father.

24. I refer to Walter Morel here as "Morel," the name by which he is most often identified in the text. As with Baxter Dawes, referred to most often as "Dawes," Lawrence's insistence on identifying this character only by his last name reflects his alignment with the universalized forces of sex, violence, and work.
25. Moretti argues that work in the *Bildungsroman* "creates a continuity between external and internal, between the 'best and most intimate' part of the soul and the 'public' aspect of existence" (*Way* 30). *Sons and Lovers* both revises and confirms this notion by repudiating certain "acceptable" forms of work in favor of others. Moretti's basic formula works here, especially if we read Paul's development as a search for an "aesthetic and humanizing work superior to one that is instrumental and alienated" (*Way* 31).
26. Freud equates "daemonic" power with a form of possession that proceeds despite the patient's wishes, robbing her of the capacity to make informed, conscious decisions (*BPP* 43). "Daemonic" power corresponds, according to Freud, to what some people feel is "better left sleeping," the emergence of the compulsion to repeat (*BPP* 43).
27. According to Brooks, "the improper end indeed lurks throughout narrative, frequently as the wrong choice: choice of the wrong casket, misapprehension of the magical agent, false erotic object choice." It's the correct or "proper" choice, he argues that generally marks narrative's conclusion" (*Reading* 104).
28. See D. H. Lawrence, *Selected Letters* (New York: Penguin, 1978), 84, hereafter abbreviated as *Letters*.
29. See Maurice Blanchot, *Friendship*, trans. Elizabeth Rottenberg (Stanford: Stanford UP, 1997), 291. Blanchot's essay, "Friendship," was written in honor of his deceased friend George Batailles.
30. See T. E. Hulme, *Speculations: Essays on Humanism and the Philosophy of Art*, ed. Herbert Read (London: Routledge, 1965), 134, hereafter referred to as *Speculations*.
31. See Sigmund Freud, *Group Psychology and an Analysis of the Ego*, trans. James Strachey (New York: Norton, 1959), 43–44. Here, Freud claims that work in common reinforces the libidinal ties between men. This work brings a change "from egoism to altruism" and enables a valid rereading to the point, originally promulgated by queer theory, that homosocial bonds between men arose over women in common.
32. See Sigmund Freud, "The 'Uncanny,'" *SE* 17 (1920): 234, 241.
33. See Georg Lukács, "The Ideology of Modernism," in *The Meaning of Contemporary Realism*, ed. John and Necke Mander (London: Merlin Press, 1962), 17–47. Here, Lukács claims that "[d]istortion becomes the normal condition of human existence" in modernism and that modernist literature consequently "deprives literature of a sense of *perspective*" (33). Modernism, then, collapses objective reality and distortion into a purely subjective realm which destroys "the complex tissue of man's relations with his environment" (28). In the context of D. H. Lawrence and modernism, I interpret this loss of perspective as a loss of meaningful space. Perspective can also apply to a novel whose structures of repetition obscure any sense of positioning or event.

Chapter 4

1. See Wyndham Lewis, "The Physiognomy of Our Time," in *The Caliph's Design*, ed. Paul Edwards (Santa Rosa: Black Sparrow Press, 1986), 73–74, hereafter abbreviated as *CD*. Subtitled *Architects Where Is Your Vortex*, the collection of articles and notes, as Lewis suggests in the preface, ostensibly critiques the state of modern art and architecture, particularly its relation to the public.
2. See Leo Bersani and Ulysse Dutoit, *The Arts of Impoverishment: Beckett, Rothko, Resnais* (Cambridge: Harvard UP, 1993), 144, hereafter referred to as *Arts*. Here Bersani and Dutoit address the question of Rothko's art, asking "[c]an seeing survive the erasure of difference?" (142). This sort of question underscores the conceptual problem of impersonality I elaborate in this book. As Bersani and Dutoit remark of Rothko's work, the erasure of boundaries is also an effacement of form, of the aesthetic itself. However, Bersani and Dutoit resolve this problem by arguing that form sustains itself in the "marks" of its very "erasure" (144).
3. See "Tradition and the Individual Talent," in *Selected Prose of T. S. Eliot* (New York: Harcourt, 1975), 37, hereafter abbreviated as *Prose*.
4. Regarding Lewis, these issues receive more comprehensive attention in Douglas Mao, *Solid Objects: Modernism and the Test of Production* (Princeton: Princeton UP, 1998), hereafter referred to as *Solid*. Attending in detail to Lewis's vast corpus of critical work, Mao's chapter on the frequently disgruntled artist traces distinct phases in Lewis's thinking about objects and their relation to the external world; he sees Lewis as having altered his priorities in 1916, where his initial critique of empiricism in *Blast I* shifted into an attack on the "imperialism of subjectivity" and its domination of objects (101). Arguing of *Time and Western Man* that Lewis's attacks on subjectivity in "defense of the object's integrity" could only go so far, Mao suggests that despite the similarities Lewis shares with figures such as Woolf regarding this matter, he still "maintains his allegiance to forceful subjectivity, which he views as imperiled rather than imperial under modernity" (98, 99). Regardless, Mao claims that Lewis "does align with a number of other modernists in insisting that the division between subject and object must be preserved for the sake of both, and that any putative reconciliations between the two would merely disguise some further domination" (101). This position later became "entangled" in *Men Without Art* (1934), when Lewis accused writers such as Virginia Woolf, Henry James, and Oscar Wilde of too closely attending in their fiction to the operations of consciousness, thereby neglecting the external world (105). Tyrus Miller argues similarly that the Great War divided Lewis's career as he remade himself into an "aggressive polemicist-critic" whose work was increasingly tied to a "logic of publicity, ideological conflict, and struggle over canonizing authority in literary criticism." See Tyrus Miller, *Late Modernism: Politics, Fiction, and the Arts between the World Wars* (Berkeley: U of California P, 1999) 69, hereafter referred to as *Late*.

5. See Bruce Hainley, "Quite Contrary: Mary Butt's Wild Queendom," *Village Voice Literary Supplement* May 1994: 21, hereafter referred to as "Quite Contrary." Other articles of interest include Jascha Kessler, "Mary Butts: Lost . . . and Found," *The Kenyon Review* 17.3 (Summer/Fall 1995): 206–18; and Lawrence Rainey, "Good Things: Pederasty and Jazz and Opium and Research," *London Review of Books* 20.14 (July 16, 1998): 14–16. See also Jane Garrity's chapter on Butts in *Step-Daughters of England: British Women Modernists and the National Imaginary* (New York: Manchester UP, 2003), hereafter referred to as *Step-Daughters*, which argues that Butts endows women with "*racialized* status" as she positions them as "generative saviors of a dying nation" (195, 189).
6. Quoted in Nathalie Blondel's biography *Mary Butts: Scenes from a Life* (Kingston, NY: McPherson, 1998), 186, hereafter abbreviated at *MBSL*.
7. Butts's interest in homosexuality has lead critics such as Bruce Hainley to deem her "an ecologist of the queer" where the term "[f]ag-hag" denotes not only a woman but also "a style of writing" ("Quite Contrary" 21). Indeed, in her 1928 epistolary novella *Imaginary Letters* (Vancouver: Talon, 1994), illustrated by Jean Cocteau, Butts pronounced herself most interested in exploring the "sensual passions of men for men" ("Quite Contrary" 11). My own article, "A Queer Eye for the Straight Guy: Mary Butts's 'Fag-Hag' and the Modernist Group," in *Modernist Group Dynamics: The Politics and Poetics of Friendship*, ed. Fabio A. Durão and Dominic Williams (Cambridge: Cambridge Scholars Press, 2008), 95–118, argues that Butts's criticism of Bloomsbury's "personalized" cultural affiliations reflects the importance of effeminate men as consumers and audiences of modernist culture.
8. See *The Diary of Virginia Woolf, Volume II: 1920–1924* (New York: Harvest, 1980), 209.
9. Mao writes that "Lewis differs from writers like Woolf and Williams most significantly, however, in that his opposition to the imperialism of subjectivity served not a left politics aimed . . . at liberating the colonized other, but rather commitments . . . aimed first at protecting the intellectually strong from the intellectually weak and second at protecting white Europe from the threats of other states and races" (*Solid* 101).
10. For a similar argument, see Andrew Radford, "Excavating a Secret History: Mary Butts and the Return of the Nativist," *Connotations* 17.1 (2007/2008): 83, 80.
11. See *The Death of Felicity Taverner*, in *The Taverner Novels* (Kingston, NY: McPherson, 1992), 346, hereafter abbreviated as *DFT*.
12. Jane Garrity, in "Mary Butts's 'Fanatical Pédérastie': Queer Urban Life in 1920s London and Paris," in *Sapphic Modernities: Sexuality, Women and English Culture* (New York: Palgrave, 2006), 233–251, argues that Butts both "yokes mystical experience with homosexuality and claims the city as queer domain" (235). While Garrity observes that for Butts gay men can function "variously as signs of degeneracy, embodiments of feminine artifice and excess, symptoms of national distress, sources of poetic inspiration, and divine conduits for primitive ritual," I would also add that, even at their most degenerate, they act as

correctives to an overly personalized literary and aesthetic culture that Butts links to urban life and space (237).
13. See Mary Butts, "Bloomsbury," *Modernism/Modernity* 5.2 (April 1998): 37, hereafter referred to as "Bloomsbury."
14. Unlike Eliot, Pound, H.D., or even Lawrence, Butts does not often explicitly mention "impersonality," though her work, as I argue here, intervenes in the discourse of impersonality I elaborate in this book, particularly as it seeks to disentangle being from personality and identity. For example, her attention to the organization of space attends her interest in classical literature as an antireflective "world" of fluid boundaries. In a 1932 journal entry, Butts wrote that "[o]nly in Homer have I found impersonal consolation—a life where I am unsexed or bisexed, or completely myself—or a mere pair of ears" (qtd. in *MBSL* 22). Here, Butts characterizes the classical world of Greek literature as a stage for impersonal escape. As with Woolf's "Street Haunting," which occasions the pleasure of leaving the "straight lines of personality," the world of Homer also facilitates the "consolation" of transcending the rigid parameters of personality, especially as defined by sex. Becoming "unsexed" or "bisexed" enables Butts the freedom to access a more essential form of being. See Virginia Woolf, "Street Haunting: A London Adventure," in *Collected Essays: Volume IV* (London: Chatto and Windus, 1967), 165, hereafter referred to as *Collected IV*.
15. See Christopher Reed, introduction to *Not at Home: The Suppression of Domesticity in Modern Art and Architecture* (London: Thames and Hudson, 1996), 9.
16. See Ann Banfield, *The Phantom Table: Woolf, Fry, Russell and the Epistemology of Modernism* (Cambridge: Cambridge UP, 2000), 110.
17. See Wyndham Lewis, *The Art of Being Ruled* (Santa Rosa, CA: Black Sparrow Press, 1989), 218, hereafter referred to as *Art*.
18. Butts, for example, appears to condone the violence towards women that occurs in texts such as *Armed with Madness*, in *The Taverner Novels* (Kingston, NY: McPherson, 1992), hereafter referred to as *Armed*, where Scylla Taverner, the "sole stay" of the (mostly gay) men in the novel, captures the jealous attention of the unruly, demented Clarence, who, in a sacrificial gesture that productively restabilizes aesthetic community, "throws" her, "ties her with his lariat," and begins shooting her (literally) with an "indifferent arrow" (7, 145).
19. See Le Corbusier, *The Decorative Art of Today*, trans. James I. Dunnett (Cambridge: MIT Press, 1987), 54, hereafter abbreviated as *DAT*.
20. See Jean-Paul Sartre's account of the development of phenomenology in relation to Husserl's critique of psychology in *Logical Investigations*, in *Basic Writings*, ed. Stephen Priest (London: Routledge, 2001), 64–65, hereafter abbreviated as *BW*.
21. See M. Merleau-Ponty, *Phenomenology of Perception*, trans. Colin Smith (London: Routledge, 1962), viii, hereafter referred to as *Phenomenology*.
22. Douglas Mao is correct in his assertion that modernism's well-known "antipathy to the commodity" has too frequently driven most critical treatments of the

modernist object, especially since the publication of Andreas Huyssen's *After the Great Divide: Modernism, Mass Culture, Postmodernism* (Bloomington: Indiana UP, 1986) (*Solid* 4). Other studies that focus on the subject of modernist literature in relation to market forces include the 1996 collection edited by Kevin Watt and Stephen Dettmar, *Marketing Modernisms: Self-Promotion, Canonization, Re-reading* (Ann Arbor: U of Michigan P, 1996), hereafter referred to as *Modernisms*; along with Rita Felski, *The Gender of Modernity* (Cambridge: Harvard UP, 1995), which takes the connection Huyssen draws between fear of femininity, mass culture, and the loss of a stable ego as a point of departure for her analysis of the aesthetics and erotics of consumption. My aim here is not to fault these studies, but to develop an alternative idiom for speaking of objects that extends beyond their consumption.
23. See Colin Smith, "The Notion of Object in the Phenomenology of Merleau-Ponty," *Philosophy* 39.148 (1964): 111, hereafter referred to as "Notion."
24. See Terry Eagleton, *Literary Theory*, 2nd ed. (Oxford: Blackwell, 1983), 3, hereafter referred to as *Literary*.
25. See Sarah Ahmed, *Queer Phenomenology: Orientations, Objects, Others* (Durham: Duke UP, 2006), 65. Ahmed also argues that "tending towards certain objects and not others ... produces what we would call 'straight tendencies'—that is, a way of acting that presumes the heterosexual couple as a social gift" (91). I would argue that the impersonal perspectives I discuss in this book tend toward objects in ways that "unstraighten" space.
26. See also Wyndham Lewis, "Relativism and Picasso's Latest Work," in *Blast* (Santa Rosa: Black Sparrow Press, 1997), where Lewis connects excessive detachment to a hypermaterialization that detracts from the work's potency as an aesthetic object. The problem for Lewis lies in Picasso's attempt to "reproduce the surface and texture of objects ... so directly so," without attending to the formal demands of their real concreteness (139). These sculptures are overly bounded and consequently lack proper form. My reading of these essays from *Blast* differs somewhat from that of Douglas Mao. Arguing that Lewis's critique of Picasso represents a particularly early phase of Lewis's thinking about objects in which pure empiricism and detachment is "insufficiently virile," Mao suggests that Lewis struggled with the difficulty of how to recast this "externalism" without authorizing the "domination of the object world" (*Solid* 93, 96, 99).
27. See Douglas Mao's discussion of the Omega Workshops in *Solid Objects*.
28. Douglas Mao also references this quotation in *Solid Objects*, 90. Mao later claims that Lewis's critique of Bloomsbury and the Omega Workshops was not so much motivated by his feelings about objects as it was his feelings about the group as amateurs. The "key difference between Lewis and Bloomsbury," Mao argues, was "that between the mythologizing of a circle of talented friends regarded as amateurs and the mythologizing of a loner whose stance was insistently professional" (*Solid* 113).
29. For Gaudier-Brzeska's comments, see the retrospective piece, written and edited by Quentin Bell and Stephen Chaplin, in the October, 1964, issue of the

art journal *Apollo* (October 1964), 287, hereafter referred to as "Ideal," which reprints the series of letters exchanged in "The Ideal Home Rumpus." Having secured the "Post-Impressionist" room at the 1913 Ideal Home Exhibition, Fry aroused the ire of his former compatriot, Lewis, who—in a letter additionally signed by Frederick Etchells, C Hamilton, and E. Wadsworth—classified himself as one of a group of "Dissenting Aesthetes" compelled to call in as much "modern talent" as possible "to do the rough and masculine work without which . . . their efforts would not rise above the level of a pleasant tea-party" ("Ideal" 287). Christopher Reed's essay "'A Room of One's Own': The Bloomsbury Group's Creation of Modernist Domesticity," in *Not at Home: The Suppression of Domesticity in Modern Art and Architecture* (London: Thames and Hudson, 1996), offers a more detailed account of this incident than I am able to offer here. The letter, also quoted in *Solid Objects*, 104, appears as well in *The Letters of Wyndham Lewis*, ed. W. K. Rose (Norfolk: New Directions, 1963), 49.
30. See Roger Fry, "The Artist as Decorator," *Colour* April 1917, 92. A "life-style" magazine, which addresses women with the money to practice the prestigious art of home decorating, *Colour* could hardly be considered a paean to heady modernist aesthetic theory. Despite the ultimate failure of the Omega Workshops, Fry's appearances in periodicals help explain what Jennifer Wicke has termed "the rapturous survival of Bloomsbury as an artistic and social movement, a fashion, a deeply desirable lifestyle." See Jennifer Wicke, "Coterie Consumption: Bloomsbury, Keynes, Modernism and Marketing," in *Marketing Modernisms: Self-Promotion, Canonization, Re-reading* (Ann Arbor: U of Michigan P, 1996), 110.
31. This is not unlike the form of ownership Walter Benjamin theorizes in his famous essay "Unpacking My Library," in *Illuminations: Essays and Reflections* (New York: Schocken, 1988). Here, he claims that "[o]wnership is the most intimate relationship one can have to objects" (60). "The phenomenon of collecting," writes Benjamin, "loses its meaning as it loses its personal owner" (67). According to this perspective, the "owner" of an object, whether it is a book or a work of art, guarantees that object a place in the world through which it achieves existence. Ownership is not simply characterized by the consumption of objects but by the desire to bring objects into a "relationship" that "studies and loves them as the scene, the stage of their fate" (60).
32. See Wilhelm Worringer, *Abstraction and Empathy* (Chicago: Elephant, 2007), 15, hereafter referred to as *Abstraction*.
33. See Ezra Pound, *Literary Essays* (New York: New Directions, 1968), 3, hereafter referred to as *Literary*.
34. See Janet Flanner, *Men and Monuments: Profiles of Picasso, Matisse, Braque and Malraux* (New York: Da Capo, 1957), 96, hereafter referred to as *Men*.
35. Matei Calinescu devotes a chapter of his *Five Faces of Modernity: Modernism, Avant-Garde, Decadence, Kitsch, Postmodernism* (Durham: Duke UP, 1987) to defining kitsch in relation to modernity's other aesthetic movements. According to Calinescu, the fact that the avant-garde actually employed kitsch and that, conversely, kitsch appropriates avant-garde "devices" testifies

to the complexity of kitsch as an aesthetic. Calinescu further declares that kitsch "cannot be defined from a single vantage point," not even through a "negative definition, because it simply has no compelling, distinct counter-concept" (232).
36. This description of the Bloomsbury group appears in Butts's essay "Bloomsbury."
37. "In Bloomsbury" appears in *From Altar to Chimney Piece: Selected Stories of Mary Butts* (Kingston, NY: McPherson, 1992), 39, hereafter referred to as *Altar*.
38. See Jane Garrity, "Selling Culture to the 'Civilized': Bloomsbury, British *Vogue*, and the Marketing of National Identity," *Modernism/Modernity* 6.2 (1999): 29, hereafter referred to as "Selling." Garrity illustrates how Bloomsbury, despite its permissive attitude towards homosexuality and bisexuality, collaborated with *Vogue* "in the promotion of a heteronormative agenda. Whenever members of the Group are represented, their captions carry the words 'wife' or 'husband of' to ensure readers of their heterosexuality" (35).
39. See Christopher Reed, "Bloomsbury Bashing: Homophobia and the Politics of Criticism in the Eighties," *Genders* 11 (Fall 1991): 59–60. Reed argues that Bloomsbury's relation to the "feminized man" leads to its critical dismissal in favor of those such as Wyndham Lewis and the Vorticists, who, for critics such as Charles Harrison in his *English Art and Modernism*, represented "the highroad of masculine accomplishment" ("Bloomsbury Bashing" 63).
40. Pound's "A Few Don'ts by an Imagiste," where Pound defines the image as "presenting an intellectual and emotional complex in an instant of time," first appeared in the March 1913 issue of *Poetry* (*Literary Essays* 4).
41. Merleau-Ponty exemplifies this "motor significance" by discussing a blind man's relationship to his stick. The stick has "ceased to be an object" for the blind man because he is no longer aware of it as distinct from himself. It is rather, "an area of sensitivity, extending the scope and active radius of touch, and providing a parallel to sight." That is, the use of the stick is now habitual, since the blind man needs not negotiate its discrete presence. The blind man only then becomes aware of it "through the position of objects" rather "than the position of objects through it" (*Phenomenology* 143). To disrupt habit, the stick and its relation to the body—the blind man's very being—would have to be rearranged. Merleau-Ponty appears to use this blind man metaphorically and symbolically. The relationship between the blind man and his stick can also represent a blind, habitual mode of relating to objects, whereby the object, or "stick," loses its discrete existence through our habitual relation to it. This relationship interestingly characterizes the Curtins' style of ownership in "In Bloomsbury."
42. See Peter Brooks, *Reading for the Plot: Design and Intention in Narrative* (Cambridge: Harvard, 1992), 91, hereafter referred to as *Reading*.
43. Butts, like Lewis and Lawrence, links action or "doing" to an impersonal aesthetic. For Butts, having repeatedly professed her admiration of Yeats, this "doing" was also linked to her interest in the supernatural and the occult. In one particular journal entry devoted to understanding the supernatural, Butts charts out a number of goals: "I don't only want to find my true will. I want

to *do* it. So I want to learn how to form a magical link between myself and the phenomena I am interested in. I want power" (qtd. in *MBSL* 100). She writes further of this "true will," connecting her quest for power to the "impersonal:" "I have an intuition that, if I ever know it, I shall have to cross the threshold of some frightful impersonal suffering before I get it" (qtd. in *MBSL* 101).

44. Pound's early poem "Au Salon" appears in *Personae* (New York: New Directions, 1990), 50.
45. Gaston Bachelard, *The Poetics of Space*, trans. Maria Jolas (Boston: Beacon, 1958) will become more prominent in Chapter 5. Devoting a chapter of his study to "corners," he states that those who are "prepared to go beyond the spider, the lady-bug and the mouse," to a point of identification with things "forgotten in a corner," meditate on the neglected, the abandoned, the "poor little dead things" that create a past (142).
46. See Janet Lyon, "Josephine Baker's Hothouse," in *Modernism, Inc: Body, Memory, Capital*, ed. Jani Scandura and Michael Thurston (New York: NYU Press, 2001), 34–35, hereafter referred to as "JBH."
47. According to Shari Benstock, *Women of the Left Bank: Paris 1900–1940* (Austin: U of Texas P, 1986), Stein was "less restrictive" socially though equally "demanding of loyalty" as she had been before her career was established. Butts's story, "From Altar to Chimney-Piece" registers this change, and is especially relevant to Benstock's claim that Stein was "particularly open to the young, to those whom she might influence, to those who could carry her cause to the younger generation" (170).
48. See Gertrude Stein, *The Autobiography of Alice B. Toklas* (New York: Vintage, 1990).
49. See the memoir Robert McAlmon first published in 1938, *Being Geniuses Together: 1920–1930* (London: Johns Hopkins UP, 1984), 204, which contains supplementary chapters and an afterword by Kay Boyle. If McAlmon's chapters tell a story of modernist "security," Kay Boyle's chapters, which narrate her own struggles to become "established," reflect a much different life of constant penury and displacement.
50. In Pierre Bourdieu, *Distinction: A Social Critique of the Judgment of Taste*, trans. Richard Nice (Cambridge: Harvard UP, 1984), Bourdieu writes that "personality, i.e., the quality of the person ... is affirmed in the capacity to appropriate an object of quality." For Bourdieu, collecting itself most evidently supports this relation, since it requires a lengthy "investment of time" that affirms the "quality of the person" (281). Furthermore, the appropriation and acquisition of objects enables a "sense of belonging to a more polished, more polite, better policed world" (77). These assertions are certainly true in specific situations, but I am arguing here that modernist texts allow us to think about objects beyond the fact of their consumption, particularly as they theorize a form of relating to objects that does not magnify the personality of the owner.

Chapter 5

1. See Elizabeth Bowen, *The Death of the Heart* (New York: Anchor, 2000), 190–91, hereafter referred to as *Death*.
2. See Elizabeth Bowen's memoir *Pictures and Conversations: Chapters of an Autobiography* (New York: Knopf, 1975), 36–37, hereafter referred to as *Pictures*, where she writes, "Imagination of my kind is most caught, most fired, most worked upon by the unfamiliar: I have thriven, accordingly, on the changes and chances, the dislocations and . . . the contrasts which have made up much of my life" (36–37).
3. Jacqueline Rose has also noted the connection between Butts's and Bowen's fiction in her essay "Bizarre Objects: Mary Butts and Elizabeth Bowen," in *On Not Being Able to Sleep: Psychoanalysis and the Modern World* (Princeton: Princeton UP, 2003), hereafter abbreviated as *ON*. She argues that both writers "chart and respond to . . . a world which, in its acute presence to the sensations—its physical quality—forces itself beyond what would normally be seen as endurable or at least sane" (90). This "hallucinatory intensity" grants "objects of the phenomenal world . . . the capacity to transfer their substance into humans" in forcing the reader into a "discomforting historical identification" (93, 99).
4. See M. Merleau-Ponty, *Phenomenology of Perception*, trans. Colin Smith (London: Routledge, 1962), 336, hereafter referred to as *Phenomenology*.
5. This claim benefits from Sharon Cameron's definition of the "personality" as relating to "self-ownership, the *of* or possessive through which individuality is identified as one's own" (italics in the original). Here, the phrase "is identified" marks "personality" as both a public aspect of existence and an article of possession. See Sharon Cameron, *Impersonality: Seven Essays* (Chicago: U of Chicago P, 2007), viii, hereafter referred to as *Impersonality*.
6. See Jed Esty, "Virgins of Empire: *The Last September* and the Anti-Development Plot," *Modern Fiction Studies* 53.2 (Summer 2007): 271, hereafter referred to as "Virgins." Esty's reading of Bowen's *The Last September* within a larger modernist and colonial frame turns on the novel's "revision of inherited bildungsroman codes" (257). Esty, to whom I am much indebted in my thinking about the relation between the *Bildungsroman* and modernist texts, argues that *The Last September* is a "specifically Ango-Irish" example of the "antidevelopment plot, crystallized in Lois's arrested adolescence." This failure to develop, he argues, along with the novel's colonial setting, are "signs of modernist fiction's recoding of social antagonism into cultural difference" (271).
7. See Maud Ellmann, *Elizabeth Bowen: The Shadow across the Page* (Edinburgh: Edinburgh UP, 2003), 16, hereafter referred to as *Shadow*. Other articles, such as Elizabeth C. Inglesby, "'Expressive Objects': Elizabeth Bowen's Narrative Materializes," *Modern Fiction Studies* 53.2 (Summer 2007), reinforce this claim that Bowen is not a modernist but a realist writer, arguing that "Bowen actively resisted abstraction by binding her own metaphysical convictions to particular places and things" (327). In this case, little is done to place Bowen's

"literary animism" within the larger context of modernism (*307*). Similarly, Brook Miller's essay from the same special collection, "The Impersonal Personal: Value, Voice, and Agency in Elizabeth Bowen's Literary and Social Criticism," *Modern Fiction Studies* 53.2 (Summer 2007), takes up the subject of Bowen's impersonality but instead equates the impersonal with modernist detachment as it "contributes to the humanist work Bowen envisions with the tradition of the English novel" (*MFS* 360). Other accounts, including Raphael Ingelbien, "Gothic Genealogies: *Dracula*, Bowen's Court, and Anglo-Irish Psychology," *English Literary History* 70.4 (2003), hereafter referred to as "Gothic"; and Hermione Lee, *Elizabeth Bowen: An Estimation* (London: Vision Press, 1982), situate Bowen within "a certain kind of ascendancy biographical writing," which, while true for texts such as *Bowen's Court*, obscure other contexts of her writing ("Gothic" 1092). In *Pictures and Conversations*, Bowen herself claimed that she was not a "'regional writer' in the accredited sense" (*Pictures* 35–36). The faulty critical tendency to emphasize Bowen's regionalist aspirations follows the difficulty of placing her within a larger cosmopolitan critical frame.

8. In response to these sorts of assessments, critics such as Neil Corcoran, in *Elizabeth Bowen: The Enforced Return* (London: Oxford UP, 2004), hereafter referred to as *EB*, spend considerable time demonstrating Bowen's "worth" as an experimental writer whose works of "fraught complexity" are "as richly challenging and satisfying as anything comparable in Woolf or Joyce" (*EB* 87). Beyond its assessment of modernism as experimental and "challenging," this positive judgment of Bowen's work does not adequately gauge the ways in which Bowen's work indeed participates in that modernism. In perhaps the best critical text to date on Bowen, however, *Elizabeth Bowen and the Dissolution of the Novel: Still Lives* (New York: Palgrave Macmillan, 1995), hereafter referred to as *Dissolution*, Andrew Bennett and Nicholas Royle credit Bowen's work with transforming the notion of character by presenting "a new and culturally disruptive poetics of personality" (*Dissolution* xvii). Still life, they suggest, figures heavily into the literary technique that Bowen herself professed to practice.
9. See Peter Nicholls, *Modernisms: A Literary Guide* (Berkeley: U of California P, 1995), 3. Nicholls's conservative assessment of modernism has a foundation in Georg Lukács, *The Theory of the Novel*, trans. Anna Bostock (Cambridge: MIT Press, 1996). Writing in 1914, Lukács credits the novel with being essentially "problematic," as having "destroyed culture," with an "imitation" which is "subjective and reflexive so far as the depicted reality is concerned" (157). The duality Lukács envisions between the subjective world of individual experience that is merely imitative and a "more adequate reality" is still a guiding assumption that underlies the current reception of Bowen's writing.
10. See Douglas Mao, *Solid Objects: Modernism and the Test of Production* (Princeton: Princeton UP, 1998), 15, hereafter referred to as *Solid*.
11. Mao most succinctly identifies the modernist problematic at stake here, the "attempt to ensure the object's extrasubjective integrity, to take part of this radical other without, as it were, resubordinating it to consciousness" (*Solid* 10).

Whereas Mao argues that modernists like Pound and Eliot guarded against this problem by favoring the "impermeability of the solid object," writers such as Bowen render an object world that guards itself from human intrusion in its very ability to emotionally dissect humans, opening them to vulnerability and invasion (*Solid* 15).
12. See Susan Fraiman's critique of this model in *Unbecoming Women: British Women Writers and the Novel of Development* (New York: Columbia UP, 1993), which includes chapters on Frances Burney, Jane Austen, Charlotte Bronte, and George Eliot. Additionally, the collection of essays, *The Voyage In: Fictions of Female Development*, ed. Elizabeth Abel, Marianne Hirsh, and Elizabeth Langland (London: UP of New England, 1983), challenges the generic formulations of the *Bildungsroman* by arguing that "[e]ven the broadest definitions of the *Bildungsroman* presuppose a range of options only available to men" (7). Both studies respond to this frequently quoted passage from Jerome Buckley, *Season of Youth: The Bildungsroman from Dickens to Golding* (Cambridge: Harvard UP, 1974), hereafter referred to as *Season*, which identifies the "broad outlines of a typical Bildungsroman plot":

> A child of some sensibility grows up in the country, or in a provincial town, where he finds constraints, social and intellectual, placed upon the free imagination. His family, especially his father, proves doggedly hostile to his creative instincts or flights of fancy, antagonistic to his ambitions, and quite impervious to the new ideas he has gained from unprescribed reading. His first schooling, even if not totally inadequate, may be frustrating insofar as it may suggest options not available to him in his present setting. He therefore, sometimes at a quite early age, leaves the repressive atmosphere of home . . . to make his way independently in the city . . . There his real 'education' begins, not only his preparation for a career but also . . . his direct experience of urban life. The latter involves at least two love affairs or sexual encounters, one debasing, one exalting, and demands that in this respect and others the hero reappraise his values. By the time he has decided, after painful soul-searching, the sort of accommodation to the modern world he can honestly make, he has left his adolescence behind and entered upon his maturity (*Season* 17–18).

13. See Franco Moretti, *The Way of the World: The Bildungsroman in European Culture* (London: Verso, 2000), 12, italics in original, hereafter referred to as *Way*.
14. See Wyndham Lewis, *The Art of Being Ruled* (Santa Rosa, CA: Black Sparrow Press, 1989), 148, hereafter referred to as *Art*.
15. Diana Fuss makes a similar claim in her discussion of "modern interiority" as it developed in the nineteenth century. See *The Sense of an Interior: Four Writers and the Rooms That Shaped Them* (London: Routledge, 2004), 9.
16. See Pierre Bourdieu, *Distinction: A Social Critique of the Judgment of Taste*, trans. Richard Nice (Cambridge: Harvard UP, 1984), 281, hereafter referred to as *Distinction*.

17. See Karl Marx, "Excerpts from James Mill's *Elements of Political Economy*," in *Early Writings*, trans. Rodney Livingston and Gregor Benton (New York: Vintage, 1975), 266.
18. See George Eliot, *The Mill on the Floss* (New York: Penguin, 1979). In this formulation, the domestic sphere of bourgeois intimacy is emptied out into the anonymity of the public domain, so that objects, once privately owned, become subject to dispossession. However, the ultimate act of dispossession occurs at the end of the novel, where Tom, after Maggie's "elopement," resolutely pronounces that "You will find no home with me . . . You no longer belong to me" (612). In opposition to the traditional closure of the *Bildungsroman*, which celebrates the stability of social connections, Maggie, its inappropriate subject like the objects of the Tulliver household, is without a home, finding no comfort in "everyday life" (*Way* 40). Not surprisingly, she dies with her brother in a flood, nature's revenge against the possibility of Maggie's becoming the appropriate subject of the *Bildungsroman*.
19. See Elizabeth Bowen, *The House in Paris* (New York: Anchor, 2002), hereafter referred to as *HP*, for a characteristic exchange, in which Karen, the tale's absent mother, addresses her own mother's callous refusal to acknowledge the secret affair that produces Leopold, her son, in reference to her feelings about home: "It made me not feel I lived here" (*HP* 176). Max Ebhart, Leopold's Jewish father, who dramatically commits suicide before he learns of Karen's pregnancy, remarks similarly of their union, "we cannot live what we are" (*HP* 181). Later, regarding Leopold, Karen laments, "But I must see someway for him to live" (*HP* 187). In each of these examples, one is only able to "live" somewhere upon acquiring the stability and immobility required for legitimate existence in the world.
20. In *Pictures and Conversations*, Bowen declares that a distrust of the boundaries of self and character plays a major part in her fiction, claiming that it is "something to have character attributed to one." Human nature is characterized by "the amorphousness of the drifting and flopping jellyfish in a cloudy tide, and secret fears . . . prey upon individuals made aware of this." As a result, the "obsessive wish to acquire outline, to be unmistakably demarcated, to *take shape*" develops (italics in original; *Pictures* 58–59).
21. See Butts's story "The House" in the collection *From Altar to Chimney Piece* (Kingston, NY: McPherson, 1992), 3–21. Many of Butts's stories and her Taverner novels specifically follow the pattern of "The House," in which conflict arises when "the wrong sort of people" enter an aesthetically privileged house (4).
22. While the narrative of Rhys's *Voyage in the Dark* (New York: Norton, 1994), originally published in 1934, foregrounds sexuality more explicitly, its protagonist, Anna Morgan (much like Portia Quayne) confronts the failure of her own *Bildung* primarily through the instability of her housing situation, which is both the outcome and cause of her sexual exploitation. See also Rhys's novels *Quartet* (1929), *After Leaving Mr. Mackenzie* (1931), and *Good*

Morning, Midnight (1939) in *Jean Rhys: The Complete Novels* (New York: Norton, 1985).
23. I take this phrase from Neil Corcoran's reading of the same situation in the novel in *Elizabeth Bowen: The Enforced Return*, 121.
24. See Gaston Bachelard, *The Poetics of Space*, trans. Maria Jolas (Boston: Beacon, 1994), 78, originally published in 1958.
25. According to the Oxford English Dictionary, Anna's usage of the word "taped" most likely means "archived" rather than what a contemporary reader is likely to assume, which is audiotaped. The first audiotape machines were not available until the late 1940s.
26. See Wilhelm Worringer, *Abstraction and Empathy: A Contribution to the Study of Style* (Chicago: Elephant, 2007), 15, hereafter referred to as *Abstraction*.

Conclusion

1. See Elizabeth Bowen, *The Death of the Heart* (New York: Anchor, 2000), 384, hereafter referred to as *Death*.
2. See Elizabeth Bowen, *The House in Paris* (New York: Anchor, 2002), 51, hereafter referred to as *House*.
3. See *Selected Prose of T. S. Eliot* (New York: Harcourt, 1975), 43, hereafter abbreviated as *Prose*.
4. See Jacqueline Rose, "Bizarre Objects: Mary Butts and Elizabeth Bowen," in *On Not Being Able to Sleep: Psychoanalysis and the Modern World* (Princeton: Princeton UP, 2003), 98, hereafter abbreviated as *ON*.
5. See T. E. Hulme, *Speculations: Essays on Humanism and the Philosophy of Art*, ed. Herbert Read (London: Routledge, 1965), 33, hereafter referred to as *Speculations*.
6. See Gaston Bachelard, *The Poetics of Space* (Boston: Beacon, 1994), 214, hereafter referred to as *Poetics*.
7. See M. Merleau-Ponty, *Phenomenology of Perception*, trans. Colin Smith (London: Routledge, 1962), 101, hereafter referred to as *Phenomenology*.
8. See Rei Terada, *Feeling in Theory: Emotion after the "Death of the Subject"* (Cambridge: Harvard UP, 2001) 4, 3; hereafter referred to as *Feeling*.
9. See Virginia Woolf, "On Not Knowing Greek," in *The Common Reader* (New York: Harcourt, 1984), 25, 27, hereafter abbreviated as *CR*.
10. See David Ellison's discussion of Virginia Woolf's impersonality in *Ethics and Aesthetics in European Modernist Literature: From the Sublime to the Uncanny* (Cambridge: Cambridge UP, 2001), 212, 210.

Index

abstraction, concept of: Bowen's resistance of, 203–4n7; empathy contrasted with, 15–16, 23–24, 123–25, 132, 165–66, 169, 171; modern design and, 35; space and, 10
activity: Freud's use of term, 92; Gaudier-Brzeska's use of term, 40, 44; Lawrence's use of term, 81–82, 85–88, 90, 92, 93, 96–101; Le Corbusier's use of term, 35–36; Lewis's use of term, 113–14, 116–17, 120–21, 124; personality and, 24–25, 26
adornment, personality and, 22, 26
affective individualism, concept of, 194n19
Ahmed, Sarah: *Queer Phenomenology*, 9, 120, 146, 183n18, 199n25
Albright, Daniel: *Personality and Impersonality*, 6, 82–83, 84, 182n11, 192n3
Alfrey, Shawn: *The Sublime of Intense Sociability*, 189n14
Altieri, Charles: "Theorizing Emotions in Eliot's Poetry and Poetics," 12
animism, 145–46, 149–50, 204n7
anti-semitism, 115–16
apostrophe, 58, 61–62, 66, 68, 73–74
Archipenko, Alexander, 40
Armstrong, Tim: *Modernism, Technology and the Body*, 34, 185n11, 186n21, 190n20
authority: artistic selection and, 11; asymmetry of, 25–26, 151; definition of, 2; fantasies of, 50; impersonality's destabilization of, 16; invasiveness of, 15; Lawrence's embrace of, 193n14; Lewis's embrace of, 1–2, 14–15, 34; loss of, 41–44; occultism and, 15–16, 27; personality in relation to, 23–24, 25, 176–77; poet as bard, 47–80; uniformity and, 33–41; violence and, 2
automatic writing, 16, 27, 185n11

Bachelard, Gaston: *The Poetics of Space*, 163, 164, 165, 171, 172, 177, 202n45
Banfield, Ann: *The Phantom Table*, 117
Barnes, Djuna: *Nightwood*, 16
Bell, Clive: *On Art*, 131
Benjamin, Walter: cinema viewed by, 48–49, 187–88n5; "Unpacking My Library," 200n31
Bennett, Andrew: *Elizabeth Bowen and the Dissolution of the Novel* (with Royle), 204n8
Benstock, Shari: *Women of the Left Bank*, 202n47
Berman, Louis: *The Glands Regulating Personality*, 185n15
Bersani, Leo: *The Arts of Impoverishment* (with Dutoit), 113, 118, 196n2; *The Freudian Body*, 90–91, 191n31
Bildungsroman: Bowen's works, 85, 149–75; centrality in modernism, 85, 112; Lawrence's works, 85, 94–96, 108–9, 110, 111, 153; personality and, 153–55;

Bildungsroman (continued)
traditional narrative structure, 94, 98, 104, 154–55, 195n27
Blanchot, Maurice: *Friendship*, 105, 108, 195n29
Blast (journal), 2, 28–29, 38, 118, 121, 181n2, 196n4, 199n26
Blondel, Nathalie: *Mary Butts*, 115
Bloomsbury group: Butts's animus against, 115, 116, 117, 129–36; homosexuality and, 201nn38–39; Lewis and, 121–22, 130, 200n30; promotion of heteronormative agenda, 201n38
Boone, Joseph Allen: *Libidinal Currents*, 83, 194n21
Bourdieu, Pierre: *Distinction*, 145, 155, 162, 202n50
Bowen, Elizabeth, 10–11; critical assessment, 152–53; *The Death of the Heart*, 15, 85, 149–50, 153–74, 175–80; *Friends and Relations*, 150; *The Hotel*, 150; *The House in Paris*, 150, 157, 160, 175, 206n19; *The Last September*, 150, 151, 157, 203n6; *Pictures and Conversations*, 170, 203n2, 206n20; political agenda, 3; subject-object investigations in works of, 115, 147–75, 176, 205n11. *See also* Death of the Heart
Boyle, Kay, 202n49
Brancusi, Constantin, 40
Brooks, Peter: *Reading for the Plot*, 91, 92, 99–100, 137, 194n21, 195n27
Brown, Judith: *Glamour in Six Dimensions*, 5–6
Browning, Robert, 32
Buckley, Jerome: *Season of Youth*, 161, 205n12
Buddhist iconography, 4
Burke, Carolyn: *Becoming Modern*, 185n11
Burstein, Jessica: "Waspish Segments," 186n21

Butts, Mary: aesthetic of impersonality, 125, 146–47, 198n14; anti-semitism of, 115–16; *Armed with Madness*, 117, 126, 127–28, 140, 198n18; *Ashe of Rings*, 115; biographical studies of, 115, 197n7; "Bloomsbury," 130, 131; British imperialism viewed in works of, 126, 132–33, 134; *The Death of Felicity Taverner*, 115–16, 126–27, 128–29; drug use, 16; fascination with violence, 2; "From Altar to Chimney Piece," 143–45, 202n47; *From Altar to Chimney Piece*, 176; "The House," 206n21; "The House Party," 115; *Imaginary Letters*, 197n7; "In Bloomsbury," 126, 129, 131–36, 140, 144; *Jacob's Room*, 115; Lewis and, 115–16; modernist role of, 115; personal experience in works of, 10–11; political agenda, 3; subject-object investigations in works of, 114–18, 121, 123, 126–29, 137–46, 156–59, 176; "With and Without Buttons," 137–42

Calinescu, Matei: *Five Faces of Modernity*, 200–201n35
Cameron, Sharon: *Impersonality*, 2, 4, 25, 50, 203n5
Carlston, Erin: *Thinking Fascism*, 59
Cezanne, Paul, 142
charisma, concept of, 25, 27
clairvoyance, 68, 185n11, 189n13, 193n8
Close Up (journal), 48
Cocteau, Jean, 115, 197n7
Cohen, Ed: *Talk on the Wilde Side*, 185–86n16
collecting, art, 125–28, 132–33, 143–44
Colour (magazine), 200n30
Comentale, Edward: *Modernism*, 2, 13, 181n2
conjuring, 16

conservatism, political: impersonality and, 3, 5, 11, 57, 188n8
Corcoran, Neil: *Elizabeth Bowen: The Enforced Return*, 204n8, 207n23
cosmopolitanism, 41–46, 57–64
cruising, itinerant, 41–44, 45–46, 117
Culler, Jonathan: *The Pursuit of Signs*, 58

daemonic power, 103, 195n26
Dante Alighieri: *Inferno*, Canto XV, 12
Dean, Tim: *Beyond Sexuality*, 4, 5–6, 9, 183n18, 191n32
Death of the Heart, The (Bowen), 153–74; as *Bildungsroman*, 85, 149–50; diary in, 163–66, 168, 172; emotion after, 175–80; hotel living, 160–70; intimacy in, 166–67; personal property in, 170–74; title of, 15
decadence, imagism and, 51
decorative art: Bloomsbury group and, 130; in Bowen's *The Death of the Heart*, 156–59; kitsch and, 128, 200–201n35; Le Corbusier's views on, 34–36, 118, 186n22; Omega Workshops, 121–22, 199n28, 200n30
Deleuze, Gilles: *Coldness and Cruelty*, 65–66, 68
democracy, Lewis's views on, 1–2, 7, 29–30, 57
depersonalization, process of, 88–91
design, modernist theories of, 117–22; collecting and, 125–28, 143–44; Le Corbusier, 186n22; Omega Workshops and, 121–22, 199n28
Dial, The (journal), 115
Doan, Laura, 191n29
Dodge, Mabel, 145
Dollimore, Jonathan: *Death, Desire, and Loss in Western Culture*, 193n14
drugs, 16
Dunikowski, Xawery, 40

Dutoit, Ulysse: *The Arts of Impoverishment* (with Bersani), 113, 118, 196n2

Eagleton, Terry: *Literary Theory*, 92–93, 95, 99, 101–2, 192n5
ecological thinking, concept of, 9, 183n18
Edwards, Jonathan, 4
Egoist, The (journal), 122
Eliot, George: *The Mill on the Floss*, 155, 156, 206n18
Eliot, T. S.: attitude toward homosexuality, 183n20; Bloomsbury group and, 130; Cameron's study of, 4; Dean's study of, 5–6; Ellmann's study of, 4–5; feelings distinguished from emotions by, 12–14; *Four Quartets*, 50; "Hamlet," 13; impersonality doctrine, 3, 6–7, 11–12, 15, 33, 45, 79–80, 103, 109, 151, 178, 188n8; "The Love Song of J. Alfred Prufrock," 5, 9, 75; political conservatism, 3, 188n8; reverence for tradition, 2, 181–82n6; subject-object investigations in works of, 205n11; theories of, 31; "Tradition and the Individual Talent," 3, 7, 11–16, 22, 24, 33, 36, 37, 40, 48, 66, 84, 86, 113, 119, 146, 179, 181–82nn5–6; "The Waste Land," 114. *See also* "Tradition and the Individual Talent"
Ellmann, Maud: *Elizabeth Bowen: The Shadow across the Page*, 152, 173–74; *The Poetics of Impersonality*, 4–5, 188n8
Emerson, Ralph Waldo, 4
emotions: death of subject and, 179–80; feelings distinguished from, 12–14; World War I aftermath and, 179–80
empathy: abstraction contrasted with, 15, 23–24, 123–24, 132,

empathy (*continued*)
180; objects and, 117, 126, 129, 134, 137, 140, 141, 144, 145, 146, 163, 165–66, 168–70, 176; self-replication and, 72; space and, 136, 151, 153; Worringer's concept of, 125
Empson, William, 4
Epstein, Jacob, 40
Esty, Jed: "Virgins of Empire," 150–51, 203n6
eugenics, 50, 63–64, 190n21
Exposition des Arts Décoratifs (Paris, 1925), 34–35

fascism: Gaudier-Brzeska's embrace of, 38–40; Lewis's embrace of, 2, 116, 181n3; Pound's embrace of, 5, 78–79; prosthetic modernism and, 34, 186n21; rhetoric of, 59; vorticism and, 37
feminism: H.D. and, 49, 50, 64, 67, 188n6; impersonality and, 10, 53–56; Lawrence's works dismissed by, 83, 192n4; Lewis's views on, 28, 29
feng shui, 121, 125, 139
film, silent, 48–49, 57, 187–88n5
flaneur, 42
Flanner, Janet: *Men and Monuments*, 125–26, 127
Forster, E. M.: *Howards End*, 157
fort/da game, 91–92, 102
Foster, Hal: "Prosthetic Gods," 186n20
Fraiman, Susan: *Unbecoming Women*, 205n12
Freud, Sigmund: *Beyond the Pleasure Principle*, 91–92, 94, 103; *The Ego and the Id*, 95–96, 194n23; *fort/da* game, 91–92, 102; *Group Psychology and the Analysis of the Ego*, 108, 195n31; H.D.'s sessions with, 75; Reik's analysis of, 190n24; *Three Essays on the Theory of Sexuality*, 65, 190n25; "The Uncanny," 110

Friedman, Susan Stanford: *Penelope's Web*, 55, 189n13, 193n8
Fry, Roger, 121–23, 200n29; "The Artist as Decorator," 122, 200n30
Fuss, Diana: *The Sense of an Interior*, 205n15
futurism, 113–14

Garnett, Edward, 87
Garrity, Jane, 191n29; "Mary Butts's 'Fanatical Pédérastie,'" 197–98n12; "Selling Culture to the 'Civilized,'" 130, 201n38; *Step-Daughters of England*, 115, 197n5
Gaudier-Brzeska, Henri: aesthetic of impersonality, 33, 34, 103, 108, 125; "Hieratic Head of Ezra Pound," 37–38; "Ideal," 200n29; Omega Workshops criticized by, 122; response to term "personality," 23, 24; sculpture of, 36–41, 44; "Written from the Trenches," 38–40
gender: decorative arts and, 34–35, 117, 118–22, 199n22; impersonality doctrine and, 49–50; impersonality's transcendence of, 10–11; personality and, 28–33, 88; poetry and, 48, 50, 56, 62–72
geometrism, 165, 176–77
Giddens, Anthony: *The Consequences of Modernity*, 89–90, 109, 193n16, 194n19
glamour, 5–6
Gourmont, Remy de: *The Natural Philosophy of Love*, 62, 63, 65, 78
Grant, Duncan, 131
Gregory, Eileen: "Rose Cut in Rock," 188n7

Hacking, Ian: *Rewriting the Soul*, 27
Hainley, Bruce: "Quite Contrary," 114, 197n7
hallucinations, 149–50, 152, 158–59, 163, 168, 203n3

Harrison, Charles: *English Art and Modernism*, 201n39

H.D.: bisexuality of, 67, 191n29; critical response to, 49–50; detachment in poetry of, 51–52, 109, 189n13, 193n8; feminism and, 188n6; impersonality doctrine, 3, 79; limits of poetic authority and, 47–80; "The Mask and the Movietone," 48–49, 187–88n5; *Notes on Thought and Vision*, 47, 49, 52–53, 55, 56, 63, 66, 73, 190n18; personal experience in works of, 10–11; political agenda, 3, 57; prose of, 189n13; *Sea Garden*, 15, 49, 50, 53–78, 109, 176, 192n34; spatiality in poems of, 46; territorial stance toward classical beauty, 63–64; theories of, 31; *Tribute to Freud*, 75, 191n31; *The Wise Sappho*, 47, 49, 53, 56, 63. *See also* Sea Garden

Hemingway, Ernest, 143

hermeneutic code, 87, 99–101, 166, 176, 178–79, 194n19

Herring, Scott: *Queering the Underworld*, 9, 183n17, 187n28

Hogarth Press, 115

Homer, 198n14

homophobia: of Lawrence, 106–7, 108; of Lewis, 2, 28–33, 117

homosexuality: Bloomsbury group and, 131, 201nn38–39; Butts's interest in, 115, 197n7, 197–98n12; Eliot's attitude toward, 183n20; feminism and, 28–29, 115, 197n7; homoeroticism in *Sons and Lovers*, 96, 104, 106, 108; of Wilde, 28–29, 30, 117, 185–16n16

Hulme, T. E.: *Speculations*, 6, 8, 12, 14, 108, 176–77

humanism, 8–9, 12, 81–82; Lawrence's views on, 87

Husserl, Edmund, 12

Huyssen, Andreas: *After the Great Divide*, 199n22

hypermasculinity, 16, 34

imagism: emotional seizure of, 52–53; of H.D., 46, 47–80, 79; masochism and, 65–67; of Pound, 6–7, 40, 54, 78–79, 100–101, 188–89n10

immortality, 102, 103, 104–5, 110, 111, 132

imperialism, 126, 132–33, 134, 197n9

impersonality: agents needed for, 51; as antidote, 19; avenues of, 16; cruising and, 41–44, 45–46; depersonalization distinguished from, 88–91; disease of, 122–29; dispossession and, 151, 155–59; doctrine of, 3; earlier studies of, 6; emotional death and, 175–80; ethical problems of, 19, 82–85; expansion of concept, 3; feng shui and, 121, 125, 139; glamour and, 5–6; H.D.'s connection to, 49–50; interior decorating and, 156–59; key contradictions of, 11; like-minded collectivity and, 40; masochism and, 65–67, 107–8; metamorphosis and, 56–57; modernism and, 1–18; parasitic relationship and, 136–42; poet as bard, 47–80; poetic emotion, 12–15, 37–39, 40, 45, 79–80, 107–8, 166; psychoanalysis and, 91–96; queer spatiality and, 9; reconsiderations of, 3–4; as rejection of individualism, 2, 6, 15; scale and, 45; shared memory and, 76; sociological concept of, 21–23; space and ideal of, 21–46; of stranger, 21, 25, 42–46, 187n28; uniformity and, 33–41; Wilde and, 30–33; works of arts as monuments, 178. *See also specific authors*

individualism: impersonality's rejection of, 2, 6, 15, 33; personality as acquisition and, 24–26, 28; psychoanalytic theories of personality, 7–11; social space and, 21–22, 27–28
Ingelbien, Raphael: "Gothic Genealogies," 204n7
Inglesby, Elizabeth C.: "'Expressive Objects,'" 203–4n7

James, Henry, 152, 196n4
Jameson, Fredric: *A Singular Modernity*, 7–8, 182n14
Jay, Martin: "Modernism and the Spectre of Psychologism," 12
Joyce, James: *Portrait of the Artist as a Young Man*, 85

Kant, Immanuel, 12
Kenner, Hugh: *The Pound Era*, 37
Keynes, Maynard, 131
kitsch, 128, 200–201n35

Laity, Cassandra: *H.D. and the Victorian Fin de Siecle*, 49–50, 51; "H.D.'s Romantic Landscapes," 191n28
Lamos, Colleen: *Deviant Modernism*, 4, 11, 183n20
Lawrence, D. H.: *Aaron's Rod*, 88; "common life" concept, 86–87, 89; *Fantasia of the Unconscious*, 86, 87, 89, 92–93; homophobia of, 106–7, 108; impersonality doctrine, 3, 79, 81, 91–92; *Lady Chatterley's Lover*, 192n4; misogyny of, 83–84; proposed lecture series with Russell, 104–5; *Psychoanalysis and the Unconscious*, 92; *Sons and Lovers*, 6, 82–112, 117, 153, 167, 173, 176, 177, 192nn3–5, 194–95n23–25; use of term "activity," 81–82, 85–88, 93, 96–101; violence in works of, 2, 87–88, 101–12, 116; *Women in Love*, 107. See also Sons and Lovers
Le Corbusier: aesthetic of impersonality, 33, 34–36, 39, 41, 42; attempted liberation of space from personality, 24; *The Decorative Art of Today*, 34–36, 118, 186n22; *Modular Man*, 186n22
Lee, Hermione: *Elizabeth Bowen: An Estimation*, 204n7
Levenson, Michael: *A Genealogy of Modernism*, 6–7, 10
Lewis, Wyndham: animism viewed by, 145–46; antipathy toward Bloomsbury group, 121–22, 199n28; *The Apes of God*, 116; *The Art of Being Ruled*, 1–2, 7, 29–30, 181n3, 182n13; *Blast* journal of, 2, 28–29, 118, 121, 181n2, 196n4, 199n26; Bloomsbury group and, 121–22, 130, 201n39; Butts and, 115–16; *The Caliph's Design*, 113–14, 116, 118, 120–22, 124, 128, 196n1; "The Feminine Conception of Freedom," 28, 29–30; "Feng Shui and Contemporary Form," 121, 125, 139; Fry and, 200n29; *Hitler*, 116, 186n21; homophobia of, 2, 28–33, 117; "The 'Homo' the Child of the 'Suffragette,'" 28; impersonality doctrine, 3, 23, 33, 39, 81, 147; *Men Without Art*, 116; misogyny of, 2, 88; "The New Egos," 28–29; "The Physiological Norm and the 'Vicious,'" 28; "Relativism and Picasso's Latest Work," 199n26; *Snooty Baronet*, 41; *Tarr*, 186n21; *Time and Western Man*, 196n4; use of term "activity," 113; violence advocated by, 193n11; Wilde viewed by, 28–29, 33, 117

Love, Heather: *Feeling Backward*, 183n21
Loy, Mina, 185n11, 189–90n18
Lukács, Georg: "The Ideology of Modernism," 195n33, 204n9
Lyon, Janet: "Josephine Baker's Hothouse," 143

Macpherson, Kenneth, 48
Mansfield, Katherine, 81–82, 84, 89
Mao, Douglas: on Lewis's antipathy toward Bloomsbury group, 121–22; on modernism's object-subject relationship, 204–5n11; on modernists' antipathy to commodity, 198–99n22; *Solid Objects*, 152–53, 187n29, 196n4, 197n9, 199n26, 199n28; on violence and production in Lawrence's works, 85–86, 87, 89
Marinetti, Filippo Tommaso, 113–14
marionette. *See* ventriloquism
Marx, Karl, 155
masochism: in H.D.'s poetry, 10–11, 16, 50, 51, 52, 64–67, 107–8; in Lawrence's works, 107; ritual and, 66–68; sexual, 16, 65–72; studies on, 190–91nn24–26
materialism: art collecting and, 125–28, 132–33, 143–44; insecurity and, 161–70; modernist design and, 118–22; object placement and, 123, 128–29, 137–42, 149–50, 156–59; phenomenology and, 119–20; Wilde's views on, 30
McAlmon, Robert: *Being Geniuses Together*, 145, 202n49
mediums, 16
Melville, Herman, 4
Merleau-Ponty, Maurice: "motor significance" idea, 201n41; *Phenomenology of Perception*, 8, 9, 10, 45–46, 64–65, 119–20, 131, 135–36, 142, 146–47, 149–50, 166, 172–73, 177, 180, 189n17

Miller, Brook: "The Impersonal Personal," 204n7
Miller, Tyrus: *Late Modernism*, 116, 196n4
Millett, Kate: *Sexual Politics*, 83, 192n4
misogyny: of Lawrence, 83–84, 88, 94; of Lewis, 2, 28, 88
Modigliani, Amedeo, 40
Moore, Marianne, 115
Moretti, Franco: *The Way of the World*, 96, 99, 112, 154–56, 160, 169, 170, 193n9
Murry, John Middleton, 81–82
Myers, F. W. H.: *Human Personality and Its Survival of Bodily Death*, 23, 26–28, 33, 185n11

Nicholls, Peter: *Modernisms: A Literary Guide*, 152, 204n9
Nies, Betsy L.: *Eugenic Fantasies*, 190n21
Noakes, Richard: "The Historiography of Psychical Research," 185n11

objectification, 43, 119, 123, 124–29, 134, 137–42, 143, 149–50, 158, 163, 176
occultism, 185n11; impersonality and, 15–16; personality and, 27
Oedipus complex, 194n23
Omega Workshops, 121–22, 199n28, 200n30
Other, the, 5

paranormal psychology, 185n11
parasitic relationships, 71–72, 136–42, 189–90n18
Paris salon life, 142–45
parthenogenesis, 62–63
Peppis, Paul, 37
personality: as acquisition, 24–26, 28; authority in relation to, 23–24, 25, 176–77; *Bildungsroman* and, 153–55; Bloomsbury group and, 129–30; cloning, 72–73; embodiment

personality (*continued*)
and, 48; failures of, 24–28; Lawrence's views on, 81–82; Lewis's views on, 1–2, 23, 28–33, 117; malleability of, 23; as mask, 30, 31, 32, 48–49; materialism and, 30–31, 149–50; meaning of term, 23–33; multiple, 26, 27, 35, 72, 184n10; necessity of, 18–19; prosthetic modernism and, 33–41; psychoanalytic theories of, 7–11; social space and, 21–22, 27–28; spatial understanding of, 23–24; taste and, 202n50; Wilde's views on, 30–31

"personality value," concept of, 21

personal magnetism, 27

phenomenology: distance, scale and, 44–46, 84; geometrism and, 176–77; impersonalization and, 8; modernist design and, 118–22; objectification and, 124–29, 149–50, 163, 166

physiology, 185n15

Picasso, Pablo, 143, 199n26

Pinkney, Tony, 83, 97–98, 100–101, 112

poetic emotion, ideal of impersonal, 11–15, 32, 37–40, 45, 79–80, 84, 86, 91, 103, 107–8, 119, 146, 166

poetry: apostrophe in, 58, 61–62, 66, 68, 73–74; of H.D., 47–80, 84, 189n13, 192n34, 193n8; impersonal personae in, 32, 58–59, 73–77, 84, 109

Pound, Ezra: *ABC of Reading*, 47, 74; "Au Salon," 142–43; Ellmann's study of, 4–5; emotion characterized by, 12; formalist aesthetic, 6–7, 51; imagism of, 6–7, 40, 54, 78–79, 100–101, 188–89n10; impersonality doctrine, 3, 188n8; masculinization of H.D.'s poetry, 73; *A Memoir of Gaudier-Brzeska*, 37, 183–84n25,
187n26; poetic persona, 32, 84, 109; sculpture by Gaudier-Brzeska, 37–38; sexuality viewed by, 65; subject-object investigations in works of, 120, 125, 205n11; theories of, 31; translation of Gourmont, 62, 63, 65, 78

Prince, Morton: *The Dissociation of Personality*, 23, 26, 34, 184n10

proairetic code, 99, 100, 101, 102, 104–5, 111

prosthetic modernism, 33–41; in Butts's works, 139–40; double logic of, 186n20; fantasies of, 16; Lawrence and, 89–90; Le Corbusier's decorative arts aesthetic and, 34–36; Lewis and, 186n21; multiple personalities and, 35; reproduction and, 62, 72; as term, 190n20; Woolf and, 44–45

psychoanalysis: H.D.'s sessions with Freud, 75, 191n31; Lawrence's views on, 86, 91–96, 102; passivity and, 75–76, 78; personality theories, 7–11

psychology: humanism and, 7–8, 12; of masochism, 190–91nn24–26; modernism and, 119–20, 180; paranormal, 185n11

public opinion, personality and, 31

queer theory: empirical perception and, 145–46; modernist impersonality and, 9, 183n17; primary challenge of, 191n32

Rainey, Lawrence: *Institutions of Modernism*, 188n6

Rebel Art Centre, 122

Reed, Christopher: on avant-garde architectural theory, 116; on Bloomsbury, 130, 131; "Bloomsbury Bashing," 201n39;

"'A Room of One's Own': The Bloomsbury Group's Creation of Modernist Domesticity," 200n29
Reik, Theodor: *Masochism in Sex and Society*, 65, 190n24
reincarnation, 27
Rhys, Jean: *Voyage in the Dark*, 85, 160, 206n22
Roof, Judith: *Come as You Are*, 83, 192n34, 193n7, 194n21
Rose, Jacqueline: "Bizarre Objects," 176, 203n3
Rotello, Gabriel: *Sexual Ecology*, 9, 183n18
Rothko, Mark, 196n2
Royle, Nicholas: *Elizabeth Bowen and the Dissolution of the Novel* (with Bennett), 204n8
Russell, Bertrand, 104

Sappho, 47, 48, 56–57, 188n7
Sartre, Jean-Paul, 45, 118–19; *Logical Investigations*, 198n20
Sea Garden (H.D.), 53–78; aesthetic articulated in, 49; authority and, 15, 50; "Cities," 57–64, 70, 71–73, 74, 78; "The Gift," 73–77, 78; "The Helmsman," 67–72, 74, 76–77; "Sea Gods," 71; "Sea Rose," 53–56, 58, 61, 63–64, 67, 71, 75; self-replication in, 109; "The Shrine," 71; spatial orientation in, 176; structure in, 192n34
secrecy, need for, 163–64, 173
Sedgwick, Eve: *Touching Feeling*, 9
self-diffusion, 6
self-possession, desire for, 24, 25, 111, 149, 150, 151
self-realization, personality and, 25–26, 89
self-replication, 71–72, 110, 136
self-sacrifice, concept of, 2, 3, 48, 181n5
Seltzer, Mark, 186n20

sexual impersonality: in H.D.'s "Cities," 62–63, 64, 71–72; in H.D.'s "The Gift," 76–77; Merleau-Ponty's views on, 64–65; multiple personality and, 27, 184n10; poetry and, 48, 191n32
sexual sublimation, 52, 108
sexual submission, 16, 52–53, 68
sexuality: of Butts, 115, 197n7; H.D.'s relation to, 191n29; in H.D.'s works, 191n32; in Lawrence's works, 6, 83–84, 90–91, 95–96, 106–8, 110; masochism, 16, 65–72; queering of, 183n18. See also homosexuality
Shakespeare, William: *Hamlet*, 13
Silverman, Kaja: *Male Subjectivity at the Margins*, 191n26
Simmel, Georg: "The Metropolis and Mental Life," 22–23, 31; *Sociology*, 21–24, 27, 31, 41, 193–94n17
Simpson, Hillary: *D. H. Lawrence and Feminism*, 192n4
Smiles, Samuel: *Self-Help*, 25, 184n7
Smirnoff, Victor: "The Masochistic Contract," 190n23
Smith, Colin, 120
socialism: Wilde's views on, 30, 31–32, 33
Society of Psychical Research, 185n11
somnambulism, 16
Sons and Lovers (Lawrence), 6, 82–112; as *Bildungsroman*, 85, 87–88, 110–11, 153, 195n25; depersonalization in, 88–91, 195n24; ethical difficulties of impersonality in, 83–85; fate of Paul Morel, 173, 176, 177; interiority vs. exteriority in, 101–4, 108; intimacy in, 167; Oedipal plot of, 93–94, 98; Oedipus complex and, 194n23; psychoanalytic reading of, 91–96, 192n5; repetitive nature of, 91–92, 96; violence in, 87–91, 101–12, 117; work in, 96–101

space, spatiality: changes in orientation, 9; cosmopolitan, 57–64; cruising and, 41–44; dispossession and, 151, 155–59; domestic restructuring, 29, 143–44, 147, 149–50, 155–59; impersonality's dynamic, 16, 21–46, 84, 151, 172–74, 176; model of narrative form, 137; objectification and, 131–36, 137–42, 156–59; perception of scale, 43; psychology and, 7–11, 78; scale and, 45; "stranger" in, 21–22, 25, 42–46, 187n28; value of impersonal, 21–22; vorticist aesthetic and, 38–41
spiritualism, 27, 185n11
Stein, Gertrude, 143–45, 202n47
Stone, Lawrence, 194n19
Strachey, Lytton: *Eminent Victorians*, 131
style, personality and, 5, 22, 26, 33, 127–29, 133, 135
suffragism, Lewis's views on, 28, 29, 30
supersensory communication, 27
surrender, concept of: abstraction and, 15; authenticity and, 54, 78, 114; community aesthetics and, 124; in Eliot's works, 7; exchange and, 50, 51; impersonality and, 181n5; masochism and, 51, 52; personality and, 48; poetic emotion and, 3; violence and, 2; Wilde on, 33
Susman, Warren: "'Personality' and the Making of Twentieth-Century Culture," 24–25, 26, 28, 29

Tennyson, Alfred, Lord: *In Memoriam*, 183n20
Terada, Rei: *Feeling in Theory*, 178–79
Tiffany, Daniel, 51–52, 75
Todorov, Tzvetan, 137
"Tradition and the Individual Talent" (Eliot): activity in, 113; assessment of impersonality, 181–82nn5–6; centrality of, 3, 7; personality in, 24; poetic emotion in, 11–16, 37, 40, 84, 86, 91, 119, 146; praise of "really new" in, 22; scale and, 36; surrender of personality in, 48; synthesis of form and content, 179; ventriloquism in, 66; Wilde's forecasting of, 33

uniformity, impersonality and, 33–41, 58

ventriloquism, 16, 49, 51, 52, 66, 70, 79, 80
violence: authority and, 2; Butts's fascination with, 2; of classical emotions, 179; gratuitous, 16; in Lawrence's works, 2, 87–88, 101–12, 116; modernist, 81–112
Vogue, 130
Vorticism, 37, 38–41, 51, 183–84n25, 188–89n10, 201n39
Voyage In, The: Fictions of Female Development (collection), 205n12

Walter, Christina: "From Image to Screen," 188n5, 189n11
Wicke, Jennifer: "Coterie Consumption," 200n30
Wilde, Oscar: Berman's typology of, 185n15; "The Critic as Artist," 32, 33; "The Decay of Lying," 32; *Decorative Art in America*, 29; *Intentions*, 30; Lewis's criticism of, 196n4; notoriety of, 185–86n16; as "personality," 28–33, 117; *The Picture of Dorian Gray*, 85; "The Soul of Man under Socialism," 30, 31–32, 33; subject-object investigations in works of, 115
women: ethical problems of impersonality, 10, 82; impersonality and, 10; violence against, 82–83. *See also* feminism

Woolf, Virginia: aesthetic of impersonality, 33, 103, 108, 125; *Between the Acts*, 45, 187n29; Bowen compared to, 152; Butts viewed by, 115; on emotional aftermath of World War I, 179–80; "Flying over London," 44–45, 46; Lewis's criticism of, 196n4; *Mrs. Dalloway*, 116; "On Not Knowing Greek," 179–80; response to term "personality," 23, 24; "Street Haunting: A London Adventure," 41–44, 45–46, 117, 176, 187n28, 198n14; subject-object investigations in works of, 115; *The Voyage Out*, 85

World War I, aftermath of, 179–80

Worringer, Wilhelm: *Abstraction and Empathy*, 15, 123–24, 132, 133–34, 165–66, 169, 171

Yeats, William Butler: Butts and, 201–2n43; "A General Introduction to My Work," 15; impersonality doctrine, 3, 15–16; "Magic," 15; "A Packet for Ezra Pound," 15, 184n26; poetic persona, 32, 84; theories of, 31